understanding **psychoanalysis**

Understanding Movements in Modern Thought
Series Editor: Jack Reynolds

This series provides short, accessible and lively introductions to the major schools, movements and traditions in philosophy and the history of ideas since the beginning of the Enlightenment. All books in the series are written for undergraduates meeting the subject for the first time.

Published

Understanding Empiricism
Robert G. Meyers

Understanding Existentialism
Jack Reynolds

Understanding German Idealism
Will Dudley

Understanding Hegelianism
Robert Sinnerbrink

Understanding Hermeneutics
Lawrence K. Schmidt

Understanding Phenomenology
David R. Cerbone

Understanding Poststructuralism
James Williams

Understanding Psychoanalysis
Matthew Sharpe and
Joanne Faulkner

Understanding Rationalism
Charlie Huenemann

Understanding Utilitarianism
Tim Mulgan

Understanding Virtue Ethics
Stan van Hooft

Forthcoming titles include

Understanding Environmental Philosophy
Andrew Brennan and Y. S. Lo

Understanding Ethics
Tim Chappell

Understanding Feminism
Peta Bowden and Jane Mummery

Understanding Naturalism
Jack Ritchie

Understanding Postcolonialism
Jane Hiddleston

Understanding Pragmatism
Axel Mueller

understanding **psychoanalysis**

Matthew Sharpe and Joanne Faulkner

ACUMEN

First published in 2008 by Acumen

Acumen Publishing Limited
Stocksfield Hall
Stocksfield
NE43 7TN
www.acumenpublishing.co.uk

ISBN: 978-1-84465-121-4 (hardcover)
ISBN: 978-1-84465-122-1 (paperback)

British Library Cataloguing-in-Publication Data
A catalogue record for this book is available from the British Library.

Ttypeset by Graphicraft Limited, Hong Kong.
Printed and bound by Cromwell Press, Trowbridge.

Contents

Abbreviations

Unless otherwise stated, works refer to the *Standard Edition of the Complete Psychological Works of Sigmund Freud* [*SE*], translated under the general editorship of James Strachey (London: Hogarth Press and Institute of Psychoanalysis, 1953–74).

AC   "Some Psychical Consequences of the Anatomical Distinction Between the Sexes", *SE* XIX: 241–58.

AN   "On the Grounds for Detaching a Particular Syndrome From Neurasthenia Under the Description 'Anxiety Neurosis' ", *SE* III: 85–117.

AO   (with Joseph Breuer) "Case Histories, 1: Fraulein Anna O", *SE* II.

ATI   "Analysis Terminable and Interminable", *SE* XXIII: 211 ff.

BPP   "Beyond the Pleasure Principle", *SE* XVIII: 1–64.

CD   "Civilization and Its Discontents", *SE* XXI: 58–149.

CH   (with Joseph Breuer) "Case Histories", *SE* II: 18 ff.

CWD   "Creative Writing and Daydreaming", *SE* IX: 141–53.

DO   "The Dissolution of the Oedipus Complex", *SE* XIX: 171–9.

DT   "The Dynamics of the Transference", *SE* XII: 99–108.

EI   "The Ego and the Id", *SE* XIX: 1–66.

EPM   "The Economic Problem of Masochism", *SE* XIX: 155–70.

F   "Femininity", *New Introductory Lectures on Psycho-Analysis*, *SE* XXII: 136–57.

FI   "The Future of an Illusion", *SE* XXI: 1–56.

FL   *Five Lectures on Psychoanalysis* [1909] Harmondsworth: Penguin, 1995.

GRH "General Remarks on Hysterical Attacks", *SE* IX: 227–34.
HPM "History of the Psychoanalytic Movement", *SE* XIV: 7–66.
HPR "Hysterical Phantasies and Their Relation to Bisexuality", *SE* IX: 155–66.
ID *The Interpretation of Dreams* [1900], *SE* IV: xxxii + 1–338, and V: 339–627.
IGO "Infantile Genital Organization", *SE* XIX: 139–45.
ISA "Inhibitions, Symptoms, and Anxiety", *SE* XX: 75–175.
IV "Instincts and Their Vicissitudes", *SE* IV: 109–40.
JPH "Some Neurotic Mechanisms in Jealousy, Paranoia and Homosexuality", *SE* XVIII: 221–32.
LH "Analysis of a Phobia in a Five-Year Old Boy", *SE* X: 1–149.
LR "The Loss of Reality in Neurosis and Psychosis", *SE* XIX: 181–7.
MO "Mourning and Melancholy", *SE* XIV: 243–58.
MM "Moses and Monotheism: Three Essays", *SE* XXIII: 1–137.
MSD "Metapsychological Supplement to the Theory of Dreams", *SE* XIV: 217–35.
ON "On Narcissism", *SE* XIV: 67–102.
N "On Negation", *SE* XIX: 233–9.
NP "Neurosis and Psychosis", *SE* XIX: 147–53.
NU "A Note on the Unconscious in Psychoanalysis", *SE* XIII: 255–66.
OA "Obsessive Actions and Religious Practices", *SE* IX: 115–27.
PEL *The Psychopathology of Everyday Life* [1901], *SE* VI.
PMH (with Joseph Breuer) "On the Psychical Mechanism of Hysterical Phenomena: Preliminary Communication", *SE* II: 3–17.
QLA "The Question of Lay Analysis", *SE* XX: 179 ff.
R "Repression", *SE* XIV: 141–58.
RM "Notes Upon a Case of Obsessional Neurosis", *SE* X: 155ff.
RRW "Remembering, Repeating, Working Through", *SE* XII: 145–56.
SC "Psychoanalytic Notes on an Autobiographical Account of a Case of Paranoia (Dementia Paranoides) [The Schreber Case]", *SE* XII: 3 ff.
SN "Sexuality in the Neuroses", *SE* VII: 269–79.
ST "A Special Type of Object-Choice Made By Men", *SE* XI: 163–75.
STC "The Sexual Theories of Children", *SE* IX: 205–26.
TE *Three Essays on Sexuality*, *SE* VII.

TI	"On Transformations of Instinct as Exemplified in Anal Eroticism", *SE* XVII: 125–34.
TL	"Observations on Transference Love", *SE* XII: 157–71.
TPM	"Two Principles of Mental Functioning", *SE* XII: 213–36.
TT	"Totem and Taboo: Some Points of Agreement Between the Mental Lives of Savages and Neurotics", *SE* XIII: xv, 1–161.
U	"The Uncanny", *SE* XVII: 219 ff.
Ucs	"The Unconscious", *SE* XIV: 159–215.
UTD	"The Universal Tendency to Debasement in the Sphere of Love", *SE* XI: 177–90.

introduction

On understanding psychoanalysis

"A chance observation": Freud's introduction to psychoanalysis

"Anna O" had problems. Not the least of her problems was that the medical sciences of her day could neither cure her, nor explain what was causing her suffering. Anna O (real name Bertha Pappenheim) developed a number of troubling symptoms between July 1880 and June 1882. Many of these seemed to be physical in nature. Anna suffered rigid paralysis on the right side of her body, then her left arm. Her vision was impaired. The posture of her head was disturbed, and she had a nervous cough. Anna suffered from a kind of eating disorder – or, more precisely, a "drinking problem". For six weeks, she could not drink water, despite suffering tormenting thirst. Anna's capacity to speak was severely disturbed. She could speak only English for eighteen months, although her mother tongue was German, and she could understand others' speech. Finally, Anna would lapse into periods of delirium or "absences", during which she would abuse and throw cushions at her carers (AO: 21–33). Yet medical examinations could reveal no physical causes for these symptoms.

European medicine in the nineteenth century had a word to describe the condition of women suffering from such strange symptoms as Anna O's: "hysteria". Yet, as French philosopher Michel Foucault (and others) has documented (Foucault 1990), the understandings and treatments for mental illnesses such as hysteria available at that time were scientifically – and ethically – very questionable. Hysteria's uncertain physical basis meant that patients would often receive unsympathetic treatment, as if their symptoms and suffering were unreal. It was Anna's good fortune, however, to come to the attention of Doctor Joseph Breuer, a colleague and a friend of another young Viennese physician named Sigmund Freud. Breuer initially had no more idea about how to treat Anna O than anyone else. Yet "a chance observation" was to change all this, and to give birth to one of the most influential movements of thought of the next century (PMH: 3).

Breuer did not dismiss Anna O's symptoms, and what Anna had to say, as so much "feminine theatre". Indeed, when Breuer learnt that in Anna's absences she would repeat certain words (such as "tormenting, tormenting . . ."), Breuer tried something different. Breuer's idea was to repeat Anna's delirious words back to her under hypnosis, encouraging Anna to "speak her mind" as fully as she could about them. In this way, Breuer hoped to become aware of the ideas in Anna's head that accompanied her absences. Anna – by all accounts an intelligent and sensitive woman – began in this way to speak again, albeit at first only under hypnosis. Responding to Breuer's promptings, over time she came to recount a sequence of poetic stories and episodes from her life (AO: 29–34). Moreover, to Breuer's lasting surprise, this act of speaking her mind had unmistakable therapeutic effects. After each session, Anna would rest more peacefully, although on the following day her absences would recur, and the process would need to be repeated. Grateful for this much relief, Anna O christened the novel therapeutic procedure the "talking cure" (ibid.: 30). It was, she joked, like "chimney sweeping" – as if talking under hypnosis somehow cleansed her mind of what ailed her.

Breuer came to learn a good deal about Anna O's life and history by carrying out this talking treatment. Anna's stories would as a rule turn on the evocation of a young girl at her sick father's bedside. And when, encouraged by the successes of the talking cure, Breuer asked Anna to recall under hypnosis the first time her symptoms had appeared, another surprise lay in store. Anna's symptoms, without exception, all seemed to have first appeared during one, deeply traumatic time in Anna's own life. In July 1880, Anna's beloved father had fallen ill with a condition that would claim his life early the following year. During the first months of her father's illness, the 21-year-old Anna devoted herself to nursing her father. It was while she undertook this melancholy vigil that Anna's own symptoms appeared. By December 1880 she was consigned to a sickbed of her own.

Let us give two examples of what Anna's reminiscences revealed to Breuer about the origins of her symptoms.

KEY POINT *Where did Anna O's symptoms originate?*

- *Anna's disturbed vision and squint*: when Breuer asked Anna to recollect when the problems with her vision had begun, she recounted an experience at her father's sickbed. Anna had been crying in grief, when her father asked the time. Anna tried to look at her watch. However, tears obscured her vision. Accordingly, she brought the watch very close to her eyes, squinting to see through her tears.
- *Anna's paralysis of the right side of her body*: when Breuer asked Anna to recall when her paralysis appeared, Anna recounted how one night, attending her father, she lapsed into a vivid dream. In this dream she envisaged a snake leaping at her father from out of the wall. Anna wished she could defend him. However, her right arm, draped over the back of her chair, was paralysed. And when Anna looked at this right arm, the fingers turned, terrifyingly, into snakes before her eyes, each bearing a tiny death's head.

Once again, Anna's act of recollecting when her symptoms first appeared had unexpected effects. What Breuer found "to our great surprise at first" (PMH: 7) was this: Anna's recollection of the incidents when her symptoms first emerged seemed to dissolve these symptoms. By June 1882, Breuer tells us, he was able to cure Anna of all her hysterical symptoms. Freud's 1909 recollection of these occurrences captures the wonder Breuer's unpredicted therapeutic success produced in him: "never before had anyone removed a hysterical symptom by such a method or had thus gained such a deep insight into its causation" (FL: 10).

Freud would spend his life pursuing the implications of Breuer's (and Anna O's) chance discovery. In his own clinical work, Freud would soon discard Breuer's method of hypnosis as "a temperamental and, one might say, a mystical ally" (FL: 26–7). Not only was Freud, by his own admission, not particularly good at hypnotizing patients. Because of the traumatic, emotionally charged content of what Anna O and others recollected under hypnosis, Freud came to hypothesize that hypnosis, by momentarily suspending the patients' resistances to recalling these painful memories, also prevented the doctor from confronting these resistances. Hence these resistances would return in patients after a period of time, sometimes more strongly than before (e.g. FL: 29–30; see Chapter 8, under the section "The Ends of Psychoanalysis").

Yet Breuer's treatment of Anna O had opened the path to psychoanalysis that Freud was to travel down. It was Anna O's case that introduced Freud to the remarkable possibility that hysterics – and, by implication, the sufferers of other neuroses – "suffer mainly from reminiscences" (PMH: 7). Moreover, Anna O's case alerted Freud to the possibility on which all psychoanalytic theory would be based: namely, that there may be thoughts and processes in people's minds which, despite being unknown to them, have a decisive say in their behaviour.

Psychoanalysis proper was born when Freud came to propose, after 1895, that Anna O's "talking cure" should be undertaken without hypnotizing the patient. The doctor should do two "non-mystical" things. First, he should assure the patient that they know more about what has caused their symptoms than they might consciously think. Second, in what is known as "free association", the patient should say the first things that come into their heads, no matter how fair or foul. In this manner, Freud advocated, a type of recollection can be engendered in the mentally ill that is lastingly curative.

Introducing metapsychology

Psychoanalysis is first and foremost this clinical practice of the talking cure. It is based on the idea that a person's – the *analysand*'s – recollection of the original cause of their illness, in the presence of their doctor – the *analyst* – is somehow therapeutic. Given that this is so, we might well ask: what can psychoanalysis have to do with philosophy and other modern movements of thought, if it can have anything to do with them at all? The German novelist Thomas Mann noted Freud's own professional opinion on the matter. In truth, Mann observed, Freud

> did not esteem philosophy very highly . . . He reproaches it with imagining that it can present a continuous and consistent picture of the world; with overestimating the objective value of logical operations; with believing in intuitions as a source of knowledge and with indulging in positively animistic tendencies, in that it believes in the magic of words and the influence of thought upon reality.
>
> (Mann, in Lear 1990: 1; cf. (e.g.) ON: 77–9)

Nevertheless, perhaps the decisive challenge psychoanalysis was to pose to other Western movements of thought came from Freud's insights into the ways in which the meaning of individuals' words and actions exceed their conscious self-perceptions. Freud's discovery of the unconscious intrinsically puts into question a central conceit of Western philosophy: the possibility of individuals' achieving total theoretical mastery (and self-mastery) in their attempts to understand themselves and the world. The effects of this blow to Western man's narcissism (which Freud famously aligns with Copernicus's and Darwin's discoveries) continue to reverberate through contemporary thought. As we shall see, some philosophers (such as Derrida) and other critics (including feminists such as Juliet Mitchell or Luce Irigaray) took Freud's challenge to heart, turning to an autocritical (or deconstructive) art of reading previous Western philosophy for its inconsistencies, slippages and hidden biases in ways that directly reflect a psychoanalytic heritage. Other twentieth-century thinkers berated psychoanalysis for insufficient scientific or philosophical rigour, or for leading us into an interpretive night where all paths lead to Freud's predetermined conclusions. Yet, ironically, as with so many of the philosophers Freud would accuse of overvaluing their theoretical systems, the movement of thought Freud himself founded would very soon come to aspire to a more or less total account of human existence and civilization. Psychoanalysis began in the clinical practice of treating analysands such as Anna O. Yet it quickly became an international institution, and a movement of thought that has affected almost all walks of modern culture, from avant-garde art to popular expressions such as "Freudian slip", "anal retentive" and others. In this way, psychoanalysis came to be not only philosophy's critic, but its competitor in giving a total account of human life and meaning. This competition of psychoanalysis with the philosophers surely goes some way towards explaining twentieth-century philosophy's continuously ambivalent relations with psychoanalysis. Whatever Freud wished, however, from shortly after psychoanalysis's conception thinkers from almost all of the major schools of thought in the last century took it up (or on), challenged, weighed and debated it: analytic philosophers of language and science, existentialists and phenomenologists, hermeneuticians, Marxists and critical theorists, feminists and poststructuralists.

Despite the distance Freud attempted to underscore between psychoanalysis and previous Western thought, commentators on his work soon noted the debt his thinking about the psychoanalytic clinic owes to philosophers such as Schopenhauer and Nietzsche. In later essays, for example "Beyond the Pleasure Principle", Freud indulges in the same type of "speculations" he typically condemns in philosophers, even resurrecting the gnomic Presocratic Empedocles on a suggested biological footing (e.g. Derrida 1987). Given philosophy's epochal centrality to Western ideas, Freud's new discipline could hardly help but intervene in many of the fields philosophers had previously assumed that they were uniquely licensed to pronounce upon. Rather than accepting Freud's many dismissive statements concerning psychoanalysis's relations to philosophy, accordingly, it is more accurate to adapt what Freud has to say in *The Psychopathology of Everyday Life* about its relationship to religious belief – namely, Freud's ambition was that one day metapsychology, the theory of psychoanalysis, should supplant metaphysics, and the thought of the philosophers (PEL: 259).

So what philosophical and other movements of thought does psychoanalysis intervene in, and what does it say within these fields? Or, from the side of these movements of thought: what questions have philosophers and others posed to psychoanalysis about its findings and procedures?

There are nearly as many conceptions of philosophy as there have been great philosophers. In his *magnum opus*, *The Critique of Pure Reason*, the Enlightenment philosopher Immanuel Kant suggested that all philosophy turns on three questions: first, the question of what humans can know; secondly, what it is right for them to do; and, thirdly, what humans can hope for. In his book on *Logic*, however, Kant added a fourth question, as if this question might "take all" – *what is a human being?* This is the question of "philosophical anthropology", from the Greek word for the human being, *ό anthropos*. It is a question central to Western philosophy ever since its inception with Socrates' famous "second sailing", recounted in Plato's *Phaedo*, away from what today is called "natural science". Interestingly enough, it is also the question that the Theban Sphinx is reputed to have asked Oedipus in the myth that inspired Sophocles' tragedy, *Oedipus Tyrannis*. For the metapsychology developed by Freud to comprehend the talking cure – a theory in which the Oedipus tale was to play a very central role (see Chapter 2) – can be understood in this way. Freud's theoretical writings develop a new, *psychoanalytic anthropology*.

The prevalent self-image of humanity in Anna O's time was that human beings (or men at least) are the "masters and possessors of nature" (Descartes). This modern anthropology develops a much older philosophical tradition paradigmatically expressed in the first book of Aristotle's *Politics*. In this book, Aristotle offers two, coordinate definitions of *ó anthropos*. Men are *zoon politikon*: political or social animals, who can only flourish when they live in company with others. But men are also *tes zoas* who have *logos*: men can speak, or as the Romans came to translate it, they have "rationality".

As the poststructuralist philosophers were to emphasize in the charged intellectual climate of the 1960s and 1970s, Freud's psycho-analytic understanding of the human being strikingly qualifies this confident Western self-conception, if it does not overturn it com-pletely. For Freud, as for the philosophers, human beings are speaking, social animals capable of rationality. The talking cure could hardly have got off the ground if we were not. Yet, unlike the philosophical accounts of human nature, Freud lays emphasis on how individual human beings become such rational beings. A newborn child who cannot even control its bowel movements is not a fully rational, social being. As every parent, nurse or carer knows, there are many wishes, impulses and thoughts an infant must "grow out of" if it is to become a func-tioning member of society. Freud's most basic supposition is this: no human being makes it from infancy to a fully "civilized" state without lingering "discontents" that date first from their initial socialization. The mentally ill, far from being somehow sub- or inhuman, are in the psychoanalytic picture only those of us who have made it with more "baggage" than others. And *the unconscious*, first of all, is Freud's term for that part of individuals' psyches that bears witness to these linger-ing resistances to the civilizing process. Never a closed box, the un-conscious is attested in their irrational inhibitions, symptoms and anxieties, not to mention the dreams and "slips of the tongue" we all make all the time. For Freud, human beings are the political animals who have an unconscious. When they speak, they make jokes and blunders, through which are intimated how the unconscious works. And when human beings sleep, they dream – typically of the most bizarre or immoral things, foreign to the dreamers' waking selves.

Freud's postulation of the unconscious is the *sine qua non* of Freud's metapsychology, and of any psychoanalytic account of the human being. But it is neither the only, nor the most controversial, of Freud's hypotheses about human nature. Probably the idea Freud is best known for is the centrality he assigned to sexuality in his understand-ing of the human psyche, and of mental illness. With the possible exceptions of Plato and Nietzsche – to both of whom Freud refers – no previous secular Western thinker had accorded such importance to human beings' erotic life. When we make a list of all their inborn drives – to breathe, eat, drink, sleep . . . have sex – Freud argues that the last one on this list "sticks out". To be sure, as the old song goes: "the birds do it, the bees do it", and so do we. Yet, strange as this sounds, Freud insists that there is something particularly problematic for human beings about doing "it". If sexuality were the most natural thing in the world for us, Freud asks, why are human beings the only animals not to have any mating season? And if sexuality were not decisive in individuals' personal make-up, why do the sufferers of mental illness so often report disturbances in their sexual lives? Many philosophers would be quick to draw a line between serious, philosophical thought – pertinent only to essential questions of being and rationality – and questions concerning the place of sexuality in our lives. Yet Freud again challenges philosophy by placing the *in*essential – the rudely impertinent and unruly body – at the centre of thought and culture. It is in fact the manner in which we negotiate (and avoid) the thorny question of sexuality that orients what human beings are, according to Freud; and this includes the philosopher. However unhappy many feminists have been about Freud's answer to his famous question "What does woman want?", psychoanalysis's questions about the importance of sexuality, and the constructed nature of our sexual identities, would make it a pivotal reference for twentieth-century feminisms.

We shall return to Freud's views on sexuality in Chapter 2. The introductory point is this: if Freud is right, in contrast to the philosophers, human beings are the animals (first) with an unconscious, for whom (secondly) sexuality is as central as it is potentially problematic. There are two further dimensions to his position that we shall confront as we proceed in *Understanding Psychoanalysis*.

Thirdly, for Freud, it is not just that we all have an unconscious, *now*. As we saw in the case of Anna O, the symptoms that trouble individuals, and that Freud argues bear witness to the unconscious, originate in episodes in individuals' histories. As for many modern philosophers, if in a completely different way, we are for Freud historical animals. Neurotics' symptoms, Freud says, "are residues and mnemic symbols of particular (traumatic) experiences". In his 1909 Clark Lectures introducing an American audience to psychoanalysis ("they do not suspect we are bringing the plague", Freud supposedly joked), Freud compares neurotic symptoms with the monuments that adorn the cities of the world, commemorating their peoples' past struggles and sacrifices (FL: 15–17). The unconscious, far from being simply a storehouse of wild drives, is accordingly also a distinctive "mnemic" or memory system, Freud contends (see Chapter 3). If sexual disturbances are so prominent in the symptomatology of the mentally ill, it is because individuals' "oral fixations", "masochistic impulses" and so on somehow symbolically "commemorate" episodes from their own sexual development – in the now-infamous terms of Freud's *Three Essays on Sexuality*, the oral, anal and Oedipal phases of their personal prehistories (see Chapter 2).

Fourthly – and most ambitiously or "philosophically" – Freud argued that psychoanalytic theory allows us novel insights into more than the instinctual development of individuals. The "ontogenesis" (birth and socialization) of individuals, Freud argued, mirrors or reproduces the "phylogenesis" or historical evolution of the human species as a whole. Joining Enlightenment philosophers such as Kant, Hegel and many of his contemporaries, Freud contended that, just as an individual develops from infancy into rational adulthood, so the history of human civilization has seen the species mature from the "infancy" of primitive beliefs and civilizations to modern, scientific society. Drawing on contemporary anthropologists (and Charles Darwin) in "Totem and Taboo" (TT) Freud in this vein presents a controversial hypothesis concerning the founding event of human civilization – the murder of the "father of the primal horde" – allegedly every bit as pivotal to human development as the infamous "Oedipus complex" in individuals' maturation. Freud's views on civilization, art and religion will form the subject of Chapter 7.

Psychoanalysis, (and) the symptom

Sigmund Freud introduced into Western ideas a radical new answer to the question of the nature of human being. Psychoanalysis took an idea – that of the unconscious mind – which before Freud had at most been intimated in literature and some vitalist philosophers. It made of this idea the basis for a comprehensive "metapsychological" anthropology, and a clinical procedure for treating the mentally ill. We noted above that several poststructuralists (thinkers such as Derrida or Deleuze) drew on Freud's challenge to inherited Western ideas for their own criticisms of previous occidental philosophy. Yet the poststructuralists were by no means the only twentieth-century philosophers who responded to the challenges posed to philosophy by psychoanalysis. As we shall see in Chapter 8, other philosophers responded differently, and more sceptically, to the bold new movement of thought. Philosophers such as Karl Popper and Jürgen Habermas, and social theorists such as Michel Foucault or Philip Rieff, were less quick to take up Freud's metapsychology on its own terms. Instead, they asked of Freud's ideas variants of the first two of Kant's philosophical questions listed above: epistemologically, how can psychoanalysis verify the remarkable things it claims about individuals' fates, and the human psyche, society, art and religion? And, thinking about what makes for good human conduct and societies, are not the practices and ideas of psychoanalysis themselves a kind of "symptom" of wider modern malaises – either the individual and social malaises caused by the breakdown of traditional religion (for conservative critics) or, for more left-leaning critics, by the continuing, restrictive hold of such traditional conceits upon us?

Although this is an introductory text, one of *Understanding Psychoanalysis*'s aims – as a contribution to the Acumen series Understanding Movements in Modern Thought – is to prompt readers to further explorations of the question of psychoanalysis's relations to philosophy, and to other modern movements of thought such as feminism, critical theory, aesthetics and the theory of culture. In the later chapters of the book, examples of engagements of leading thinkers from these disciplines and fields will be introduced and analysed. These accounts are for the most part uncritical on their own terms, given the primarily exegetical calling of *Understanding Psychoanalysis*. Yet readers who look can discern an ethical defence of psychoanalysis developed at the book's end, one that reinforces what we think a clear exposition of key psychoanalytic ideas and their limits also makes evident: if psychoanalysis is supposedly long dead today (see Chapter 8), its challenge to us remains, and should do, for some time yet.

Understanding Psychoanalysis has three parts, culminating in the encounter of psychoanalysis with the critics and the philosophers. Part I examines the thinking of Sigmund Freud, the "father" of psychoanalysis, in detail. Starting with his earlier "dynamic", "economic" or biological account of the mind (Chapter 1), we proceed via his theory of sexuality and the drives (Chapter 2) to the "topographical" theory of the unconscious as a memory system, and Freud's *magnum opus, The Interpretation of Dreams* (Chapter 3). Our understanding of Freud provides the basis for Part II's chapters on Freud's two great successors, Melanie Klein (Chapter 4) and Jacques Lacan (Chapter 5). Chapter 6 examines the critical engagements of feminists with psychoanalysis, from Deutsch to Irigaray, centring on Freud's patent confusion about "what women want".

Part III then returns to the questions we have posed in this introduction, about psychoanalysis's ambivalent relations with the philosophers and other modern movements of thought. Chapter 7 examines Freud's claims concerning art, religion and civilization, and how they have been received by later psychoanalysts, philosophers and cultural theorists. Chapter 8 turns to philosophers' and social theorists' challenges to psychoanalysis, asking how it can justify its claims to truth in the age of advanced neuroscience and psychopharmacological medications, whether psychoanalysis is in terminal decline or crisis, and what its ethical and sociopolitical significance today might be. It is in this context that our closing defence of psychoanalysis emerges: a defence that among other things recommends a rethinking of the terms and need for today's ritualized (re-?) "killings" and "bashings" of the man long physically dead named Sigmund Freud.

If we were to summarize the attitude that animates *Understanding Psychoanalysis*, we would point to a wonderful phrase of the twentieth-century Greek philosopher Cornelius Castoriadis. Castoriadis once commented that all great thinkers "think beyond their means". They may not have all the answers, however ardently the acolytes that inevitably besmirch their names wish. Their greatness consists in opening up new fields of enquiry, or reopening old questions in new ways. It is the animating conviction of the authors of this book that Freud was, in this sense, a great thinker. It is our task here to indicate the paths that have emerged from Freud's "excessive" thought. The psychoanalytic attempt to rationally comprehend the unconscious opened up a new field of theoretical enquiry, one that surprised its very proponents, let alone the hosts of critics who were duly to appear. One need only look at the history of *The Interpretation of Dreams*, which Freud considered his greatest work, to see living testimony to a thinker thinking beyond his means. Freud could never finish his *magnum opus*. He returned to it throughout his life, adding new examples, and revising and qualifying earlier formulations.

For us, then, dogmatic Freudians – no less than dogmatic followers of anyone else – betray Freud's scientific aspirations. They also miss the greatest challenge Freud posed to other movements of thought in the twentieth century. Klein, Lacan and feminist critics form the subject matter of Part II because they did not stick slavishly to the Freudian orthodoxies of their times. Instead, they addressed the many questions and shortcomings Freud's *oeuvre* bequeathed to people interested in human psychology, mental illness, and the wide-ranging areas Freud wrote about. Part II highlights how Klein, Lacan and feminists respectively drew upon, developed but also criticized Freud's *oeuvre* in the light of later clinical research, and theoretical and social developments.

Part III of the book, finally, aims not only to introduce students to psychoanalysis's contributions to theoretical debates about art, religion and civilization. Our emphasis is on the questions philosophers and critics have posed to psychoanalysis, and the "issue" philosophers and later psychoanalytic thinkers have taken with Freud's ideas.

In "The Future of an Illusion", Freud puts into the mouth of an exasperated interlocutor a response that well expresses the anxieties Freud's attempt to bring reason to the most irrational parts of the human soul continues to provoke:

> On the one hand, you admit that men cannot be guided by their intelligence, they are ruled by their passions and their instinctual demands. But on the other hand, you propose to replace the affective basis of their obedience to civilisation with a rational one. Let he who can understand this. To me, it seems that it must be either the one thing or the other . . .
>
> (FI: 46)

One thing Freud's thinking indicated, as Lacan formulated it, is that anxiety is *the one affect that does not deceive.* In this context, we can understand part of Lacan's meaning by saying that the anxiety Freud provoked in his contemporaries, and ours, indicates that psychoanalysis "touches a nerve" or two in modern Western culture, threatening to upset many of the sanctified "either–ors" ("to me . . . it must be *either* the one thing *or* the other . . .") that our civilization had set up to explain the world.

We began this introduction with Anna O, in whose mantic utterances ("tormenting, tormenting . . .") Joseph Breuer heard a stifled attempt to communicate, and a plea for help. Psychoanalysis begins with the confrontation of such symptoms, whose very existence, when we think about them, confounds many of the ways we have inherited to think about the world. At the beginning of the scientific age, Descartes had agued that for a thing to exist, it must be capable of being known, ideally with clarity and distinctness. What Breuer and Freud came to find, with the symptoms of the unconscious, was that there are more things existing in heaven and earth than were dreamed of in Descartes's philosophy. Anna O's symptoms, and the symptoms of the cast of female hysterics Freud would treat in the ensuing years, only repeated in so far as their cause was *not* known. If Anna could remember – and communicate – the traumatic episodes in which the symptoms first appeared, they would cease. Of all the things that the twentieth-century "ordinary-language philosophers" were to discover people could "do with words" (J. L. Austin), none tops this act of dissolving psychological symptoms. Indeed, its centrality to Freud's breakthrough brings psychoanalysis very close – too close, for many – to a professional faith "in the magic of words and the influence of thought upon reality . . ." (Thomas Mann) which puts the philosophers' (m)antics to shame.

So let us close this introduction by proposing a hypothesis that can stand at the metaphorical gates of *Understanding Psychoanalysis*. If Freud is right, philosophers' difficulties in accounting for psychoanalysis reflect the attempts of psychoanalysis to account rationally for an objectively perplexing "thing". This is a field of "objects", like Anna O's symptoms, subjects' knowledge of which changes these very subjects. As we shall see in Chapter 8, this claim by itself arguably means that psychoanalysis eludes classification in either of the two types of intellectual enquiry sanctified by the modern world, which still divide university faculties today. It is not a natural science, as Popper, Nagel, Ricoeur or Grunbaum agree. Yet nor is it, for this reason, a discipline that can be safely embosomed within the interpretive or "human sciences" such as criminology, sociology and economics, as neuropsychoanalysts such as Mark Solms or Eric Kandel rightly protest. Like Anna's symptoms which called psychoanalysis into being, that is, psychoanalysis itself has something like a "symptomatic" status in the modern world's self-understandings. And like the proverbial symptom the neurotic wishes ardently he might ignore, so we can surmise that it will not cease troubling us until we come to terms with it, which means working through both its shortcomings and its truths. Put more strongly, psychoanalysis, if anything, poses an ethical challenge to subjects, and to modern civilization. It represents in the bosom of modern medicine and our "therapeutic" culture an unlikely refiguring of the Greeks' injunction to *gnothi seauton* (know thyself) that continues to address itself to us as individuals, and as a discontented civilization. It is with the aim of heeding this injunction, and so of making a small contribution to coming to terms with the modern "symptom" called psychoanalysis, that we offer this introductory text.

part I

Sigmund Freud, the father of psychoanalysis

one

Where it was: Freud's biology of the mind

From the pleasure principle to the reality principle

In the decade following Breuer's treatment of Anna, Freud confirmed for himself Breuer's claim about the curative value of analysands' recollections in a number of other cases of female hysteria (Emmy von N, Lucy R, Katherina —, Elizabeth von R) (CH). Eschewing Breuer's reliance on hypnosis, it was in these cases that Freud developed the method of free association and, *a fortiori*, clinical psychoanalysis. But why might the spoken expression of forgotten traumatic incidents be a therapeutic experience for individuals? It is one thing to do something; another to know what you have done. Such an unexpected clinical finding, Freud saw, could be made sense of only by a far-reaching account of the mind. Yet the categories of Freud's metapsychology did not come to him all at once, by the time of his first theoretical writings in the early 1890s. Freud would continue to revise them until well after the traumas of World War I.

Sigmund Freud was born in 1856, the youngest son of a pious Jewish wool-merchant, and the only son of his father's second wife. At the time of Breuer's treatment of Anna O (1880–82), Freud was beginning his professional life as a physician in Vienna. Freud's training as a physician, as well as the unquestioned cultural prestige the natural sciences enjoyed in late nineteenth-century Europe, pointed him in the direction of his earliest writings. In these texts, as throughout the ensuing decades, Freud proposed that what the psychoanalytic clinic revealed about the human psyche could be theorized in the terms of a biological account of the mind.

Recall that Anna O described the effect of the talking cure as like chimney sweeping. Implied in Anna's description is the idea that somehow mental energy, held in by restrictive forces, is released by the spoken recollection of earlier trauma(s). As Jonathan Lear comments, Anna's idea, however flippantly intended, influenced the theoretical formulations of the young Freud, and thereby psychoanalytic metapsychology (Lear 1990: 35–6).

KEY POINT *A précis of the 1895* Project for a Scientific Psychology

Here the young Freud postulates that observable psychological phenomena depend on the neural structure of the brain. The *Project* posits three "systems" of "neurones", separated by "contact barriers" (which restrict the passage of energy (Q) from each neurone to those adjacent to it in the neural network):

- *The "Φ-system"*: neurones involved in perception of the external world, through which the Q involved in receiving external stimuli flows without resistance.
- *The "Ψ-system"*: neurones which resist, and retain permanent traces of, Q as it flows through them. The Ψ-system is the part of the brain involved in memory. (Interestingly, Freud locates what he will call the ego here (see below).)
- *The "Ω-system"*: a much more enigmatic postulate, the Ω-system contains no Q, but by registering the workings of the other systems, supplies the qualitative dimension of conscious experience (what it is like to be conscious): what philosophers of mind today call *qualia*.

In everyday speech, we call people who are angry or anxious "pent up". When they express themselves in angry words, gestures or actions, we say they are "blowing off steam". The young Freud's founding metapsychological wager draws on the mechanistic sciences of his day which argued that, at base, the behaviours of all living organisms can be understood according to a kind of universal principle of "blowing off steam" (PMH: 8).

In several key texts, Freud asks us to consider the case of "an almost entirely helpless living organism" (IV: 119). Such organisms have only the most basic abilities to respond to their environment. The stimuli the organism receives from the external world activate its nervous system, and generate reflex responses. However, if at any time these stimuli become too great, the organism must either remove (itself from) the source of stimulation, or perish. The nervous system of even such an organism, claims Freud, "is an apparatus having the function of abolishing stimuli which reach it, or of reducing excitation to the lowest possible level . . ." (IV: 120). This function of reducing nervous "excitation" is what Fechner named the biological "principle of constancy" (EPM: 159). What we call the pain of any organism, Freud adds, is the qualitative affect of a quantitative overstimulation of its nervous system. This overstimulation produces a heightened tension inside it, and the reflex impulse to reduce the offending stimulation. Fechner's principle of constancy, Freud for this reason argues, can be renamed "the pleasure principle". Pleasure involves at this very basic level the release of painful, pent-up tension within the organism.

All this mechanistic biology has the most telling relevance for human psychology, Freud maintains. The reason is that the newborn human infant is evidently almost entirely under the sway of the pleasure principle, very like our "almost entirely helpless living organism". Attended to nearly constantly by its carers, it at first has no sense of the distinction between itself and the outside world. When needs do arise for it, as Freud intriguingly posits in *The Interpretation of Dreams*, infants seem capable from very early on of "hallucinating" their satisfaction (ID: 565–6). Infants do this by recalling the "mnemic images" of earlier satisfaction(s), whenever a new source of pain arises. Freud's newborn, like a Leibnizian monad, thus has no doors and windows – its wishful thoughts, coupled with the instantaneous attendance of its carers, omnipotently sate its instinctual needs.

Yet all good things must come to an end. The child is forced to discover that the external world does exist. The external world imposes itself upon the child as the sum total of things which the child cannot "dream up". If the child is chafed by its clothing, for example, no amount of wishing will remove this somatic source of pain. Something in the child's environment must be altered. In a "realist" refrain central to Freud's thought up to such later texts as "Civilization and Its Discontents" (see Chapter 7), growing up for Freud involves learning to cope with our constitutive inability to instantly get everything we want. Due to the recalcitrance of the external world to its every whim, the child must develop what Freud calls the "reality principle", a principle that significantly modifies (although it does not negate) the impulsive demands of the pleasure principle.

External things place demands upon the nervous system of the
infant. But by developing perception, memory and motility, it becomes
capable of recognizing, fleeing or fighting these demands. However, in
an absolutely basic principle of psychoanalysis, Freud's realism about
the harsh intractability of the external world is matched by an even
harsher view about the potential dangers to the human being of their
own, internal drives. If psychoanalysts are popularly depicted as tire-
somely asking analysands about how they "feel" about things, rather
than events, the basic reason is this. According to Freud's biological
understanding of the mind, our drives, like external objects, place a
"demand for work" upon our nervous system: when we feel hunger,
there is a rise in internal tension which, if it becomes keen enough, is
painful. Our first ideas, Freud maintains, are the "representations"
(*Vorstellungen*) of these instinctual needs. However, like Oedipus, who
can only try and fail to flee the words of the oracle that has stated his
destiny, so each of us can only fail if we try to fight or flee from our own
drives. If we flee, we take them with us. If we snuff them out, we damage our own selves thereby (IV: 119–21).

The child can sate its internal needs by obtaining appropriate
objects, or its first others might get them for it. Yet satisfying objects
can be scarce. And children are capable of experiencing more than one
instinctual demand at a time. The insistence of internal demands in
potential contradiction with what the child can readily obtain, for
Freud, underlies the development of a further, higher capacity.

> **KEY POINT** *What is called thinking?*
>
> - When needs persist, and objects cannot be obtained, the infant must develop the capacity for the "binding of psychical energy". It cannot achieve pleasure by instantly jumping to conclusions, or actions. On top of the capacity for action, it needs now to learn to hold back action, "tolerating an increased tension of stimuli while the process of discharge is postponed" (TPM: 221).
> - Thinking, then, is "an experimental kind of action" made possible by this new capacity. "Do my ideas match anything in the external world?", the child begins to ask. Or, more precisely – drawing on its stock of memories – "do my remembered ideas about how the world is correspond to what I can perceive now?" (see Chapter 5).
> - Secondly, the child learns to make elementary hypotheses. "If I do x," it wonders, "what then?" And, considering the options, "what if I instead acted in ways y or z? Which outcome might be more satisfying in the long run?"

With the development of thinking, our little child has become a strategist. It can now play off different drives, and defer impulses to act on the basis of calculations as to where greater satisfactions lie in the medium to longer terms. From monadic immersion in the "pleasure principle", it has become capable of what our economists call "rational choice", aiming to maximize pleasure, over time, in the conditions of a world it did not create.

Can a psychical agency serve three masters?

Alas, Freud does not preach good news for our reality-testing child. For what happens, he asks, if the satisfying of one of its instinctual wishes, for whatever reason, involves courting other dangers? As every fairytale depicts, the hero cannot save the princess without slipping by the guards and humbling the villain. Likewise, becoming a civilized adult means restraining or renouncing many of the drives with which we are born. As we shall examine in Chapter 2, many infantile drives are deemed distasteful or immoral by our societies, and so are incapable of satisfaction without censure: from unrestrained bowel movements to unchecked displays of affection towards siblings. In Freud's understanding, then, the human psyche always stands under the threat of becoming overburdened. We are all torn from very early in our lives between at least two masters. On one side, there are the demands of our drives or "libido", which would ideally brook no dissatisfactions. On the other, there are the demands of social reality, which check the abandoned acting out of all our fondest wishes.

The ego is Freud's name for the part of the psyche that takes on the difficult profession of trying to keep both these "masters" content. The ego "occupies an intermediate position between the external world and the [individuals' drives] and . . . attempts to humour all its masters at once . . ." (NP: 147). In developmental terms, the ego is "that part of the psyche which has been modified by the direct influence of the external world acting through perception-consciousness" (EI: 25). It is the psychical bearer and agency of perception, memory and motility, representing "what we call reason and sanity" (*ibid.*) against the imperious, inconsistent demands of our libido. In common parlance, Freud's ego is the "self" we all think of ourselves as being: in control of who we are, what we say and do, and who or what we do it with.

But what, Freud asks, will the good little ego do when it comes to those libidinal drives whose satisfaction would involve conduct prohibited by its elders, and accordingly court punishments or the loss of love?

KEY POINT *Repression and its relation to the unconscious*

Freud's answer is that the offending instincts will effectively be struck from the conscious record. The child's developing ego wants to know nothing about them. The problem is that:

- at this point of its development, it knows only how to respond to threatening external things – by fight or flight. Accordingly, it makes what philosophers call a "category mistake", responding to its own prohibited wishes as if they were threatening objects in the external world. Unable to fight, it tries to flee them. This is the psychological process that Freud calls "repression" (R: 146–7);
- and, as we have reflected, to flee one's drives is as impossible as Oedipus' flight from his own destiny. Repression in Freud's understanding is thus always failed repression;
- the repressed wishes do not disappear, as the good little child hopes. These wishes remain "in the back of its mind", or, to (re)introduce Freud's paradigmatic term, these repressed wishes become *unconscious*.

The unconscious wishes are from this point kept at a distance from the demands of external reality. Accordingly they revert back to the exclusive sway of the pleasure principle and of fantasies that, like the infant's earliest hallucinations, stage their fulfilment without need to change the external world. Freud calls the repressed unconscious drives of individuals *the id*. When rendered in English, this looks innocuous enough. But in German, what Strachey translates as the id is the neuter pronoun "it" (*Es*). Having repressed its illicit drives, these drives appear to the ego like an "it", Freud is indicating. From the perspective of the ego they seem a "foreign body" (PMH: 7) – or, as Lacan will capitalize it, some alien Thing. As we shall see in Chapter 7, the origin of psychoanalytic understandings of the "uncanny" in literature, and of our enjoyment of horror films, lies here. Reflecting the key psychoanalytic principle we cited above – that first our own internal demands are potentially most disturbing – for such psychoanalytic criticism, what we see in the monstrous Things of horror films are our own repressed it or "id" impulses returning from the screen to overwhelm us.

However, Freud's account of the ego and its relation to the id was never wholly unequivocal (see Chapter 5). As the important 1914 article "On Narcissism" shows, after 1910 Freud qualified his account (presented so far) of the ego as the psychological agency of reason and sanity. In our introduction, we saw that psychoanalysis began with the clinic of hysteria. By the 1910s, Freud had treated analysands suffering from phobias (like Little Hans) and obsessional neurosis (like the Ratman) (see below). He had also confronted the apparently untreatable symptoms of psychotics (as in the *Memoirs* of Judge Schreber). Alongside Jung, Freud was struck by the evident megalomania of psychotics, in whose delusions they would become literally the centre of the universe. How could such symptoms occur, Freud came to ask, if the ego were not only the agency adapting the child's wishes to external reality, but also itself a possible object of such wishes and psychical "cathexes"? Recalling the myth of Narcissus, who fell in love with his own image in the waters of the fountain, Freud began to argue that the ego is a very early, perhaps even primary, *love-object*. Recalling the child's initial inability to distinguish between itself and the world, Freud in some papers posits a "primary narcissism" (ON: 100; IV: 136; EI: 28) that preceded the child's attachments to others and to external things.

In Freud's second, post-1914 account, the ego is not simply a psychical agency that uses the body's perceptual organs to orient the individual in relation to objects. Freud now adds that "it is seen in the same way as any other object . . . it is not merely a surface entity, but also the projection of a surface" (EI: 26). The individual comes to distinguish this body-object from all other objects because it is the only object that hurts when it is struck, cut and so on. The child comes to identify its "self" with it, and in this way to shape its sense of individual identity. As the child is made to renounce pursuit of certain of its now-prohibited drives, the decisive question is how it can bear up to these necessary renunciations. We have seen one side of Freud's answer – infants repress the offending drives. The other side, which Freud's second account of the ego develops, is this: individuals identify with the objects for which they have been made to renounce desire. Forced by external, social reality to renounce our desire to have these objects, we instead model how we look, behave, speak and so on upon them. The little boy will now "be all grown up like Daddy". This, if Freud is right, is why brothers and sisters often share so many mannerisms, or sons often have similar postures, gaits and so on to their fathers. It also casts an interesting light on the old saying about figures such as James Bond: women want to *have* them, and men want to *be* them. In a series of beautiful formulations, Freud writes: "The character of the ego is a pre-cipitate of abandoned object cathexes, and . . . it contains the record of past object choices . . ." (EI: 29). And "[in mourning] the shadow of the object falls upon the ego . . ." (MO: 249).

Ironically enough, given the title "The Ego and the Id", the most important development this essay introduces into Freudian metapsy-chology is a third psychical agency, *the superego*. The superego is closely aligned with the conscience of individuals. Yet it is not identical with it, despite some of Freud's own formulations. The superego is that part of the ego which is shaped by the child's identification with its first love-objects – usually its parents or carers. At the most decisive point of its socialization (what Freud calls the Oedipus complex (see Chapter 2)), the child must renounce its dearest wishes concerning these figures. In order to cope with this heaviest libidinal burden, it accordingly identifies with one or other of them, coming to see itself as if "through their eyes" – or as it imagines they see it. The superego is that critical voice we continue to hear throughout our lives, particularly in times of strain, and which says such generally unhelpful, aggressive things such as what Freud's father once said to him: "That boy will never amount to anything!" The superego is also that critical *gaze* that people very often adopt when they look at themselves in a mirror: one in which they are always too fat, unattractive and so on. As Freud argues in "The Ego and the Id", the superego is effectively a third master, alongside external reality and the id, that the unfortunate ego must try to humour (EI: 28–39; ON: 93–6; MO: 247–8).

The onset and nature of mental illness

Psychoanalysis is the impossible profession, Freud once joked. We have seen how the task of each of our egos is difficult enough, if Freud's metapsychology is true. It is little wonder, given the terms of Freud's theory of the mind, that individuals so often develop forms of mental illness. The enigmatic symptoms of mental illness are where psychoanalysis began. Unlike other philosophies of mind, for psychoanalytic theory the orienting goal is to generate a set of categories exacting enough to diagnose and respond clinically to the diverse mental illnesses from which human beings suffer. So how does Freud explain the nature of mental illnesses, given the metapsychological framework we have so far developed?

First of all (and this is worth underscoring, since people still accuse Freud of "blaming the parents"), Freud holds that the onset of mental illness always involves the individual's internal reality: their own unconscious drives. As we have emphasized, for psychoanalysis, it is one's internal wishes that are most potentially disturbing for one's mental health. In the case of the onset of a mental illness, this insight is easy enough to confirm – because not everyone who, for example, attends at the bedside of their dying father develops symptoms like Anna O.'s. What does Freud think happens when someone like Anna falls ill?

"Mental health", for Freud (although his more famous description is "ordinary unhappiness"), is that state of psychical affairs wherein an individual's ego has succeeded in "mediating" relations between the id, the superego and the external world. The individual gleans enough satisfaction from his relations with the external world that the level of nervous stimulation in his psyche does not reach too high a level. The superego's aggressively critical judgements are kept at bay because the individual is achieving enough, and the id's imperious urges are not troubling her overly (because she, for example, is content in her love and family lives). To adapt Kipling, the healthy person is changing what can be changed, living with what she cannot, and her ego has wisdom enough (mostly) to tell the difference.

Illness will befall this "balanced" individual, Freud postulates, if or when something upsets this happy state of affairs. There may be some change in the person's external circumstances: the loss of a job or a loved one, or the end of an affair. However, to emphasize again the key psychoanalytic postulate, it is the effect of this loss on his "inner life" that matters. Freud indicates this by using the word *Vorsagung* (forsaking) to describe this external loss (which Strachey somewhat misleadingly renders as "frustration") (NP: 151). Secondly, there may be an internal change in the individual's libidinal make-up, as for example with the onset of puberty, or menopause in women.

In either type of case, Freud says, a "damming up of libido" occurs. And the illness is the disturbance in the individual's relation to the external world that this "damming up" produces:

> Every neurosis disturbs the patient's relation to reality in some way . . . it serves him as a means of withdrawal from reality and . . . in its severest forms, it . . . signifies a flight from real life. (LR: 181)

As we say today, the individual at this point of *Vorsagung* threatens to become "dysfunctional". Yet Freud's diagnostic categories are more subtle than this. For him, there are not only mental illnesses of varying severity. There are three qualitatively different types of mental illness: the neuroses (hysteria and obsessional neurosis); the psychoses; and the perversions. Freud understands the manifest differences between these illnesses in terms of the framework his biological account of the mind provides:

> The pathogenic effect [in different illnesses] depends on whether, in a conflictual tension of this kind, the ego remains true to its dependence on the external world and silences the id or whether it lets itself be overcome by the id and therefore turns away from reality. (NP: 151)

In the first case, there is a neurosis, and in the second, the individual will have become psychotic. Freud's claims about the onset of mental illnesses can hence be formulated as shown in Table 1.1.

Table 1.1 The onset of illness

Illness	Neuroses	Psychoses
Impoverishment of . . .	The id	Individuals' sense of external reality
By means of . . .	Repression (*Verneinung*)	"Disavowal" (*Verleugnung*)

The difference between the mechanisms involved in the onset of illness in neurosis and psychosis can be illustrated by referring to the case of Elizabeth von R. Elizabeth was a hysteric who suffered a variety of symptoms. Free association revealed that one of the sources for her suffering concerned Elizabeth's illicit admiration for her sister's husband. When this sister unexpectedly died, Elizabeth found herself thinking at the funeral, despite herself: "Now he is free to be with me" (CH: 15; LR: 184). Because this wishful thought so deeply shamed her, her memories of the situation which had provoked them (her sister's funeral) were repressed:

> Neuroses originate from the ego's refusing to accept a powerful instinctual impulse from the id or to help it find a motor outlet, or from the ego's forbidding an impulse the object at which it is aiming. (NP: 150)

A psychotic in Elizabeth's situation, Freud by contrast explains, might have "disavowed" the very fact that her sister had died, since it is this event that led her into temptation. In psychosis, that is, the conflict between the id and reality leads to the disavowal of parts of the world whose confrontation, because of the wishes they provoke, would be too traumatic. Freud puts this point by saying that psychotics suffer a failure of "object cathexes". If "paying attention" to the outside world involves the expenditure of psychic energy, as we saw, with the onset of psychosis, the individual's ego ceases paying the toll. This is why psychotics so regularly suffer delusions such as Judge Schreber's, that the world has ended (ON: 76; see Chapter 5). Characteristically, Freud maintains that there is truth to these metaphysical delusions. The psychotic's individual relation to the external world has indeed ended. The delusion is a psychological truth misrepresenting itself as a truth in metaphysics, in a way that goes towards explaining Freud's hesitations about philosophy (see introduction; PEL: 258–9).

The onset of neurosis and psychosis accordingly involves a disturbance in the individual's relation with reality. Yet, Freud specifies, each mental illness has two phases. It is only in the second phase of mental illnesses that the individual's symptoms become manifest. As strange as this sounds, Freud contends that the symptoms of the mentally ill are the individual's attempts at a cure (NP: 151). They function to maintain (in the neuroses) or to restore (in the psychoses) the individual's relations to external reality, under the changed conditions of the illness.

Table 1.2 The onset and the manifestation of the mental illnesses

Illness	Neuroses	Psychoses
Impoverishment of . . .	The id	Individuals' sense of external reality
By means of . . .	Repression (*Verneinung*)	"Disavowal" (*Verleugnung*)
Damming up of . . .	Object libido	Ego libido
Symptoms/attempts at (self-)cure	Return of the repressed	Delusional formations

The full table of Freud's diagnostic understanding of neurosis and psychosis is as shown in Table 1.2.

To take the psychoses first: with the onset of illness there is a "damming up" of psychical energy. Yet in the neuroses, this "dammed-up" energy finds substitute outlets in unconscious fantasy – like the "hallucinated satisfactions" of the young infant. In the psychoses even this mechanism fails, and the tenuous link unconscious fantasies' "mnemic images" maintain with the object-world cannot hold. The libido dammed up by the precipitating *Vorsagung* is instead "cathected" to the individual's ego as a narcissistic love-object. This is how Freud explains the hypochondria so often symptomatic before a full-blown psychosis – anxieties that the person's body has been poisoned, violated, or is extremely vulnerable to physical corruption. The psychotic's bizarre delusions, Freud maintains, represent her best attempt to rebuild or "recathect" her relations to the world, given this complete collapse of her object cathexes. The manifest problem is that "this fresh libidinal cathexis takes place on another level and on other conditions than the primary one" (ON: 86–7).

The most striking feature of these delusions is their *paranoid* content. The psychotic's ego is elevated within their delusions to the centre of their universe, albeit as a kind of universal victim: the object of the intrusive surveillance and malign intentions of one, or a host, of persecutors – whether God, the CIA, aliens, or one's doctor. For the psychotic, it is as if the superegoic voice and gaze which all subjects experience internally (see above) has become part of the external world, from whence it confronts the individual with hateful omniscience. In Chapters 4 and 5, we shall examine in detail the principal mechanism that Freud argues is involved in the formation of these persecutory delusions: *projection*.

In Chapter 7 of "The Unconscious", finally, Freud contrasts how neurotics and psychotics stand with regard to language. One typical manifestation of psychosis is the attribution of "magic powers" to words. Just as the newborn cannot distinguish between what it hallucinates and external reality, so psychotics typically treat words like things, and "treat concrete things as if they were abstract ideas" (Ucs: 199). Words can and do, metaphorically, transmit ideas "between people's minds". But few of us maintain that others can physically put ideas in our heads. Yet exactly such "delusions of influence" are a common psychotic fear. Similarly, a hysteric wrestling with her wish to reproach her lover with "looking askew" at other women might develop a symptomatic compulsion to roll her own eyes. Yet a psychotic in this very situation, Freud recounts, complained that her lover had physically "twisted her eyes", as if this metaphor had "become flesh" in her hypochondriac symptom:

> She could not understand him at all, he looked different every time . . . ; he had twisted her eyes, now they were not her eyes any more, now she saw herself through different eyes
>
> (Ucs: 197–8)

KEY POINT *On the psychoses*

- The psychotic denies a part of reality that provokes forbidden wishes. Then he sets about reconstructing, through delusions, his relation to the external world of objects and others. What we see as the psychotics' symptoms are hence their best attempt at a psychological "cure".
- But the means the psychotic has at his disposal are "patently infantile" (CD: 86). He is unable to anchor his sense of reality in anything outside his own ego.
- His delusions for this reason invariably turn upon the axis of his own relations with (a) more or less all-seeing and all-knowing double, devoted to persecuting him, onto whom he has in truth "projected" his own foreclosed impulses, as a film projector projects images on to a screen.
- Unable to accurately stabilize the distinction between his thoughts and wishes and external reality, he treats words as things, and comes painfully to embody the "figures of speech" that might have mediated his relations with others.

The neuroses: anxiety, inhibitions and symptoms

Unlike the psychotic, the neurotic sides with reality against the id at the onset of his illness. Accordingly, the manifestations of neurotics' illnesses (at the second stage of their development) are remarkably different from psychotics'. In the words of the title of an important late essay, neurotics are subject to "inhibitions, symptoms, and anxiety" (ISA) – but not to delusions.

Freud's hypotheses concerning the role of anxiety in the neuroses are probably the least controversial among these three. Many non-psychoanalytic clinicians today diagnose patients with "anxiety disorders". Freud would find such a diagnosis of no help at all. The reason is that anxiety, according to Freud, is present in all mental illnesses. At base, anxiety functions psychologically as a signal that the individual's psyche is in some danger – or, in the terms of his biological account of mind, that there is heightened tension within the psychical apparatus (ISA: ch. VII). Neurotics are often only too aware that they are anxious: it is this "free-floating anxiety" that has led them to see a doctor. Their problem is that they do not know what is causing their anxiety, and this is what the "anxiety disorder" diagnosis misses. We shall say more on anxiety in Chapter 2, when we consider hysterical attacks.

The role of inhibitions in neuroses, Freud argues, can equally be explained in terms of the psyche's elementary function in service of the pleasure principle. Inhibitions are, as we say today, "places" where neurotics "don't go": from physical places to topics of conversation or painful memories. Hysterics such as Elizabeth von R avoid with disgust certain topics (for example, sexuality), because confronting them stirs up illicit or competing wishes their ego would rather not confront. Neurotic inhibition is clearly manifest in cases of phobia, as we shall see in a moment. It is also apparent in a variety of sexual maladies: from impotence in men or frigidity in women, to the inability to enjoy the act (ISA: ch. I).

Freud argues that neurotics' symptoms, finally, are "compromise formations", attempting to resolve conflict between the superego, the ego and the id (e.g. SN: 78). We saw above how, confronted with a pro-hibited wish, the child represses this wish and "identifies with the prohibitor": usually its parents, teachers, siblings and so on. But the repressed id-wishes do not disappear, Freud maintains. Abiding by the pleasure principle, they continue to demand satisfaction, in any way they can. While, then, neurotic symptoms are the results of com-promise between the ego's censorship and this insistence of the id (e.g.

ISA: 98), the "compromise" takes the form of "substitutive satisfactions" (R: 154). The ego maintains its censorship on the direct expression of the wish: Elizabeth did not leap at her dead sister's newly free husband. But the id must have its satisfaction, too. The result is that neurotic symptoms are both sufficiently unlike the original wish-fulfilment that the ego cannot recognize it as threatening any longer, and sufficiently like it that the psyche gets a return of pleasure from the symptom's repetitions. For this reason, Freud argues that symptoms involve "the return of the repressed" (esp. R; Ucs: ch. III).

To illustrate these theoretical propositions more concretely, let us look at one of Freud's famous case studies, the case of the young child, Little Hans.

KEY POINT *Understanding Little Hans (LH; ISA: ch. IV)*

What were Hans' symptoms?

- A phobia of horses, especially of being bitten by them.
- A resulting fear of going into public places.

What was "free association" able to reveal about the cause of the phobia?

- Hans had seen a horse fall in public, and he had also seen his friend fall down while playing with a horse.
- At the time the symptom appeared, Hans had "mixed feelings" – what Freud will call "ambivalence" – towards his father. On the one hand, he loved him very much. On the other hand, he saw his father as a rival for the affections of his mother.

How did Freud interpret Hans' phobia?

- Hans' rivalrous wishes concerning his father jeopardized his familial relations, risking the loss of his parents' love, and punishments.
- Accordingly, Hans displaced his prohibited hateful feelings for his father on to horses: as if he wished his father would fall down, like the horse he had seen fall.
- In this way, a "compromise formation" was achieved which allowed Hans to continue relations with his father (whom he could not avoid), at the cost of his inhibition about going anywhere near horses (which he could usually avoid).

Besides phobia, the two major categories of neurosis Freud systematically examines are *hysteria* and *obsessional neurosis*. We encountered hysteria in Anna O and Elizabeth von R, and shall look at it further in Chapter 2. In order to understand Freud's claims that neurotic symptoms are compromise formations involving substitute satisfactions for repressed id-wishes, let us look now at obsessional neurosis. The classical case of obsessional neurosis in Freud's *oeuvre* is that of "the Ratman", an educated young man who came to Freud in 1907 (see Chapter 3). The Ratman suffered from a host of disturbing thoughts and symptoms. He was plagued by the irrational fear that bad things might happen to his father (who was already dead), or that his lover might die or become terminally ill. He experienced compulsive aggressive impulses, such as the suicidal wish to cut his throat, or – contrastingly – equally compelling "protective" impulses, such as the need to put his cap, protectively, on his lover's head. Sometimes these opposed aggressive and protective wishes would alternate: he would actively undo some protective action (like removing a stone from the road where he knew his beloved's carriage would pass) only moments after he had undertaken it, or be plagued with doubts that he had performed such well-meaning acts. Finally, the Ratman became preoccupied with understanding every word anyone said to him, goaded (again) by an equally intrusive doubt whether he had succeeded in this endeavour (esp. RM: 187–91, 222–3).

How does Freud understand these obsessional symptoms? First of all, as with little Hans, Freud argues that what is at stake in the Ratman's neurosis is his own violent and aggressive wishes towards his father and his beloved, however much he initially resisted this interpretation. The Ratman's strange compulsions, Freud argues, represented "reaction formations" that functioned to protect his conscious self from confronting these infantile, anti-social wishes. Such wishes would present themselves to him as if from nowhere, in the form of dispassionate, "scientific" hypotheticals, isolated from all his other thoughts: as when people wonder about something like "what if . . . (say) it didn't rain tomorrow . . . ?" To cite the Ratman's own suicidal impulses when his beloved went away: "*what if* one were visited by the command to cut one's throat with a razor blade . . . ?" (RM: 187). What indeed! If one were psychologically visited by such masochistic commands, Freud proposes, they might well disturb one's conduct in various ways. As one tried to pray for the well-being of loved ones, one might find oneself repeatedly interrupted by these terrible "commands" (RM: 191–2, 241) – like the raven in Poe's poem who knocks so insistently upon the hero's chamber door. A similar fate might befall you as you tried to understand others' words, so like the Ratman you would momentarily lose concentration, and be troubled by the compulsive doubt that you had misunderstood.

Or consider the compulsive nature of the prohibitions from which obsessionals like the Ratman suffer. The obsessional who, like Lady Macbeth, cannot sleep unless she repeatedly washes her hands (or opens and re-shuts the bedroom door . . .) might well be performing a hygienic or necessary action. What is irrational is when she feels herself compelled to do it again and again, plagued by doubts that – although she secured the tap for the nth time only an instant before – the tap might nevertheless have come loose, so she must check it again. The only way obsessionals' compulsion to repeat their symptomatic activities can be comprehended, Freud contends, is if we see these actions as responding to a danger to the individual's psyche – witness Lady Macbeth's heightened anxiety as she frantically attends to her imagined "damned spot". The point to stress again is that the danger is an internal danger, since there was after all literally "no blood on Lady Macbeth's hands", however things stood for her metaphorically.

Freud's interpretation of obsessionals' symptoms as "compromise formations", then, at the very least, is striking and elegant. In what Freud calls the "tempo" of their compulsive repetitions, obsessionals play out the conflict between the person's prohibited, hateful wishes and the reaction formations against these (RM: 191, 238–41). But how does this account stand with Freud's formulation that symptoms are "substitutive gratifications"? Lady Macbeth hardly appears happy. It is the unhappiness of obsessionals such as the Ratman that brings them to analysis. In order to understand this Freudian idea, we need to emphasize the "substitutive" component in Freud's idea of "substitutive satisfaction". Since the direct expression of the obsessionals' hateful wishes is prohibited by the ego, these wishes adopt indirect or metaphoric forms. More than this, in cases like the Ratman, the ritual-like repetitions of the symptomatic defences against the prohibited wishes in particular start to resemble what they repress. Remember that unconscious id-wishes are freed by repression from any need to be tested against external reality, hence remaining subject exclusively to the pleasure principle. Remember also that for Freud the pleasure principle is at base a mindless, reflex-like principle whose demands compel the organism under its sway, until such time as it develops higher capabilities. The compulsive tenor of the protective rituals of obsessionals, Freud argues, reflects the compulsive character of the infantile impulses they are pitted against. Moreover, these symptoms, when successfully completed (as when, for instance, the Ratman was able to say his prayers so quickly that no evil thought could intrude), provide the individual with a satisfaction oddly reminiscent of the quiescence one achieves after sexual enjoyment – so they can now sleep, relax, or go on living as normal. As we might say, in the obsessionals' symptoms, the repression of (sexual or aggressive) enjoyment has, uncannily, given way to the eroticized enjoyment of repression.

Summary

- Far from a wilful obscurantism, Freud's metapsychology is based on the most advanced natural sciences of his day.
- Freud contends that the psyche operates according to the "pleasure principle" with the function of keeping excitation from external sources, or internal drives, as low as possible.
- Initially, the infant is wholly under sway of the pleasure principle, insured by its parents' love against the need to develop a sense of the external world, and temper its wishes in response to it. Instead, it hallucinates its own satisfactions, based on its first memories of satisfaction.
- This "Edenic" scenario is unsustainable. The external world imposes itself as everything the child cannot "dream up". The ego is the psychical agency that develops to mediate between the infant's libidinal demands and external reality, although in Freud's later work it also becomes its own love-object.
- Since the child has many, competing drives, many of which are aesthetically or morally prohibited in its community, it must renounce certain of these wishes. Repression is the device that answers to this need, by treating its own drives (falsely) as if they presented external threats, and fleeing them. The result is that these repressed drives repeat, seeking according to the pleasure principle to "return" to find means of satisfaction.
- Mental illness is that state which occurs when the individual's ego becomes unable to mediate the conflicting demands of its illicit wishes and the external social world. In psychosis, the ego sides with the wishes of the id, disavowing parts of reality that provoke unacceptable wishes within it, before reshaping its sense of the world in its "ego-centric" delusions. In neurosis, the ego sides with reality, at the price that its repressed wishes, nurtured by unconscious fantasies, return to trouble it in symptoms.
- Symptoms are "compromise formations" between the ego and the repressed drives, embodying forms of satisfaction of repressed

wishes that are sufficiently unlike the original, repressed wish to avoid provoking anxiety, and evade censorship by the ego.
- The compulsion to repeat these symptoms, particularly evident in obsessional rituals, reveals the infantile origin of the motives that underlie them, which are "regressively" prey to the pleasure principle.

two

Sexuality and its vicissitudes

Introduction: why sexuality?

If psychoanalysis had a dime for every time someone asked "why is sexuality so central to your metapsychology?", the "impossible profession" (Freud) might be as lucrative as many critics imply it is. Freud knew his 1905 *Three Essays on Sexuality* would provoke outrage. Attitudes towards sexuality were much more austere in the "Victorian" era than they now are, however much ink Victorians spilt upon it. Yet the spontaneous disgust Freud's hypotheses about sexuality provoke remains. There is something comforting and "commonsensical" about Jung's break with Freud, which turned centrally around this issue. Jung thought psychoanalysis should not accord primacy to the sexual drives. Why should sexuality be singled out, given the panoply of symptoms exhibited by the mentally ill (cf. ON: 79–81)? Others have raised different questions: does not Freud's focus on sexuality reflect his own fixations? Was not the "Oedipus complex" discovered in Freud's self-analysis, a circumstance Freud is otherwise dubious about? If Freud is the "father" of psychoanalysis, did he not bequeath to the movement of ideas he spawned many of his own neuroses?

In this chapter we shall examine Freud's controversial views on sexuality. Freud held on to these views until at least 1919, when he introduced the hypothesis of the death drive (Chapters 4 and 7). In this chapter we shall see that, whether we finally agree with them or not, Freud's views on sexuality are neither simplistic nor simply vulgar. Indeed, these views are arguably so challenging less because they cynically reduce everything spiritual to sexuality than because they show the many ways "a person's sexuality reaches up to the highest peaks of their spirituality", as Nietzsche once opined.

Evidences, clinical and metapsychological

However far-ranging Freud's metapsychology is, its clinical starting-point remains paramount. Psychoanalysis is always applied – incidentally its principal difference from philosophy. So when we ask "why sexuality?" concerning Freud's theory of the drives, we should not be surprised that the chief reasons Freud gives come from the free associations of analysands. The theory follows what this clinical basis of psychoanalysis brought to light. What the testimony of analysands attested, Freud reports, was that a key feature of the neuroses is disturbances in individuals' sexual functioning. Indeed, these observations led him to "this thesis: if the *vita sexualis* [sexual life] is normal, there can be no neurosis" (SN: 274).

The centrality Freud attributes to sexuality appears very early on, in his writings on female hysterics such as Anna O, Elizabeth von R and Dora (see Chapter 6). "If the psychical traumas from which the hysterical symptoms arose were pursued . . . by means of the treatment developed by Breuer and me", Freud later reflected on these cases, "experiences were eventually reached which belonged to the patient's childhood and related to his sexual life". These experiences invariably involved a traumatic component (PMH: 3–9). More than this, if these sexual experiences were not recalled by analysands, Freud claimed that it was impossible "either to elucidate . . . the way in which [their symptoms] were determined, or to prevent their recurrence" (SN: 273).

Principal among these symptoms were hysterical attacks, like Anna O's delirious absences (see Introduction). As meaningless as such "hysterics" seem, Freud argues, analysands' free associations show how they are intelligible as the "actings out" of unconscious fantasies staging the fulfilment of repressed sexual wishes. As Freud begins his "General Remarks on Hysterical Attacks", hysterical attacks are "nothing else but fantasies translated [or converted] into the motor sphere, projected onto motility, and portrayed in pantomime" (GRH: 229). One woman Freud introduces suffered attacks during which one hand would tear at her clothing, while the other would press her clothing against her side. Her associations revealed that, in this hysterical attack, she was acting out both parts of an unconscious fantasy wherein she struggled against a man trying violently to undress her. Another analysand suffered from attacks that would begin with being shaken by convulsive movements, including rubbing her thighs together. She would then get up, move into another room, sit down and begin reading, before responding to some imaginary remark. Her associations, Freud confides, revealed she was acting out in reverse her repressed fantasy of being approached by a gentleman who would proposition her as she sat reading on a park bench, then lead her away to make love.

On the basis of such clinical evidence, Freud hypothesized that the somatic (bodily) "conversion symptoms" of hysterics represent a kind of continuation of hysterics' sexuality by other means – in line with his definition of symptoms as substitute satisfactions in Chapter 1 (SN: 278).

KEY POINT *Stages in the formation of conversion symptoms (adapted from HPR: 232–3)*

1. Children's earliest instinctual satisfactions are "autoerotic", reflecting their initial "monadic" inability to distinguish between their own bodies and the external world (see Chapter 1).
2. Next, this autoerotic satisfaction becomes attached to one or several fantasies.
3. The autoerotic act is then renounced because of social prohibitions (which make its performance likely to lead to painful consequences), but the fantasies are repressed.
4. With a *Vorsagung* (Chapter 1), the repressed fantasies return, either unchanged or reshaped in response to the individual's changed environment.
5. The acting out of the symptom may then (through, for example, the rubbing together of the thighs) reinstate the original autoerotic satisfaction.

Freud's position allowed him to explain the heightened anxiety evident in hysterical attacks, with their disturbed breathing, sweating, tremors and so on. Hysterical attacks, Freud contends, are the indirect actings out of a sexual act. The sexual act has long been compared to a "minor epilepsy" in many cultures (GRH: 234). Just so:

> in further support of this view, I may point out that in normal copulation . . . the excitation expends itself, among other things, in accelerated breathing, palpitation, sweating, congestion, and so on. In the corresponding anxiety attacks of our

neurosis we have before us the dyspnoea, palpitations, etc. of copulation in an isolated and exaggerated form . . .

(AN: 111)

In time, Freud claimed that other forms of neurosis, such as Little Hans' and the Ratman's (see Chapter 1), confirmed his hypotheses concerning the role of sexuality in the neuroses. Yet Freud's claims about sexuality also draw on several other, non-clinical observations concerning the human condition.

On sexuality and reproduction

In response to widespread criticisms of his theory of sexuality, Freud repeatedly claimed the lineage of his theory of sexuality in Plato's celebrated account of *Eros* in the *Symposium*:

> as for the "stretching" of the concept of sexuality . . . anyone who looks down with contempt upon psychoanalysis . . . should remember how closely the enlarged sexuality of psychoanalysis coincides with the *Eros* of the divine Plato . . .
>
> (TE: 134)

In Plato's *Symposium*, the Priestess Diotima gives the culminating theoretical account of *Eros* – desire, which includes (but is not reducible to) sexual desire. *Eros*, Diotima claims, is that drive in each of us that strives towards immortality. For non-philosophers, this can be seen in how our sexual drive pushes us to reproduce – our children will outlive us, as will the species. The first of Freud's observations in defence of the special status he accords to our sexuality points, like Diotima, to the function of sexuality in the reproduction of the species. In Chapter 1, we saw how for Freud the ego brings the individual's drives to heel in the name of its individual adaptation to reality. Freud's Diotimaian question concerning sexuality is this: how can sexuality fit with the ego's individualistic ends, given that it is the one bodily drive that functions to reproduce the species? None of the other drives – hunger, thirst, respiration and so on – share this feature. For these reasons, Freud claims that our sexuality splits or divides us:

> The individual does carry on a two fold existence; one to serve his own purposes and the other as a link in the chain, which he serves involuntarily, an appendage to his germ plasm . . .

the mortal vehicle of a (possibly) immortal substance – like the inheritor of an entailed property.   (ON: 78; cf. IV: 125)

On the absence of a mating season

If the previous observation points to a feature of sexuality common to all higher animals, the second Freudian observation singles out human sexuality. Humans are the only creatures who do not have a mating season. People show every sign of wanting to cavort all year around, as if their sexuality were somehow decoupled or "cut" from the natural function of reproducing the species. The Christian author Saint Augustine, reflecting on exactly such "Freudian" points, concluded that human sexuality was surely divine punishment for Adam's sin in the garden, a truth underlined by how the male sexual organ is the one part of the body men cannot consciously control – notably including when they dream (see Chapter 3).

On the latency period

Freud observes in "Moses and Monotheism" and elsewhere that human beings have a singularly long "latency period" between birth and sexual maturity (MM: 77–9; TE: 176–7). No sooner have children learnt the difference between the sexes than they show every sign of wanting nothing to do with the opposite sex. (In Australia, young girls cite "boy's germs" as sufficient reason for their aversion, and boys vice versa.) Freud notes that neither hunger nor our other drives undergo any such latency – nor could they, if individuals are to survive. How does Freud understand this curious phenomenon? In "The Two Principles of Mental Functioning", Freud argues that it provides a further, good reason as to why sexuality, of all the drives, might be so closely caught up with the pleasure principle, and accordingly the unconscious (TP: 222–3). All the other drives must continually be tested against reality as the child becomes an adult. But sexuality – at least as long as we do not assume it appears all at once at puberty – remains throughout the latency period insulated from such reality testing:

> [W]hen . . . the process of finding an object begins [in the case of sexuality], it is soon interrupted by the long period of latency, which delays sexual development until puberty . . . [the result is] that the sexual instinct is held up in its psychical

development and remains for longer under the dominance of the pleasure principle, from which in many people it is never able to withdraw . . . (TP: 222)

At this point, though, we have reached the nub of the issue: for many people, Freud's presumption that "finding an object" begins before puberty will seem abhorrent at worse, and certainly in need of further argument.

The perversions, and what they reveal

Freud's *Three Essays on Sexuality* (TE) is his longest statement on sexuality. The *Three Essays* challenges two long-sanctified views about human sexuality:

- The idea that human sexual evolution is linear and unproblematic, tending by nature and necessity towards heterosexual reproductive activity.
- The idea that children have no sexuality until they reach puberty.

Kant, in his *Critique of Pure Reason*, introduced what has since been called *the transcendental argument*. Transcendental arguments have this form:

1. X is (where X is an observable phenomenon).
2. Y is the (only possible) precondition of X (this is the controversial premise).
3. Thus Y must be the case.

Freud's *Three Essays* present a kind of transcendental argument based on evidence taken from the psychoanalytic clinic. The "X" Freud sets out to explain is, first, the sexual perversions: sadism (where the agent enjoys hurting their partner), masochism (where they enjoy being hurt by them), fetishism (where they enjoy seeing or touching some particular part(s) of others' bodies, or even their shoes, clothes, etc.), voyeurism (where sexual enjoyment comes from seeing others), exhibitionism (where enjoyment arises from exposing oneself to others' gaze) and paedophilia.

Freud's concern is that the perversions, however people morally or aesthetically judge them, pose intriguing theoretical questions about human sexuality. How is it that some human beings can sexually desire animals, children, fetishes, or enjoy engaging in violent forms of sexual activity? And why, again, does (say) our desire to eat exhibit similar, strange aberrations? Freud argues that theoretical reflection upon the perversions forces us to concede "that we have been in the habit of regarding the connection between the sexual instinct and the [normal, heterosexual] sexual object as more intimate than in fact it is" (TE: 147–8). This is the founding claim of Freud's theory of sexuality. We might suppose that individuals' choice of a member of the opposite sex as their love-object is the most natural thing in the world. The problem for this view is that some people do enjoy forms of sexual activity in which the sexual object is not a member of the opposite sex, and the sexual aim evidently has little to do with reproduction. Just as human beings do not have a mating season, that is, the existence of perversions would seem to prove that our sexual drives are not as geared towards the natural ends of reproduction as we might suppose.

But could not someone say: "It is true that the perversions attest to some people's ability to desire abhorrent things. But isn't this why we call them 'perverts'? Why infer anything about normal sexuality on this basis?" Freud's response comes through his analysis of a much less morally or aesthetically contentious sexual phenomenon. When couples make love, they indulge in foreplay – however brief. For example, they kiss. And what is in a kiss? When people kiss they get sexual enjoyment by pressing together the mucous membranes of their mouths and tongues, parts of the body usually only serviceable for the "ego-instincts" of eating and drinking (TE: 156). Similarly, people typically enjoy merely seeing their partner naked, or being seen by them, as part of sexual foreplay. Sexuality also involves some playful component of aggression or the desire to subjugate the other to one's will and charms. Sexual encounters may not even culminate in intercourse at all, as President Clinton reminded the world.

Freud's point is that, with foreplay, normal sexuality is made up of components that also feature in the perversions, and which involve more than just the genitals. "No healthy person . . . can fail to make some addition that might be called perverse to the normal sexual activity" (TE: 158). The desire to see one's partner naked, or to stroke his hair, for example, is perfectly normal, but will become a perversion if it becomes the principal aim of a person's sexual activity, overriding all shame, and providing more compelling enjoyment than intercourse itself. There is thus no absolute difference between perverse and "healthy" sexuality, Freud observes, as if perverts were wholly inhuman monsters. What differentiates all but the most aberrant forms of perversion (e.g. paedophilia or fetishism, where the sexual object is different) is instead that in the perversions, sexual actions that usually feature as preliminaries to genital intercourse "usurp" its place altogether:

> [P]erversions are sexual activities which either (a) extend . . . beyond the regions of the body that are designed for sexual union or (b) linger over the intermediate relations to the sexual object which should normally be traversed rapidly towards the final aim . . . (TE: 157)

The perversions, Freud contends, are rightly thought of as "the negative" of the neuroses that bedevil more normal subjects (TE: 165). Many of the anatomical "extensions" involved in perverse sexual activities, Freud means – like the "eroticization" of activities (such as seeing, touching or defecation) and organs (such as the anus, hair and so on) usually considered asexual – also feature in the conversion symptoms of hysterics, and the compulsive symptoms of obsessionals. Recall how, in one of Freud's examples above, the hysterical attack featured the autoerotic rubbing together of the girl's thighs. Equally, recall how in obsessionals' symptoms, the subject's very defences against their illicit wishes become the source of quasi-sexual enjoyment (Chapter 1) – just as in masochism, subjects perversely enjoy being punished by their partner, including the paraphernalia of handcuffs, whips, chains, blindfolds and so on.

So, thinking again of Freud's transcendental argument, given that the "X" Freud reflects upon in the *Three Essays* is sexual foreplay and the perversions, what does Freud conclude that about the nature of sexuality to explain them?

KEY POINT *Three principles of Freud's theory of sexuality*

1. Human sexuality is not unproblematically calibrated to heterosexual reproduction. If heterosexuality is the ideal most fully in accord with the "reality principle", the achievement of this ideal can in no case be taken for granted: "We are . . . warned to loosen the bond that exists in our theories between instinct and object. It seems probable that the sexual instinct is in the first instance independent of its object; nor is its origin likely to be the object's attraction . . ." (TE: 147–8).

2. Human sexuality is a "complex" phenomenon, in that it comprises more than one "component drive". These include the drives to see, touch and

to master, all of which feature in foreplay, and become dominant in the perversions. Nor should we discount the preponderant role played by fantasy (and thus the imagination) in sexuality.

3. On the basis of 1 and 2 Freud maintains that human beings are animals who, uniquely, have to be taught what, whom and how to desire. Our many component drives must be "soldered" together (TE: 148); and our sexuality as a whole must be directed, through nurture, to its final object(s).

4. What mental illness attests is that the component drives that are thus united can also always fall back apart into these separate components (TE: 162), or – depending on the individual's upbringing – these components may never achieve subordination to the normal aim of heterosexual coupling.

The drives (versus the instincts) and their vicissitudes

Freud's 1915 essay "The Drives (*Triebe*) and Their Vicissitudes" is a further, decisive contribution to Freud's theory of sexuality. It is premised on what the *Three Essays* have argued:

> [T]his much can be said for the sexual drives: they are numerous, emanate from a great variety of organic sources, act in the first instance independently of one another, and only achieve a more or less complete synthesis at a later stage . . .
>
> (IV: 125–6)

The problem is that if the drives are in this way numerous, and not automatically set in their ways, psychoanalysis will need a precise set of terms to track their different "vicissitudes", and how it is that they do not always make it to "more or less complete synthesis". To generate such a set of terms is the first task that "The Drives and Their Vicissitudes" sets itself.

KEY POINT *Four "Terms Which Are Used In Reference to the Concept of a Drive . . ." (IV: 122–3)*

1. *The source*: the source of a drive is the organ or part of the body whose "demands for work" are represented in the psyche by the *Triebe*.
2. *The pressure*: the "motor factor" of a drive is "the amount of force of the measure of the demand for work it represents". All drives exert a "demand for work" on the individual's psyche.

3. *The aim*: the aim of a drive is in all cases, as per the pleasure principle, satisfaction: "removing the state of stimulation in the source of a drive".
4. *The object*: the object of a drive is "that in regard to which and through which [the drive] can achieve its aim". As the *Three Essays* established regarding the perversions, this is the most variable component of human beings' drives. These drives "are not originally connected" with their object(s): "they become assigned to it" (IV: 123). Famously, Freud calls the process whereby a drive becomes strongly attached to one object "fixation" (see R: 148 and below). Objects may:

- be parts of the individual's own body, or others', or animals', or inanimate things;
- be changed as the individual develops;
- satisfy a "confluence" of drives (as for example, the mouth for eating and kissing).

With this vocabulary to describe the different "vicissitudes" of the drives in place, "Drives and Their Vicissitudes" centrally examines two such vicissitudes. Freud's hope is that tracking these vicissitudes will go further towards explaining how the sexual perversions and symptoms of neurotics are possible. The first "vicissitude" examined at length is the reversal of a drive into its opposite. A drive with an active aim may turn into one whose aim is passive, says Freud. For example, the desire to master one's beloved can turn into the desire, passively, to be mastered by her. Interestingly, Freud uses grammatical language to describe this process: in the case of masochism, Freud says, the verb involved ("to master") has changed from the active voice to the passive voice. We shall see in Chapter 5 what Lacan makes of such Freudian "metaphorics". The second vicissitude Freud examines closely in the essay is the turning of a drive, so its object becomes the individual's own self. Masochism, Freud says in this paper, is sadism with its object changed (but see EPM for a later, contrasting, account). The drive to do violence now has as its object the individual's own body, rather than that of its sexual partner. Equally, in exhibitionism the scopic drive to see the other becomes the drive to be seen by them. These transformations, then, are necessarily games "only two (or more) people can play". The exhibitionist needs an other to play the role he would play (that of the active subject) in voyeurism. The masochist needs his other not to inflict pain upon, but to inflict pain upon him.

Freud's account of these transformations to which drives' aims and objects are subject in "Drives and Their Vicissitudes" arguably raises as many questions as it settles. If the reversal of a drive's aim, or the changing of its object, is being adduced as an explanation of the possibility of perversions and neurotic symptoms, we wonder in particular what nature the drives themselves must have, such that they can be so protean or pliable. One thing Freud's essay does underline in this connection is the following point, which is also decisive for the way Freud thinks to bring together his biological metapsychology with his clinical, interpretive work (see Chapter 3). The drives are not the same thing as natural instincts, as Strachey's deceptive translation of *Triebe* as "instincts" conceals. Rather, says Freud:

> a *Trieb* appears to us as a concept on the frontier between the mental and the somatic, as the psychical representative (*Vorstellungen*) of the stimuli originating from within the organism and reaching the mind, as a measure of the demand made upon the mind for work in consequence of its connection with the body. (IV: 121–2)

Just as human beings have no mating season, and their drives are not naturally bound to their objects, so Freud maintains that these drives too are less wholly bodily than uneasily situated at the "frontier" of the mental and the physical, the linguistic and the somatic. Lacan, later, takes up this thought as decisive for understanding psychoanalysis. He suggests that, if the drives are subject to such strange vicissitudes as Freud discloses, the only possible explanation for this must be that these vicissitudes reflect the effects of the drives' somatic "demand for work" having been caught up in the "unnatural" laws of language to which the drives' *Vorstellungen* become subject. However idle Freud's "grammatical" description of the reversal of a drive into its opposite might seem, that is (cf. SC: ch. 3), it is in this language that the truth of the unconscious is revealed. We shall return to these matters in Chapters 3, 4 and 5.

The riddle of the Sphinx – what is infantile sexuality?

So for Freud, the sexual drives are multiple, "decoupled" from any natural object, and subject to the most uncanny vicissitudes, located as they are on the frontier between the mental and the somatic. Freud's second controversial claim in the *Three Essays* is his argument that children have a sexual life. There are moral and psychological reasons why this truth has been denied, Freud argues, although he suggests that parents and carers have long been familiar with it. The moral reasons concern societies' understandable, but Freud thinks overprotective, investment in the idea of children's moral and sexual innocence (cf. SEC). The psychological reason – in itself interesting given Freud's accounts of repression and the latency period – is the phenomenon of *infantile amnesia* (TE: 174–6). Despite learning one or several foreign languages in their first years, people typically don't remember many of their own experiences from before their fifth or sixth years.

So what does Freud say concerning the imputed *vita sexualis* of infants? As we saw in Chapter 1, according to Freud the human child from very early on "pleases itself" by recalling the "mnemic images" of earlier gratifications. Its first sexual satisfactions are similarly auto-erotic, Freud claims, on the model of an activity like thumb-sucking. Using the terms of "Drives and Their Vicissitudes", the sources of such enjoyments (in this case, the mouth) and their objects (in this case, the thumb) both belong to the child's own body. Now, nobody denies that many infants do suck their thumbs. But why does Freud argue that such activity is "sexual" and, indeed, compare it with the propensity of young children to masturbate – an activity whose sexual nature seems less controversial? Doesn't Freud collapse the distinction between sexuality and non-sexual activities in an unacceptable way?

In order to understand Freud's answer, let us consider the case of thumb-sucking in more detail. The source of the satisfaction is the mucous membrane of the mouth. This part of the body is typically used by the child for eating (and for wailing its discontents). Yet when the child sucks its thumb, these egoistic functions of the mouth are evidently not in play. The child is using its mouth, and something (its thumb) is entering and leaving it, like food when it eats. But this entry and eviction of the object is repeated without any nourishment occurring. If we accept that the psyche is governed by the pleasure principle, Freud reasons, this repeated act must aim at some satisfaction. But this satisfaction must be non-functional and, Freud reasons – in line with his wider theory of infantile psychology – be "determined by a search for some pleasure which has already been experienced and is now remembered" (TE: 181): namely, its nourishment at the mother's breast. The child's evident need to repeat the satisfaction also indicates that a very strange type of sensation must be in play: "a peculiar feeling of tension, possessing . . . the character of unpleasure . . . a sensation of itching and stimulation, which is centrally conditioned and projected onto the erotogenic zones . . ." (TE: 184). Other examples Freud cites of this "unpleasurable pleasure" (or, in French, *jouissance*) include the evident delight children take in riding on swings or on trains, together with the sensations produced by the child's holding in its faeces, and playing with its genitals. The sensual thumb-sucking involves a "complete absorption" of the child's attention "and leads either to sleep or even to a motor reaction in the nature of an orgasm" (TE: 180). Freud hypothesizes that it is the infantile precursor of the later enjoyment adults will find in genital sexual activity. "No one who has seen a baby sinking back from the breast and falling asleep with flushed cheeks and a blissful smile", Freud comments, "can escape the reflection that this picture persists as a prototype of the expression of sexual satisfaction in later life" (TE: 182).

So Freud's contention is not the implausible one, that all children's behaviours are sexual. Infantile sexuality extends only to those activities that a child repeats, absorbed, having sated its functional needs. Moreover, Freud comments that nature gives infants "safe provision" to ensure that there are what he calls "predestined erotogenic zones" (TE: 183, 184). Infants' sexual activities initially "attach themselves to . . . the functions serving the purposes of self-preservation and seem not to become independent until later", Freud contends (*ibid.*: 182). In particular, those parts of the body serving these functions, wherein things enter it (the mouth, as in nourishment) and exit it (the genitals, as in urination and the anus, as in excretion) are subject to what Freud calls "eroticization". In addition to these autoerotic zones, Freud adds, infants in the first years of life evince two component drives concerning objects external to their own body: a scopophilic drive to actively see certain objects (or, passively, to be seen by them) and a sadistic drive to destroy and control things. The multiplicity of infantile erotogenic zones and drives, Freud contends, represent the "pre-historical" antecedents of later tendencies subjects exhibit towards perversions or neurotic symptoms:

> In [hysteria for instance] repression affects most of all the actual genital zones and these transmit their susceptibility to stimulation to other erotogenic zones (normally neglected in adult life) which then behave exactly like genitals.
> (TE: 183)

Think, for instance, of Anna O's symptoms, which affected her speech, a paralysis in her right side, or we could also cite Elizabeth von R's legs, which "joined in the conversation", experiencing sharp pain, as Elizabeth's treatment continued (CH: 148). The infant, Freud famously says, has an innate "aptitude" for becoming "polymorphously perverse", especially if the child is subject prematurely to seduction by an adult or older child (TE: 191).

As we have said, the founding claim of Freud's theory of sexuality is that human beings are creatures who need to learn how to desire. Natural bodily changes, Freud details, map out an itinerary of various libidinal "stages" children typically go through, in which one or other autoerotic and component drives will attain pre-eminence. However, Freud maintains that the way a child is nurtured is decisively important in how it proceeds through these organically conditioned stages. The principal means by which infants' multiple sexual drives are brought to heel, Freud maintains, is through the force of social law. "Shame, disgust and morality" (TE: 191) are brought by parents and carers to bear upon the child to force him to renounce the earliest aims, objects and sources of his drives (*ibid.*: 225–8). Now he is a "big boy like Daddy", the child will be served notice, "you can't do *that*". Moreover, "it is dirty . . . wicked . . .", "if you persist, then there will be consequences . . .".

In the *Three Essays*, Freud famously maintains that infants pass through three stages of sexual development before the latency period and, with puberty, sexual maturity (see Table 2.1). Each is named after the source predominant in it: the oral, anal and phallic stages. Each, though, is also profoundly unsatisfactory for the infant, leaving them suspended in what Freud famously calls "ambivalence" towards their objects: since to eat or master an object tends to destroy it; and in the phallic or "Oedipal" phase, as we saw with Little Hans, the child wrestles with "mixed feelings" for his parents.

Freud's stress on the importance of nurture in each of these stages is tied to his diagnostic concerns, and his central clinical claim that the origins of neurotic disorders can always be traced back, by free associations, to traumas affecting infantile sexual life. The final synthesis of the drives with a heterosexual love-object may always misfire, neurotics' symptoms and perverts' activities attest. And why might things go wrong in these ways, given Freud's metapsychology? Recall that in Freud's biological account of the mind, pain results from the overstimulation of the individual's nervous system. In the same way, Freud argues that individuals' sexual development will be upset if a particular, infantile activity becomes overstimulated (ISA: 89), perhaps due to premature seduction, but also if they unwittingly witness the sexual activity of parents, as in the case of the Wolfman (see Chapter 3). What occurs in such traumatic events, Freud contends, is that the drives predominant at that point of the infant's development will become

Table 2.1 The phases of infantile sexual development

Phase	Oral (until 2–3 years old)	Anal/sadistic ("the terrible twos")	Phallic/Oedipal phase (3–6 years)	Latency period	Adult/genital
Source	Mouth	Anus/child's motor capacities	Penis/clitoris		
Aim	Organ satisfaction	Organ satisfaction/mastery of environment	Organ satisfaction		Reproduction
Non-sexual function attached to	Nutrition	Defecation	Urination ("micturition")		
Object	Mouth/mother's breast	Anus, faeces/other(s)	An other		An other
Gender of object	On sense of distinctions self/object, male/female	Bisexual	Female (the mother)		The opposite sex (or in homosexuality, one's own)
Activity/ies	Thumb sucking, sucking of nipple or bottle	• Holding in faeces • Cruelty to others • Exhibitionism ("look at this, Mummy . . .")	• Masturbation • Bed-wetting		Intercourse
Attitude towards objects	Ambivalence (to eat/drink object is to destroy it)	Ambivalence (to master object is to destroy object)	Identification with parent of one sex; desire for the mother; ambivalence towards father		

Table 2.2 The sexual theories of children

Phase	Oral	Anal/sadistic	Phallic/Oedipal
Theories of birth/marriage	Not applicable (child cannot yet speak)	Babies are produced by kissing, or eating certain objects; by defecation; by urinating in front of each other; by urinating in the other's toilet, or by violently overpowering one's partner	Children are produced by the girl exchanging her penis/being castrated, in exchange for a child
Categories of (boy) child's thinking	Not applicable	Activity versus passivity (i.e. no stable sense of male/female sexual difference)	Having a penis (being male) versus being castrated (being female)

fixated. Although the child may later repress them, it will nevertheless be continually subject to "regressing" back to these unmastered forms of infantile sexuality, should it later undergo some *Vorsagung* and fall ill (Chapter 1).

One of the more endearing features of Freud's essays on infantile sexuality is his stress on how infants' development is both a practical and a theoretical process (see Table 2.2). Freud's child does not simply passively undergo things (STC; IGO; TI). It is always trying to understand the world into which it has been thrown, drawing on its limited scope of memories and capabilities. Freud's infant, we might say, is a spontaneous scientist, theorist, or even philosopher (see Chapter 4). The motives children have for their "research projects" are deeply egotistical. The most important question for infants, which Freud ironically calls "the riddle of the Sphinx" (TE: 194–5), is "where do babies come from?" Behind these dispassionate enquiries, Freud argues, is the anxiety that another child might appear, and compete with their privileged place in the parents' affections (STC: 212–19). The principal problem for infants pursuing these researches is that they typically have no knowledge either of semen or of intercourse. A further problem facing young boys, Freud argues on the basis of cases such as Little

Hans, is that until they discover otherwise, males narcissistically assume that girls have a penis just as they do. Even when they are confronted with the fact that girls, and their mother, lack this special appendage, young boys exhibit a marked tendency to disavow such anatomical lack (*ibid.*: 215–19). The result is that the content of these infantile sexual theories can appear very humorous to us "enlightened" adults.

The little boy (of Oedipus, madonnas and whores)

To clarify Freud's understanding of infantile sexuality, let us focus here on Freud's understanding of the little boy, leaving his career-long hesitations about femininity to Chapter 6. For children of both sexes, Freud argues, the most important phase in their libidinal development is the phallic or Oedipal phase (see Table 2.1) between the child's fourth and sixth year. Freud's (in)famous idea is that the fate that befell Oedipus in Sophocles' *Oedipus Tyrannis* (Oedipus unwittingly killed his father and slept with his mother) expresses all (male) children's erotic wishes at this stage of their libidinal development. For Freud, the central issue deciding the boy's subsequent mental health and sexual development is how the child resolves his "Oedipus complex" of amorous wishes towards his mother, and aggressive envy of his father. Its adequate resolution sees the child stabilize his own gender identification (for the boy, with his father) and, via the incest taboo which the dissolution of the complex sets in psychological place, also his "object-choice" (EI: 31–8; DO; AC). The result is that when the latency period ends at puberty, the boy will be ready to desire women of his own generation, and not of his own family. One Freudian definition of neurotics, by contrast, is that they are those subjects who have incompletely resolved their Oedipus complex, and so remain prone to sexual dysfunctions with women, and problems with "authority", in whose prerogatives they repetitively see the "imago" of the feared and envied father.

KEY POINT *Freud's account of the (male) Oedipus complex and its resolution (esp. DO)*

- In this phase of his sexual development, the primary source of the little boy's sexual enjoyment is his penis.
- The child normally has as yet no clear sense of what intercourse is. The aim of his sexual activities is bed-wetting and masturbation.

- The little boy's primary fear at this stage – based upon his own memories of weaning and defecation, if not on the warnings of his elders – is losing the special organ involved in these activities.

The active and passive Oedipus complexes

The "complex" of conflicting wishes in the boy's Oedipus complex typically contains both active and passive wishes, Freud argues.

- The active Oedipus complex is best known. The boy, identifying rival-rously with his father, takes his mother as his sexual object, with the active aim of "loving" her in his father's place. Little Hans, for instance, at one stage wished he might sleep in his mother's bed like Daddy – without having any idea about intercourse.
- The passive Oedipus complex is less well known. For Freud the boy's sexual identity and object-choice are not yet stabilized – this will only occur with the *resolution* of the Oedipus complex. The bisexuality of the earlier anal phase (see Table 2.1) is carried into this phase in the passive wish to be loved by the father.

The resolution of the Oedipus complex

In both the active and passive Oedipus complexes, the achievement of the boy's sexual aim necessitates his acceptance of his possible castration:

- If he pursues his active aim to replace his father, he faces the prospect of provoking his fathers (imagined) reprisals, including losing "it".
- If he pursues the passive aim, because to be loved by the father will involve taking on a passive position, a comparable blow will be struck to the child's narcissism.

Faced with this unacceptable double bind – "damned if you do, damned if you don't" – the little boy gives up his Oedipal designs.

With the resolution of the Oedipus complex, the boy identifies with his father, who until this point had been his rival. Importantly (see Chapter 1 and Chapter 7), it is this identification that forms the basis of his superego (see Chapter 1):

> The authority of the father or the parents is introjected into the ego, and there it forms the nucleus of the superego, which takes over the severity of the father and perpetuates the prohibition against incest, and so ensures the ego from the return of libidinal object-cathexes [towards the mother or sister(s)].
> (DO: 176–7)

Secondly, in taking on this prohibition, the boy's sexual wishes concerning the mother are repressed. The aim of these wishes towards her will instead now be inhibited (another vicissitude of the drives), so the boy's conscious feelings towards his mother (and sisters) from this point on will be solely affectionate, however things stand in the unconscious. In the terms of Freud's essay, "On the Universal Tendency to Debasement in the Sphere of Love", the sexual and affectionate (or "anaclitic") "currents" of the post-Oedipal boy's feelings towards his mother are separated when the Oedipus complex is resolved (UTD: 180–83). In the short term – in what stands as Freud's explanation of the otherwise puzzling latency period – the boy's penis is "de-cathected" or de-eroticized, and his Oedipal wishes are repressed. Yet when the boy goes through puberty, his object-choice will also have changed: from wishing to love his mother, he will instead be driven to choose a substitute for this first "lost object" (e.g. Bion 1967: 169–70). Typically, this might be someone who resembles her in some way – her hair colour, way of speaking or acting, and so on. However, Freud's "Universal Tendency to Debasement in the Sphere of Love" makes it clear that, if the man is to desire a woman sexually, she should absolutely not too closely evoke his first love-object (UTD: 185–7). In this remarkable essay and its precursor, "A Special Type of Object-Choice Made By Men", Freud is particularly interested in a "special type of object-choice" many men make of lovers whom they can neither respect nor affectionately love. Freud's analysis starts from a common enough symptom: that of a male's impotence with his regular sexual partner. This sexual inhibition looks like a simple case of his losing interest in her, or "wanting to sow his wild oats". Freud, however, argues that what is actually at stake in such male impotence is not that the man has fallen out of love with his partner. What has instead occurred is that, with the "routinization" of the love relationship, the man's partner has come too closely to evoke the "mnemic images" of his mother. Far from loving his partner too little, he loves her too much: so much that her presence evokes his long-repressed incestuous wishes. The result, evident in the boy's inhibitions, is that he now can no longer approach his beloved sexually without the prospect taking on an incestuous colour, and attracting all the repulsion the original prohibition of incest commands.

For this reason, Freud laments, "where [such men] love they do not desire, and where they desire they cannot love" (UTD: 187). In order to re-experience sexual desire for a woman without evoking such repressed incestuous wishes, they are compelled to choose a "debased" partner – someone whom they feel to be intellectually, morally or culturally beneath them. Only if "this condition of debasement is fulfilled, [can] sensuality . . . be freely expressed, and important sexual capacities and a high degree of pleasure can develop" (UTD: 187).

Summary

- In contrast to all previous philosophers excepting Plato and Nietzsche, Freud accords decisive psychological importance to sexuality principally because of the clinical testimony of hysterics. Their free associations attested to their symptoms' origins in traumatic childhood events in which conflicting sexual wishes were evoked, and that hysterical attacks are symptomatic "actings out" of illicit sexual wishes.
- For Freud, sexuality is so psychologically powerful (and potentially disturbing) because it is the one drive that binds individuals to the species, beyond the "ego instincts" of hunger, thirst or respiration.
- Yet individuals' sexual development towards the final aim of reproducing the species is a fraught process. The infant naturally develops multiple autoerotic and "component drives", including the drives to devour, to master and to see. These drives are neither innately coordinated nor all initially geared towards a member of the opposite sex.
- Infants must be taught how to desire, through their relations with their first others (parents, siblings, carers). This is a process in which the drives undergo multiple vicissitudes (such as repression, drives' turning around upon the subject's own body, aim-inhibition, reaction formation and so on) that can "fixate" perverse forms of sexual behaviour and "object choices", and neurotic symptoms.
- The decisive moment in infants' "libidinal education" is the "Oedipus complex", in which the male child (aged 4–6) develops aggressive feelings towards the father, charged by its wish to monopolize the mother's affections.
- This complex of sexual and aggressive wishes is dissolved when the boy realizes that, if he persists in rivalry with his father, he risks punishment, including imagined castration.

- The "castration complex" propels the male child into identifying with his father, and choosing female sexual object(s). Typically, the women he will desire will be substitutes for the mother, of his own generation. However, they must never become so similar to her in his mind that his repressed Oedipal wishes are evoked, in which case he may experience inhibition with her, and then need to seek out "debased" sexual objects (prostitutes, pornography and so on).

three

To slip, perchance to dream: Freud on the unconscious

Remembering Signorelli

If dreams are "the royal road to the unconscious", Freud did not stumble upon this road straight away. His discovery of the unconscious came via another route: the unlooked-for byway of the talking cure. As Freud puts it in "The Question of Lay Analysis", psychoanalysis seemed to stumble upon a modern confirmation of ancient beliefs in the magic power of words to effect changes in the real world (QLA: 187). To understand this chance discovery, Freud turned to the mechanistic biology pre-eminent in the culture of his time (Chapter 1) and his theory of the drives (Chapter 2). Yet the primary evidences upon which Freud based his theoretical conclusions remained linguistic: the spoken clinical testimony of analysands. When Freud asked his analysands to free-associate, phenomena emerged that seemed to point him away from the solely natural-scientific approach he desired. Instead, they recommended a primarily interpretive theory of the psyche (see Chapter 8). Analysands would recount their dreams, as if these were somehow connected to their malaises. Moreover, Freud's analyses of neurotics' symptoms pointed towards the specific importance of language in shaping neurotics' symptoms, as well as their cure. We glimpsed this in Chapter 1, when we considered the strange symptom of the psychotic who felt her deceptive boyfriend had "twisted her eyes", or the metaphorical "blood on Lady Macbeth's hands". The point can be illustrated further by returning to the Ratman case, and considering what might be in this name Freud bestowed upon him.

KEY POINT *Why did Freud call the "Ratman" the "Ratman"?*
(Rat = Ratte = Spielratte*)*

As we saw in Chapter 1, the "Ratman" suffered from an obsessional neurosis manifested in compulsive symptoms. Why did Freud dub him the "Ratman"? Freud's rationale comes from the young man's "great compulsive fear" (RM: 165):

- This fear hailed from a story he had been told by a captain, while serving in the army. This captain, who "took pleasure in cruelty" (RM: 166), recounted an oriental punishment whose culmination was rats boring into the criminal's anus.

This story is shocking enough. But its immediate effect on the Ratman was very peculiar:

- The cruel captain advised him that he was in debt to "Lieutenant A" for a small postal fee. Although our young man knew that this was not truly so, he immediately felt compelled to pay Lieutenant A anyway, lest the rat punishment happen to him.

How does Freud explain this bizarre symptom?

- The rat story provoked the young man's unresolved Oedipal ambivalence towards his dead father (coupling rivalry towards him with anal eroticism, characteristic of the "passive" Oedipal complex (Chapter 2)).
- The cruel officer recalled his father to the Ratman (his second association to the rat story was that the punishment should happen to his father), who had cruelly prohibited the young boy's infantile sexual activities (principally, his masturbation).
- His father, who like the Ratman had been in the army, had once racked up a debt ("*Ratte*") in a game called "*Spielratte*" (gambling debt); and our young man also suspected that his father had acquired syphilis (through sexual misdemeanours) during his time in the military.

Freud thus contends that in his unconscious the young man "inaugurated his own rat currency" (rat = *Ratte* = *Spielratte*) around which his symptoms turned. In reaction against the repressed wishes provoked by the cruel captain's rat story, the Ratman identified with his dead father, taking on absurdly a proxy of his father's *Spielratte* debt (*Ratte*) as reparation for his own criminal impulses ("you will be a great man or a great criminal", his father had once opined) (RM: 205), lest the anal rat punishment happen to him.

How was Freud to account for such phenomena, with their apparently linguistic character? Given Freud's metapsychological apparatus, already discussed, the answer might seem clear enough. Consider, for example, another of the evidences Freud encountered in the clinic, the famous "Freudian slips" or "parapraxes" ("practices beside themselves"), like that of the man described in *The Psychopathology of Everyday Life* who says "I hereby declare this meeting *closed*" when his conscious, professional role was to *open* it (PEL: 59). Here, as in neurotics' compromise formations, the man's illicit wish to be done with the whole affair has put egg on his ego's face. Yet this explanation defers the deeper question, of how such an illicit wish could trouble this subject's speech at all. According to long-standing philosophical and cultural precedents, words are "higher things" – the bearers of intellect, soul and spirituality. Yet the drives Freud associates with the unconscious are anything but spiritual, when they are not evil. As we commented in the Introduction, in the modern culture Freud inherited, these older dichotomies (body–mind/spirit) were reflected in the disciplinary division between the natural sciences and the interpretive human sciences. The symptomatic challenge Freud's clinical discoveries posed to these inherited oppositions emerges further when we examine another famous case from *The Psychopathology of Everyday Life*: Freud's own "chance" forgetting of a proper name on a train ride to Herzogovina. While on this journey in 1898, Freud forgot the name of a painter who painted frescoes of "The Four Last Things". Although the correct name was on the "tip of his tongue", Freud could recall only the names *Botticelli* and *Boltraffio*. What did Freud's free associations on this matter reveal?

KEY POINT *Why did Freud forget "Signorelli"? (PEL: 1–7)*

- Freud had been talking to his companion about the customs of the Turks living in *Bosnia* and *Herzogovina*. Freud was (favourably) struck by the confidence the locals placed in their physicians, even when the doctor was forced to convey the very worst: *"Herr* [sir], what is there to be said? If he could have been saved, I know you would have saved him . . ."
- This thought about death was connected in Freud's mind with another thought that Freud tells us that he, consciously, did not want to pursue: the great importance the Turks place on sexual health, so one had said to a colleague: *"Herr,* you must know that if *that* comes to an end then life is of no value."
- This thought reminded Freud of the news he had heard in Trafoi about a patient of his who had committed suicide because of a sexual disorder.

So, Freud argues, his forgetting of Signorelli was not senseless, but revealed the activity of his unconscious. The final motive concerned this last, dead patient and sexuality. Yet, as in a symptom, this motive was not all that was

---

repressed – what was lost to his consciousness was the name of a painter, albeit one who painted a fresco about such "last things". Why?

- The vital thing is that the name "Signorelli" was repressed because it had become "placed" in an "associative" linguistic "chain" with this repressed thought. It concerned the syllables in the word "Signorelli", in particular *"Signor"*, the Spanish equivalent of *"Herr"* ("Mister" or "Sir"). In Freud's associations, this *"Signor"* evoked the sayings of the local patients: "Herr, you must know . . ." which so troubled him, since they recalled the suicide of his patient. Because "Signorelli" was thus so closely linked to the repressed, Freud says that it had been "drawn down" into the unconscious and forgotten.
- Yet the repressed returned in substitutive linguistic forms. The *"Herr"* invoked in *"Signor*-elli" was associated with *"Her*-zogovina", and thus *Bosnia*. Hence the two names that Freud could recall shared the first syllable "Bo-" with "Bosnia": *"Bo*-tticelli" and *"Bo*-ltraffio". The first name, "Bottic-elli", shares the *"-elli"* suffix with the forgotten "Signor-elli". The second, "Bol-*traffio*", evoked *"Trafoi"*, in turn indirectly connected in Freud's mind with the repressed thought, because this was where he heard the bad news about his dead patient.

Hence, pictorially:

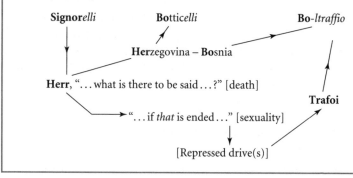

Freud's topographical account of the psyche

Freud's account of the vicissitudes of the drives allows him to explain how many symptoms (for example, obsessionals' compulsions) are the indirect expressions of repressed drives. Yet none of these vicissitudes (reversal of aim, turning around of object upon the ego, repression, aim-inhibition and so on) can help us with this case of Freud's forgetting of "Signorelli". For what Freud's analysis of this case supposes is that people's repressed sexual or aggressive drives are "caught up" in the linguistic formulations of their memories and self-understandings. When these drives are formed, Freud's analysis suggests, they become "associated" with certain words, such as "*Trafoi*" or "*Herr, if that is ended . . .*". These word-representatives of the drive(s), in turn, have different kinds of relations in the person's mind with other words (e.g. "*Herzogovina*", "*Boltraffio*" and so on). Some of these relations are rational, but others are less clearly so: like relations based on sound ("*Herr*" and "Her-", "Boltraffio" and "Trafoi"); or on meanings across different languages ("*Signor*" and "*Herr*"); or the common place these words have in otherwise unrelated, but personally significant, sentences ("*Herr*" in both ". . . what is to be said . . ." and ". . . if *that* is ended"). The key to Freud's analysis is that – in what he calls *secondary repression* (as opposed to the "primal repression" of the illicit sexual and aggressive wishes themselves) – many of these associated ideas, like the innocent name "Signorelli", are accordingly repressed by the individual. They become guilty by association. In our example, only "Botticelli" and "Boltraffio" were sufficiently distant from the repressed chain of words that they could reach Freud's conscious mind in place of the forgotten "Signorelli".

In Chapter 7 of *The Interpretation of Dreams*, reflecting on these types of analytic phenomena, Freud develops a "topographical" account of the psyche, different from the biologically based account of the psyche we have examined in Chapters 1 and 2. Drawing on ideas first developed in correspondence with his friend Fliess, Freud argues that the psyche is a kind of "mnemic" (remembering) apparatus. This apparatus has two functions. The first function, associated with "the system perception-consciousness", is the ability to perceive new things in the changing external world. This function is connected with the "access to motility": the individual's ability to fight, flee, or pursue what it perceives. The second function, equally crucial to the operation of the reality principle and the individual's maturation, is to record in memory significant aspects of the external world so that the ego might avoid painful and experience pleasurable things in future (Chapter 1). There are a host of things a person at any one time will be able to remember by simply redirecting their conscious attention: for example, what they had for breakfast, their pet's name, job, stock prices and so on. Freud calls these things *preconscious* (he abbreviates this to Pcs). They are generally "filed" in ways we recognize as rational: according to the rules of logic and of the linguistic community we live in, or – in the case of experiences – according to rational considerations such as when and with whom we experienced them.

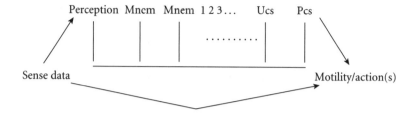

Figure 3.1 Freud's topographical model of the psyche (ID: 537)

How then does the unconscious enter Freud's "topographical" model of the psyche? Freud's claim is that everything we experience simultaneously leaves a variety of "records" or "*Mnems*" in the psyche:

> The first of these *Mnem.* systems will naturally contain the record of association in respect of *simultaneity in time*; while the same perceptual material will be arranged in later systems in respect to other kinds of coincidence; so that one of the later spheres, for instance, will record relations of coincidence; and so on with the others . . .   (ID: 539)

Freud asks us to picture the mind, on this basis, as shown in Figure 3.1. The sweeping arrow in the diagram below the mnemic systems indicates the course taken by a perception that produces an immediate action: say, fleeing a threat. We perceive the threat (on the left) and act immediately (on the far right). The "Mnem", "Mnem 1", "Mnem 2" . . . lines signify the different ways in which the perception (let us say it is a snake) will be classified in memory, in terms of: how it looked, when we saw it, where, how, with whom, and so on. Freud's argument is that the same perception of the snake of our example will be "filed" in a number of mnemic systems, according to: when it was seen, what it looked like (snake, lizard, pole . . .), who we were with when we saw it, how it affected us, but also according to the words that share linguistic features with the word that describes it (sn*ake–rake–cake* . . . *snake–snag–snack* . . . etc.).

So note that the unconscious (Ucs), in this topographical Freudian model, is one such mnemic system. Located on the right-hand side of the diagram, it guards access to the preconscious, and with it, access to the sources of motility. The preconscious carries "word-presentations",

Freud specifies: "the conscious presentation comprises the presentation of the thing plus the presentation of the word belonging to it". The unconscious, by contrast, is a mnemic system that contains "presentation of the things alone" (Ucs: 201–2). Freud's idea is that, when an idea is repressed, the preconscious cathexes of energy are withdrawn from it, and with them, their rational or logical links with other ideas. The unconscious accordingly involves an unholy confusion of tongues, arranging words-presentations as if they were things – not according to rational rules or considerations, but like a bad poet, according to how they sound. This is why analysands themselves cannot understand the meaning of their symptoms, and why Freud could not at first remember "Signorelli". This name had been severed from its rational links with other ideas (like "the painter who painted the 'Last Things'") on grounds of its phonic associations (*Herr* → Signorelli) with the representatives of repressed wishes.

KEY POINT *The five special characteristics of the system-Ucs, or "primary process" thinking (Ucs: 186–8)*

Freud contrasts the "primary process" thinking characteristic of the system-Ucs with the "secondary process", rational thought (mostly) characteristic of the system-Pcs.

1. The representatives (*Vorstellungen*) of repressed drives, cut free of rational, logical links, are independent of each other. They exist side-by-side in the individual's unconscious and can be logically contradictory. While one cannot rationally wish for both A and not-A, as philosophers underline, in the unconscious we do this all the time.
2. There is no negation, nor any degree of doubt in the system-Ucs. As we shall suggest in Chapter 5, negation is a more advanced mental process to deal with things with which the psyche "disagrees" than the type of thinking characterizing the system-Ucs.
3. The energy that is "cathected" or "bound" to drive-representatives in the unconscious is much more mobile than that attached to preconscious ideas. (We shall return to the two mechanisms Freud specifies here about how the quantities of affect can move around: *displacement* and *condensation*.)
4. The processes of the unconscious are timeless. The memories or drive-representatives are not ordered rationally in this temporal sense either: things remembered from yesterday can be linked in the unconscious mind with events that occurred in the individual's childhood. Nor does the passage of time age these earlier memories: "they have no reference to time at all" (Ucs: 187).

5. The system-Ucs lacks any ability to distinguish representations of internal/psychical ideas and outside reality – as in early infancy and also in the process of repression. Insulated from reality testing, "their fate depends only on how strong they are and on whether they fulfill the demands of the pleasure–unpleasure regulation" (*ibid.*).

For all the apparent differences between Freud's topographical and the dynamic biological account of the psyche we developed in Chapters 1 and 2, Freud always maintained that his two metapsychological perspectives were complementary. The reason is that each of the interpretable mnemic representatives of our external experiences and internal drives carries with it a quantity of "cathected" energy. A correct psychoanalytic interpretation releases the energy bound up with some repressed memories or idea(s). This is how Freud thinks that we can explain the central mystery of the psychoanalytic clinic: how an act of speech can produce effects on the analysand's body and psyche, dissolving her symptoms. Psychoanalysis as the practice of interpreting the unconscious, if Freud is right, is accordingly a practice located somewhere between hermeneutics and the natural sciences, in a way that has caused philosophers continuing epistemological problems (see Chapter 8).

With both the dynamic and topographical perspectives on the unconscious in place, we are now in a position to travel directly down Freud's royal road.

. . . Perchance to dream

The dynamic account of dreams as the fulfilment of wishes

Freud's account of dreams is among the richest but most difficult parts of his *oeuvre*. The basis of his account is typically clear and distinct. "The meaning of every dream is the fulfillment of a wish . . . there cannot be any dreams but wishful dreams," Freud announces in *The Interpretation of Dreams*, after surveying and critiquing earlier religious and philosophical views (ID: 134). Dreams do not predict the future, nor do they give us direct insight into the "other world", as many of these views maintain. When looking at the contents of a dream, Freud proposes, we should effectively simply "prepend" to these contents: "I wish that . . . [dream contents a, b, c . . .]." Consider the dreams of small children. Freud recounts how a child who, during the day, was denied her wish to eat strawberry cake, dreamt that night of savouring the most delicious cake. It does not take a contemporary Joseph to see that this dream provided the young girl with a substitute satisfaction, like a symptom. But Freud's interpretation goes further. Recall from Freud's account of earliest infancy in Chapter 1 his claim that children from very early on hallucinate fulfilments of their wishes. Sleep itself represents an approximation to reactivation of interuterine existence, Freud claims (MSD: 222). Our dreaming activity, he maintains, is a regressive reactivation of the hallucinatory means of "wish-fulfilment" of these first days, unchecked by the reality principle.

Having stated the thesis that dreams stage the hallucinatory fulfilments of wishes in *The Interpretation of Dreams*, Freud immediately recognizes: "I feel certain in advance that I shall meet with the most categorical contradictions" (ID: 134). One objection that was to trouble Freud throughout his career is that people have nightmares or "anxiety dreams". These cases seem deeply opposed to any idea that dreams fulfil wishes. Although in "Beyond the Pleasure Principle" Freud later hesitated on this (see Chapter 4), in *The Interpretation of Dreams* he argues that anxiety dreams in no way contradict what his theory would lead us to expect. Recall how Freud's metapsychology is built around the postulate that human beings have competing wishes, and that many of these wishes – principally infantile sexual or aggressive wishes – contradict the individual's reality-testing, moral self-image. The drives that an individual represses are those drives the attainment of whose aim would produce pain instead of pleasure. Anxiety dreams in this light become intelligible as dreams that stage too directly the satisfaction of transgressive unconscious wishes. The ego, whose defences against the id are lulled when the person falls asleep, eventually responds to the hallucinated fulfilment of the id's wishes in the dream as if responding to a real, external threat. When the resulting anxiety becomes overwhelming, the sleeper indeed wakes to avoid the perceived danger (ID: 556–7, 580–85).

As we saw in Chapter 1, Freud argues that even to pay wakeful attention to the outside world requires all the psychical effort involved in reality-testing. At its most basic, then, sleep for Freud is the periodic withdrawal of this psychical effort of attention, so "the batteries can be recharged". As the case of sleepers being forced to wake by anxiety dreams indicates, so Freud contends that the most basic wish at play in our dreaming activity is simply the wish to continue sleeping. We can see this also in cases where some external interruption (e.g. the sound of one's alarm clock) is more or less instantaneously woven into our dreams (as, say, a church bell, school bell, part of a movie, etc.), so we can continue sleeping. However, if the aim of the wish to sleep is to wholly withdraw our "cathexes" from our daily concerns, why do we dream at all? Why isn't all sleep dreamless sleep? Well, for Freud, the fact that we do dream attests that the organic wish to wholly "shut down" stands arrayed against other wishes in the psyche that refuse to be wholly silenced when we go to sleep.

Freud specifies two types of wishes that conspire against a night of undisturbed, dreamless sleep. The first are wishes we carry with us from the previous day or days, "the day's residues":

> Observation shows that dreams are instigated by residues from the previous day: thought-cathexes which have not been submitted to the general withdrawal of cathexis [to objects and concerns with external reality], but have retained in spite of it a certain amount of libidinal or other interest.
>
> (MSD: 224)

These residues will be the types of thing that emerge more or less freely when analysands are asked in the clinic to free-associate regarding the various elements of their dreams (see below). Freud calls such chains of thought the "latent contents" of our dreams, in contrast to their "manifest contents".

KEY POINT *The distinction between the latent contents and manifest contents of dreams*

- The manifest content of a dream is what we experience as we sleep: usually a series of images that seem to form a coherent sequence, such as a movie – albeit one in which we are invariably the star.
- The latent content of a dream are the "dream thoughts" that underlie and inform the manifest dream contents. They can be uncovered by asking the dreamer, as in the clinic, what the various elements within the manifest contents "remind" them of.

In *The Interpretation of Dreams*, Freud specifies that the day's residues which inform the manifest contents of our dreams come particularly from wishes, concerns or chains of thought that have remained incomplete in the waking day. We might not all get as vexed as Freud's child was that we cannot eat strawberry cake. But perhaps an important conversation was interrupted by chance. Or perhaps we have been obliged to "sleep on" some unresolved work or personal problem. It is from the broken fabric of such interrupted events that the manifest content of dreams is woven (ID: 551–2, 554).

The second type of wish involved in our dreams, Freud however stresses, is unconscious wishes – the types of wish that will not emerge instantly in the clinic. Freud hypothesizes that, however vexing the dream day's unfinished business, by itself it will not be sufficient to overcome the general shutting down of the psychical apparatus involved in sleeping. If it is "to figure as constructors of dreams", this unfinished business of the "dream day" must find "reinforcement which has its source in the unconscious . . . impulses" (MSD: 224). The day's residues must form some "link" or "connection" with unconscious wishes that date from much earlier than the previous day (*ibid.*: 226). There is in this way a "temporal regression" involved in the construction of dreams. The manifest content of the dream will be the result of a kind of superimposition of the repressed unconscious wish with the unfulfilled, preconscious wishes of the dream day. In colloquial terms, two unfulfilled wishes are much better than one when it comes to the formation of dreams. Indeed, if the dream were solely the direct expression of a repressed unconscious wish, it would never make it into our conscious life, any more than a dream based solely on the day's events. However weakened the ego's vigilance against the id is when we sleep, it still maintains a "censorship" of our dreaming activities. This censorship is like the censorship political regimes exercise on the criminal actions or seditious statements of their subjects. Any too direct hallucinatory staging of the fulfilment of such wishes would hence be censored, just as it is the failure of the censorship that Freud argues leads to our having anxiety-provoking dreams (see above). Freud's hypothesis is that, since we do dream, we must suppose that the manifest content of any dream is the result of the psyche having it both ways – the dream "gives expression to the unconscious impulse in the material of the previous day's residues" (MSD: 226).

The topographical account of dreams: Freud's psychoanalytic theory

The second major objection facing Freud's claim that all dreams are wish-fulfilments is that so many of adults' dreams seem absurd – not signifying fulfilled wishes, but so much sound and fury. Surely the sleeping psyche is simply burning off energy, so that the products of

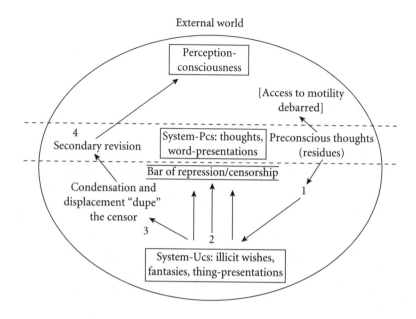

Figure 3.2 The metapsychology of dreams

Notes:
1 The system-Pcs day's residues are "drawn into" the system-Ucs.
2 Ucs wishes are "linked" to day's residues to form the "dream wish".
3 The dream work of condensation and displacement takes place.
4 Dream content becomes conscious as a hallucinated sense-perception.

this process have no rhyme or reason? Freud accepts the idea that the dreaming psyche is burning off energy. Yet he disputes the implication that the products of this "letting off of steam" have no meaning. In psychoanalysis, when an analysand "free-associates" on the manifest content of the dream, he claims, we very soon find that even the most apparently random products of a dreamer's mind have manifold connections with their wider thoughts and concerns. Each dream has a plethora of "latent contents", to use Freud's technical term. Once we acknowledge this, the enigma posed by the manifest absurdity of dreams concerns the relations between the manifest content of the dream and the individual's latent dream thoughts.

When we examine these relations for any dream, Freud argues, it soon becomes clear that a complex process is involved in its construction. Freud calls this process the dream work. The dream work can be envisaged as in Figure 3.2, which can also form the basis of our understanding.

At point 1 of the process shown in Figure 3.2, the preconscious "day's residues" are debarred access to motility, since the person is asleep. Instead, a link between them and the unconscious impulses is established, thanks to the easing of the communication between the Pcs and the Ucs associated with being asleep. This is a regression, Freud specifies, since the preconscious thoughts are rational, and expressible in sentences such as: "I wish that I had been able to solve that maths problem" or "I wish I had said more", and so on. However, when the "text" of these thoughts (ID: 324, 388) is "drawn into" the unconscious, it takes on "the irrational character possessed by everything that is unconscious". At this point, Freud contends, certain "considerations of representability" present themselves. These "considerations" follow from how the "text" of the rational Pcs chains of thought cannot all find "means of representation" in the more primitive system-Ucs (ID: 314). The dream thoughts, Freud specifies, "stand . . . in the most manifold logical relations to one another. They can represent foreground and background, digressions and illustrations, conditions, chains of evidence and counter-arguments . . ." (ID: 312). By contrast, we have seen that the system-Ucs contains the separate, a-logical "thing-presentations" tied to repressed wishes. Faced with the task of "translating" dream thoughts involving connectives such as " 'if', 'because', 'just as', 'although', 'either–or', and all the other conjunctions without which we cannot understand sentences or speeches", Freud argues that the system-Ucs simplifies this original text: "When the whole mass of these dream-thoughts is brought under the pressure of the dream-work . . . its elements are turned about, broken into fragments and jammed together – almost like pack ice . . ." (*ibid.*: 312). To describe this process, Freud asks us to imagine what a journalist would do if asked to reproduce a "political leading article" (*ibid.*: 340) wholly by means of illustrations – say, in a cartoon strip. First of all, they might scan their mind for concrete "figures of speech" that would allow the abstract ideas of the article to be presented pictorially. Every language has such "figures of speech", Freud notes, which "in consequence of the history of their development, are richer in associations than [more abstract] conceptual ones" (*ibid.*). To describe how fine some politician's rhetoric was, our political cartoonist might for instance evoke the "lofty heights" of his speech. The politician could then be depicted speaking on the heights of some mountain range, and the idea would have been successfully "translated" while respecting the relevant "considerations of representability". In the same way, Freud argues that, in the formation of dreams:

> A good part of the intermediate work done ... which seeks
> to reduce the dispersed dream-thoughts to the most succinct
> and unified expression possible, proceeds along the line of
> finding appropriate verbal transformations for the individual
> thoughts ...   (ID: 340)

So let us grant Freud that the nouns and verbs of the Pcs dream thoughts are in this way "packed into" more concrete figures of speech, wherever this can be done. Freud gives us many examples: a girl's dream represented someone "hurling invectives" at her in the pictorial form of someone throwing a chimpanzee and a cat at her, making use of a German linguistic convention which "pictures" animals with invectives. A man's dream represented his "being retrenched" by way of digging a trench in his garden. What though does Freud think happens to the logical relations between the things and actions the Pcs dream thoughts describe? How can these be pictured? Mostly, Freud argues, "it is only the substantive content of the dream-thoughts that [the Ucs] takes over and manipulates" (ID: 312). Nevertheless, the system-Ucs does use several primitive means available to it to try to represent higher-order logical connections between the preconscious dream thoughts. For example, a relationship of cause and effect can be represented in the dream work by the successive presentation of two wholly different scenes, or one dream figure transforming into another in front of our dreaming eyes; or the "distance" in time of an event represented in the dream can be represented by *spatial distance* – those people are now "so far away from us", and so on.

As these examples show, the import of "considerations of representability" for understanding Freud's interpretation of dreams can hardly be overstated. Dreams, for Freud, are distorted texts that, using "figures of speech" as a way of translating the linguistic dream thoughts, finally present themselves as sense-perceptions (at point 5 in Figure 3.2, "Perception-consciousness") in a way that convinces the dreamer of their external, spatiotemporal reality. Freud for this reason opens Chapter VI on the dream work by comparing dreams to picture puzzles or rebuses:

> Suppose I have a picture puzzle, a rebus, in front of me. It
> depicts a house with a boat on its roof, a single letter of the
> alphabet, the figure of a running man whose head has been
> conjured away, and so on. Now I might be misled into raising

objections and declaring that the picture as a whole and its component parts are nonsensical. A boat has no business to be on the roof of a house, and a headless man cannot run ... *But obviously we can only form a proper judgment of the rebus if we put aside criticisms such as these of the whole composition and its parts and if, instead, we try to replace each separate element by a syllable or word that can be presented by that element in some way or another ...* (ID: 277–8)

We could not then be further mistaken than to imagine, as people often do, that dreams represent coherent narratives which unfold wholly at the sensory level, like a feature film. This is the principal reason why they seem manifestly absurd, like so many bad movies, or movies by David Lynch. Dreams are, in their way, coherent and meaningful products of the human psyche. Yet their coherence lies in the linguistic text of the dream wish, as it is pieced together out of the linguistic content provided by the Pcs dream thoughts. The sense we do sometimes get that the manifest pictorial contents of our dreams form a pictorial story Freud argues is a lure serving to lull the ego's censorship. It represents the deceptive result of a kind of supplementary process concealing the dream but itself "not to be distinguished, [Freud] says, from our waking thoughts" (Lacan 2006: 426). This is "secondary revision" (point 4 in Figure 3.2).

KEY POINT *What is secondary revision? (ID: 488–508)*

Secondary revision is a final process of revision that hinders our waking ability to recollect, and interpret, our dreams. Secondary revision "fills up the gaps in the dream-structure with shreds and patches". Its result is that "the dream loses its absurdity and disconnectedness and approximates to the model of an intelligible experience", concealing in partcular its linguistic constitutuion (ID: 490). In Lacan's gloss: "no better idea of this function's effects can be given than comparing it to patches of color wash which, when applied here and there on a stencil, can make stick figures ... in a rebus or hieroglyphics look more like a painting of people" (2006: 426).

So what then happens at points 2 and 3 of Figure 3.2? The "text" of the dream thoughts has been reduced to more concrete, pictorial figures of speech. But we are still far from the point at which the secondary revision repackages the elements of the dream into the semblance of a pictorial narrative. At point 2, Freud tells us, the dream wish is formed. This dream wish "gives expression to the unconscious impulse in the material of the preconscious day's residues" (MSD: 226). In an important footnote added in 1926 towards the end of Chapter VI of *The Interpretation of Dreams*, Freud complained that people too often confuse the latent contents of the dream with its unconscious wish (note 2 at ID: 506–7). Nevertheless, as Slavoj Žižek has recently emphasized (Žižek 1989), the dream wish is not what a person will produce when asked to free-associate on the manifest elements of his dream. As with Freud's famous dream of Irma's injection, the latent thoughts will typically concern the person's workaday life. In the dream of Irma's injection, for instance, Freud's preconscious wish was to be excused from culpability when his patient's, Irma's, health did not improve under his care (ID: 107–21). To use a metaphor, these preconscious wishes are for Freud instead like the materials the artist-unconscious has on its palette in order to make conscious its otherwise censored, illicit wishes. However, as in the "Signorelli" case, Freud emphasizes that these repressed dream wishes will always be of an infantile, sexual or aggressive nature, very different from the desire to "save face" in front of one's colleagues, as in Freud's Irma dream.

At point 3, with the dream wish having now "met" the pre-packaged, simplified dream thoughts, the psyche distorts or "transvalues" the dream thoughts to give indirect expression to this wish in a manner that further confounds the ego's censorship. It does this through two processes, condensation and displacement.

KEY POINT *Condensation and overdetermination*

- When an analysand free-associates on the manifest contents of her dream, she will always produce quantitatively more thoughts than the number of manifest contents in the dream.
- These manifold latent thoughts, in order to make it into the dream, must accordingly be subject to a process of selection. In particular, only those elements that "link up" with more than one chain of latent dream thoughts will make it into the manifest content of a dream. Each of these "condensed" dream elements, Freud says, is overdetermined.

In order to illustrate condensation, consider Freud's famous *dream of the botanical monograph* (ID: 282–4). The manifest content of the dream was this:

I had written a monograph on an (unspecified) genus of plant. The book lay before me and I was at the moment turning over a folded colored plate. Bound up in the copy there was a dried specimen of a plant.

What did Freud's free associations reveal? First, resisting the lure of "secondary revision", Freud divides the dream into its individual linguistic elements. He then associates on each of these in turn:

- "*monograph*": Freud had seen a "monograph" on a type of plant the day before in a bookshop. Moreover, "monograph" reminded Freud of his own monograph on cocaine, and of his friend Dr Königstein who had assisted the young Freud in his research for it. Freud had had a conversation with Dr Königstein the previous evening about the payment of medical services which, he confides, lay close to the illicit dream wish;
- "*botanical*": the word "botanical" recalled the name of Freud's colleague Dr Gartner [Gardener], the "blooming" looks of Gartner's wife which Freud had recently remarked, and to two of his analysands, one named "Flora" and a second [Frau L] to whom Freud had "told the story of the forgotten flowers" (the details of which do not concern us here).

Freud's thoughts concerning Gartner recalled a conversation he had had with Dr Königstein in which Flora and Frau L had been mentioned. "Forgotten flowers" recalled to Freud's mind his wife's favourite flowers, and his own "jokingly" favourite flower, the artichoke. "Artichoke" then recalled to him an episode from his childhood "which was the opening of his own intimate relations with books [monographs]".

Each of the dream elements, we can see, has "copious links with the majority of the dream-thoughts". What such cases compel us to hypothesize, Freud says, is that

A dream is constructed . . . by the whole mass of dream-thoughts being submitted to a sort of manipulative process in which those elements which have the most numerous and strongest supports acquire the right of entry into the dream-content – in a manner analogous to election by *scrutin de liste*.
(ID: 284)

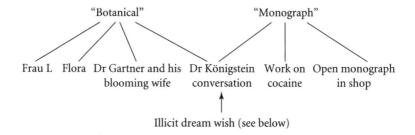

"Botanical"   "Monograph"

Frau L   Flora   Dr Gartner and his   Dr Königstein   Work on   Open monograph
                 blooming wife   conversation   cocaine   in shop

                                            ↑
                         Illicit dream wish (see below)

Figure 3.3   The condensations in the "botanical monograph" dream

In the case of the dream of the "botanical monograph", the work of condensation can be represented as in Figure 3.3.

Famously, alongside condensation, Freud lists displacement as a key mechanism of the dream work.

KEY POINT *What is displacement? (ID: 306–9)*

- Freud tells us that displacement is the "transference ... of psychical intensities" between elements of the already-simplified dream thoughts. It illustrates the "mobility of cathexis" that Freud associates with the unconscious.
- The evidence that displacement has occurred in the dream work is that what psychoanalysis shows to be the most important dream thoughts (those closest to the unconscious wish) are completely unrelated to the events or actions that appear to be the most important in the manifest contents of a dream: "In the course of the formation of a dream these essential elements, charged ... with intense interest, may be treated as though they were of small value, and their place be taken in the dream by other elements, of whose small value in the dream-thoughts there can be no question" (ID: 306).

The botanical monograph dream also illustrates what Freud means by "displacement". Freud tells us that the dream thoughts all turned on his important conversation with Dr Königstein. This conversation, as he confides, had invoked illicit wishes he is not at liberty to disclose, given the censorship of his own times. Yet the manifest dream is about a botanical monograph, a folded plate and a dried specimen of plant! Nothing could seem further from any illicit sexual wishes, or even Freud's conversation with Königstein. Displacement, Freud emphasizes, plays a particularly important role in the distortion of the unconscious dream wish. Since the latent content of the dream is in this way "displaced", the dream wish whose fulfilment is being indirectly represented simply does not come to the attention of the censor, just as it usually completely eludes the sleeper on waking.

An illustration: the Wolfman's "primal scene" dream

Given the complexity of Freud's understanding of the dream work, we close by considering one complete Freudian dream analysis. The dream in question comes from Freud's psychoanalysis of "the Wolfman". Alongside Little Hans and the Ratman (and Dora and Schreber, whom we have still to meet), the Wolfman analysis is one of Freud's great case studies. As *The Interpretation of Dreams* puts it, this case history presents not only a psycho*analysis* of the individual elements in the dream. Freud also performs a "synthetic" *reconstruction* of the dream, in light of the analysis's full disclosure of the dreamer's unconscious wishes.

At the heart of the Wolfman's analysis was a recurrent dream he had had over many years. The key elements of the manifest content of the dream were as follows:

> Suddenly the window opened, outside of which was a large tree. The tree had many branches. 6 or 7 wolves were perched upon them. They were not moving. The wolves sat still, looking in through the window at the dreamer. They each had large white tails. The overwhelming affect of the dream was one of fear.
>
> (cf. WM: 29)

Here, as elsewhere, Freud's interpretation proceeds on the basis of the Wolfman's free associations on each of the dream elements. These associations disclosed the "latent contents" of the dream: the dream thoughts. As the analysis bore out, these latent thoughts turned on two associative chains:

- a childhood memory of the door opening at Christmas time to reveal a tree with presents on the branches (WM: 35–6, note 2 at 42–3); and
- childhood fairytales that had made a strong impression on the Wolfman, about wolves who eat little goats, hide in trees, but who end by having their tails chopped off as punishment for their misdeeds (*ibid.*: 29–32, 41–2).

The Wolfman's psychoanalysis revealed, however, that the unconscious dream wishes behind the dream concerned the analysand's infantile sexuality, and in particular his unresolved Oedipus complex. Specifically, the Wolfman's infantile sexual development was deeply affected, Freud contends, by his witnessing at a very young age the spectacle of his parents having sexual intercourse (WM: 36–8). Although he was too young to comprehend the spectacle (see Chapter 2), this event was to have a lastingly traumatic effect upon him as he matured sexually. The Wolfman's sexual development suffered from a fixation at the anal phase. His own amorphous sexual wishes became fixated around a series of wishes characteristic of this infantile stage: the wishes to see his mother and father doing "it", to be castrated (so his father might do it to him, according to the "passive" Oedipus complex), and to be devoured by his father (on the basis of a sadistic/oral understanding for which to love is equivalent to "gobbling up" the beloved).

Figure 3.4 shows how Freud understands the dream work in this case. The force of these repressed wishes distorted the Wolfman's latent dream thoughts concerning the Christmas tree and the story so as to give rise, in their place, to the horrifying insistent dream of the wolves on their braches, gazing in fixedly at him.

Summary

- Freud couples his dynamic, biological account of the psyche with his "topographical" account. The topographical account sees the psyche as a "mnemic" (memory) device with two "systems": the system-Pcs (containing rationally associated memories, ideas and "drive representatives") and the system-Ucs (the unconscious). The unconscious is a mnemic system characterized by "primary process" thinking, in which "drive-representatives" are treated separately, as "thing-representatives" not subject to reality-testing, which may thus contradict each other, are timeless, and able to be linked, according to the most apparently tenuous links, with preconscious ideas.
- The royal road to understanding the primary processes of the system-Ucs is the interpretation of dreams. Freud's account of the construction of dreams, based upon his contention that dreams always stage the fulfilment of wishes, brings together his dynamic and topographical accounts of the psyche.

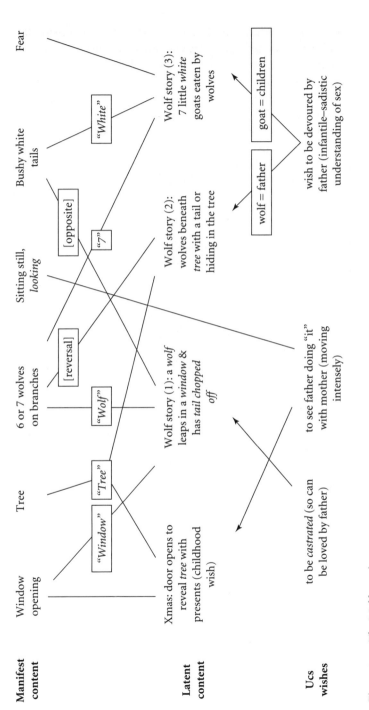

Figure 3.4 The Wolfman dream

- The preconscious dream thoughts, made up of the dream day's cognitive "residues", are "drawn into" the unconscious, then "sifted" into more concrete pictorial language. Hence their manifold logical relations are simplified into the types of relations that can hold between pictured things (considerations of representability).
- The dream wish then "links" with the unsatisfied preconscious wish from the dream day. This simplified "text" becomes the contents out of which this wish will form its indirect hallucinated satisfaction in the dream's manifest contents.
- In the process of condensation, only those elements of the latent content connected to many (or most) of these latent thoughts make it into the manifest content of the dream. Because of displacement, by contrast, the elements seemingly central in this manifest content are generally not those that are most important in the original preconscious thoughts. The process of displacement highlights the distorting impact of the intersection of the repressed dream wish on the latent dream thoughts. In order to reach consciousness, this wish must "transvalue all [the] psychical values" from the day's residues. In particular, the latent thoughts most closely connected to this illicit wish must themselves disappear from the manifest content, or be relegated to a seemingly incidental place in the dream.
- In the process of "secondary revision", finally, the contents of the dream are given a last "once-over", so the dream is made to appear as a coherent pictorial story capable of convincing the dreamer that its manifest contents are real, and he can continue sleeping.

part II

Freud's children

four

Precarious love: Kleinian object relations theory

Introducing Klein and "object relations"

We have now examined the foundations of psychoanalysis, laid down by Sigmund Freud. Part II of this book will consider developments of psychoanalytic theory after Freud. Melanie Klein's object relations approach to psychoanalysis represents one of the most original trajectories to have emerged in psychoanalysis after Freud. Klein discovered psychoanalysis in Budapest. But it was only after moving to London that her work took on its distinctive, original character. Perhaps, Juliet Mitchell suggests, this was because of the peculiarly practical and "nononsense" culture of England, in which divergence from orthodoxy was better tolerated than on the European continent. However that may be, Klein was explicit about her departures from Freudian orthodoxy. As we shall see, Klein offers a vivid account of this psychology: one that focuses much more than Freud's on the violent and erotic relation between the infant and its mother. In this relation, Klein holds, the erotic desire to possess the mother goes hand in hand with wanting to cut her up, rob her body of its good contents, poison her with excrement, and destroy her.

Yet Klein's analysis of children opens the way to a particularly sympathetic account of the infantile psyche, and the problems children face in the normal course of their development. Kleinian object relations theory also opens up new insights into adult psychology, and pathologies such as schizophrenia and depression. According to Klein, these signal a regression to childhood states visited during the Oedipus complex. But in her diagnostic picture what she calls the *schizoid* and *depressive* positions assume centrality, rather than Freud's familiar "phases". Finally, object relations theory underscores the role and character of "fantasy" in relations between the ego and its objects – an emphasis that connects Klein and her followers to a philosophical genealogy comprising Kant, Hegel, Schopenhauer and Nietzsche. The connection between human being and the object world is forged through representation (*Vorstellung*) or the imagination. In philosophical parlance, meaning is imbued in worldly things, and the mind grasps its objects, by virtue of an active capacity (or "faculty") of reason, so that, in the words of Jorge Luis Borges:

> A man sets out to draw the world. As the years go by, he peoples a space with images of provinces, kingdoms, mountains, bays, ships, islands, fishes, rooms, instruments, stars, horses, and individuals. A short time before he dies, he discovers that the patient labyrinth of lines traces the lineaments of his own face. (Borges 1999: 327)

Child analysis and the play technique

Klein's chief clinical *modus operandi*, from which her discoveries about the child's psyche are drawn, she calls the "play technique". Klein developed this technique to treat children with language disturbances, or who are not yet able to speak. The technique involved introducing to the child a number of simple toys:

> little wooden men and women, usually in two sizes, cars, wheelbarrows, swings, trains, aeroplanes, animals, trees, bricks, houses, fences, paper, scissors, a knife, pencils, chalks or paints, glue, balls and marbles, plasticine and string.
> (Klein 1987: fn. 4, 230)

This range of toys is generic enough to act as a conduit for the child's imaginary or fantasmatic projections. Klein's interpretations were formulated on the basis of her attention to how the infant played, and how children treat the objects of their play. Her operative assumption was that the child transfers emotional attachments to loved ones on to the toys, thus enacting emotional situations – or fantasized relationships – through play. The analyst's role as interpreter is to relay back to the child what they are doing, thus presenting to their conscious awareness what the unconscious communicates by means of the game. The analyst must hence remain affectively neutral, no matter how violent or abject the child's behaviour:

> [T]he analyst should not show disapproval of the child having broken a toy; he should not, however, encourage the child to express his aggressiveness, or suggest to him that the toy could be mended. In other words, he should enable the child to experience his emotions and phantasies as they come up.
>
> (Klein 1987: 42–3)

Klein stressed such procedural prescriptions in order to ensure scientific repeatability, and inure the procedure against the undue influence of suggestion (see Chapter 8). These principles also served the goal of analysis: to cure the child's disorder. To this end, Klein provided each child their own exclusive drawer of toys – an equivalent measure, for Klein, to the adult analysand's personal record of associations, shared only with the analyst.

Klein drew analogies between what a child does in play, and what an adult does with language and in dreams. Klein's analysis of play is like Freud's analysis of dreams and analysands' spoken testimony, drawing upon the same principles of free association, the primacy of the unconscious, and the "transference" – the analysand's affectively charged attitudes towards their analyst (see Chapter 8). The child's play enables it to express the symbolic relations and meanings produced by its fantasies, like – Klein claims – the structures found in adult dreams. Klein insists, however, that, as with Freudian dream analysis, the interpretation should not only rely upon a generalized "translation of symbols". It should take its bearings from the milieu given by the child's emotional engagement with the toys. In this way, as with the interpretation of dreams, the interpretation of the child's unconscious becomes possible only within the clinical situation, in the dialogue between the child and the analyst, as mediated by the child's toys and its play with them.

Klein's writings give numerous examples of how the interpretation might proceed. For instance, a key event might involve the destruction of a toy – representing the wish to destroy a sibling or parent. This event might be followed by an attitude of regret, because the toy had stood, in the child's imagination, for this person. In communicating to the child this analogy between destroying the toy and wishing to harm the person whom the toy represents, Klein would frequently observe an initial heightening of anxiety in the child, which would then subside, freeing them to produce more associations and material for analysis.

The structure and development of the psyche

The child at play, as a psychoanalytic motif, pre-dates Kleinian object relations. Famously, in "Beyond the Pleasure Principle" (1920), Freud analyses his grandson's play with a wooden spool, repeatedly pushing it away (exclaiming *fort!* [gone]), and pulling it in (exclaiming *da!* [here]). In this "*fort-da* game", Freud argues, the wooden spool has come to stand for the child's mother. In the repetitive play, the child manages his feelings of distress at separation from the mother by hurling the substitute from his cot ("*fort!*") and reeling it back in ("*da!*") at his pleasure. Importantly, Freud argues that this game also expresses a type of destructive impulse central to his postwar work, the famous "death drive" (see Chapter 7).

KEY POINT *Freud on the death drive*

In "Beyond the Pleasure Principle", Freud argues that two types of drives govern the psyche:

- *Eros* sustains the life of the organism by connecting psychic energy with its "objects" (the breast, food, etc.), seeking pleasure through the discharge of tension.
- *Thanatos*, or the death drive, accumulates tension, disconnecting and destroying alliances in order to achieve a "greater" equilibrium beyond the organism in death.

Freud's theory of the death drive made sense of new clinical phenomena with which Freud had grappled, namely:

- the transference, whereby the analysand relives her relations to her first others through the analyst (see Chapter 8);
- the reappearance or "metastasis" of hysterical symptoms after their successful interpretation; and
- the traumatic "war" neuroses: returned World War I soldiers would dream repeatedly of their trauma-inducing experiences at the front.

The death drive is one of Freud's most controversial concepts. It split Freud's followers down two lines: those who accept the death drive as one of psychoanalysis's most pivotal concepts, and those who see it as obscure and metaphysical (for instance, Otto Rank, David Rapaport, Ernest Jones). Both Klein and Lacan (see Chapter 5) regarded the death drive seriously, although each accords to it a different significance. While Lacan viewed the death drive from the perspective of his theoretical structuralism, Klein saw it as galvanizing the formation of the self.

The schizoid position

For Klein, the ego is brought into being by its "object relations" – or its relation to the "part objects" of its earliest drives, such as the breast, face or voice of the mother, who is not yet conceptually unified as a whole object for the infant. Object relations exist for the child from the first time it feeds, and the relation to this object (initially the breast) is characterized by the mechanisms either of "introjection" or "projection" (see Chapter 2), as Freud had argued in "On Negation" and "Drives and Their Vicissitudes":

> Expressed in the language of the oldest – the oral – instinctual impulses, the judgement [of the child regarding its first objects] is: "I should like to eat this," or "I should like to spit it out"; and, put more generally: "I should like to take this into myself and to keep that out" . . . the original pleasure-ego wants to introject into itself everything that is good and to eject from itself everything that is bad. What is bad, what is alien to the ego and what is external are, to begin with, identical.
>
> (N: 237)

As for Freud, so for Klein: in the child's first months there is no clear boundary between the mother and the child. The child introjects the nourishing ("good") breast, with which it forms a positive identification. Klein contends that the "good breast" object comes to form the primary core of the child's ego. On the other side of the coin, the child identifies feelings of discomfort such as indigestion or hunger with the "bad breast". These bad internal feelings are projected outwards in the child's fantasy on to this "bad" "part object", which becomes for it the source of absolute danger: "an uncontrollable over-powering object" (Klein 1987: 179). It is from this splitting of the bad and good objects, Klein argues, that the "death drive" emerges. It is "felt as a fear of annihilation (death) and takes the form of fear of persecution" in the child. Because of the still-basic stage of mental development of the child, each of its "good" and "bad" feelings is exaggerated by the child, so that at one extreme they experience the fearful, persecuting "bad breast", and at the other, the "inexhaustible and always bountiful breast – an ideal breast" (*ibid.*: 182). It is a matter of heaven and hell, as it were, with little in between.

The upshot of this scenario is that the child unknowingly identifies in the same real "object" (the mother) both its most valued and integral core – the fantasmatic good part object – and the greatest threat to its integrity – the fantasized bad breast. In order to secure their sense of self, the child will thus draw upon its oral sadism and – in fantasy – raid the mother's body for its good contents: "suck dry, bite up, scoop out and rob the mother's body" (Klein 1987: 183). At the same time, Klein holds, the child launches fantasized attacks upon the bad breast by drawing upon its emergent anal-sadistic impulses, hurling its own excrements into the mother, as weapons. The child attempts to appropriate all that is nourishing or good from the mother, and to control her from a distance by means of the parts of its own self that it has projected on to her "bad" breast. However, Klein argues, the infant's ego soon becomes depleted by this ambivalent, fantasmatic traffic of love and hatred between itself and its objects. Indeed, unlike Freud, Klein dates the Oedipus complex – with its ambivalence towards its first others – to this early, schizoid phase of childhood development. Because of its own attacks against the (m)other, the child begins to fear the mother's retaliation, which is anticipated in evermore anxiety-producing fantasies regarding the bad breast. Ultimately, Klein says, the child fears being incorporated entirely by the mother, an infantile fear that manifests as castration anxiety (and later claustrophobia in adults).

The child escapes this persecutory dialectic only when it comes to appreciate that the mother is actually one whole other – and so that what it had taken to be the "good object" and the "bad object" are one and the same. This stage is marked by the child's experiencing of regret about its fantasized attacks against the mother, and the onset of what Klein calls the depressive position.

The depressive position

According to Klein's account, the depressive position catalyses the resolution of the Oedipus complex. In it, the superego is installed, and the child comes to accept its proper position in the family. The task of this resolution for Klein, however, is not only for the child to take up its social position in relation to the father, in exchange for renouncing its claims upon the mother. For Klein it signals the child's acknowledgement of the mother's completeness, through the conceptual integration of the "good" and "bad" part objects. The "task" of the depressive position is the incorporation of the whole loved object – rather than the part object that characterized object relations during the schizoid position. With this integration of the object, love and hate come to coexist for the child, so it learns to cope with ambivalence towards the loved one.

KEY POINT *Mourning and melancholia in Freud*

Klein's account of the depressive phase develops through central reference to Freud's "Mourning and Melancholia".

- When a significant object (such as a parent or lover) dies or departs, the ego must undergo a process of adapting to this new reality, one that takes time, and whose failure results in melancholia.
- Initially, the subject will over-invest (or "hyper-cathect") libido into the object by way of introjection. This will appear to others as a state of self-absorption and dwelling upon one's loss.
- In the normal case, however, the ego's work of mourning "incorporates" the lost object by way of identification, and in this way the loss is compensated for.

In the depressive phase, the child incorporates or comes to identify with the whole "loved object" (the mother). Such integration of the whole object signals new difficulties for the child. It must incorporate the whole good object (mother), overcoming the schizoid wish to destroy her and the fear of destroying its own self thereby. Most importantly, the child must negotiate its own guilt in relation to the good object regarding past aggressions enacted toward the object in the schizoid position. The ego is ultimately unable to sustain the degree of violence and instability that characterizes the schizoid position. Eventually it must become organized enough to gain a greater purchase upon reality, through an understanding of the object/mother as integrated rather than split. Unlike in Freud (and, as we shall see, Lacan), there is no third term involved in this process for Klein: no father who will intervene to stabilize the dangerously intimate relation between the mother and the child. Rather, a solution to the schizoid impasse is galvanized by the child's own fear that it might destroy the good object, reflected in the mother's decreasing availability to it during the period of weaning.

With these points established, we can chart the differences between Klein's account of the Oedipus complex and Freud's, which we examined in Chapter 2.

KEY POINT *Klein's disagreements with Freud over "Oedipus"*

1. The Oedipus complex emerges and is dealt with in the child's first two years for Klein, which, as we have seen already in Chapter 2, is far earlier than for Freud.
2. The object of both desire and fear for the infant is different for Klein. Rather than the father, it is primarily the mother who also incorporates the father's penis, and other objects such as faeces and rival children.
3. Following from this, it is the father who is castrated by the mother, not the reverse.
4. The mother is the predominant internalized model for the superego rather than the father, who is relatively peripheral.

What is the significance of these differences?

- The father's (or equivalent) prohibition is not required to catalyse the dissolution of the Oedipus complex.
- The superego is engendered by the child's refinement of these primary relations and is not installed in response to the repression of the child's Oedipal wishes.
- Because she lacks Freuds's pivotal concept of *Nachträglichkeit* (or *retroactive effect*), the superego is for Klein constructed cumulatively from very early infancy, instead of being installed late and then reorganizing previous experience.

This shift from the schizoid to the depressive position is occasioned for Klein by the mother's increasing absence as the child grows up. Crucially, the child sets out to repair the damaged mother, who had previously borne the brunt of the child's aggressive and appropriative impulses. The child wishes now to protect the loved object, but – because of the truth of its sadistic impulses – feels unable to do so without also endangering it:

> the ego becomes fully identified with its good, internalized objects, and at the same time becomes aware of its own incapacity to protect and preserve them against the internalized, persecuting objects and the id. This anxiety is psychologically justified. (Klein 1987: 119)

Klein's argument here becomes clear when we reflect again upon the function of play for the child. For instance, when a child damages and then attempts to repair a toy, Klein posits that this activity reflects the psychical activity of making reparations to the internal "good" object. Likewise, Klein cites the instance of a child "in the wars" – or victim to seemingly accidental, yet self-inflicted, injury – as a further case of acting out internal psychic events through which the child wishes to keep in check its own destructive capacities. As with Freud's grandson in "Beyond the Pleasure Principle", Klein argues that the children she analysed were able to alleviate their anxiety about the absent mother in the depressive phase through play. There is, however, one key difference between Freud's conclusions about his grandson's activity and Klein's account of what the child achieves through play. Whereas for Freud the *fort-da* game represented an attempt to master the mother through playfully – and sadistically – sending her away and then bringing her back, for Klein the situation is reversed. Because the child initially understands itself to be omnipotent ("the whole world"), the child supposes it has already sent the mother away with its attacks against her. Worse still, the child fears her return as the "bad mother". Play thus functions in the depressive position as a mode of reparation of the loved object – and of mastery of the sadistic impulse – rather than as an attempt to master the object.

This also demonstrates the extent of the ego's development in the depressive position. During the depressive position the child comes to desire the whole object rather than part objects. This involves a capacity to tolerate increased amounts of frustration, beyond simply enacting its aggression upon the object through fantasized attacks. In turn, this increased tolerance leads to new anxiety contents, and a refinement of the defence mechanisms such that imagos of objects (or fantasmatic complexes relating to an object) rather than actual objects come to be split:

> Ambivalence, carried out in a splitting of imagos, enables the small child to gain more trust and belief in its real objects and thus its internalised ones – to love them more and to carry out in an increasing degree its phantasies of restoration on the loved object. (Klein 1987: 143)

Under these conditions, the child is finally able to establish within itself the imago of the whole object: the superego, which (see Chapter 1) represents the voice of conscience and social law. Yet this effect of stabilization and resolution is only apparent. The schizoid structure is still always a possibility – albeit usually a latent one – for the psyche. This is because the superego, as the "integrated" and "organized" loved object, serves both as the ego's ultimate protection against attack and, at times, its most vicious aggressor. For this reason, Klein (like Freud and Lacan) stresses how the superego is inherently liable to attack the ego: as in everyday references to the "gnawing of conscience" which for Klein "testifies to the relentless 'persecution' of conscience and to the fact that it is originally conceived of as devouring its victim" (Klein 1987: 123).

In order to make clearer our understanding of Klein's account of childhood development, let us look at her most famous case study, "Little Dick".

The case of Dick

Klein's treatment of four-year-old "Dick" in 1929 gave rise to her best-known, and most frequently criticized, paper, "The Importance of Symbol Formation in the Development of the Ego". In "Dick", Klein confronted a child who exhibited no affective relation to those around him (including his mother and nurse), no interest in toys or play, and for whom words appeared to have no meaning. From the object relations perspective, Dick's history before entering Klein's clinic had all the hallmarks of an infancy destined for psychological difficulties. Attempts to breastfeed him had been aborted early and he had rejected replacement foods, so that at one point Dick approached starvation. Since then he had been plagued with poor digestion and haemorrhoids. Thus Dick's oral sadism had been excessively stimulated by painful indigestion, at the same time as his ability to appropriate the "good breast" was inhibited. In addition to this, his mother was cold to him, partly because of these early difficulties in bonding, and because it was clear to her that he was "abnormal". Finally, Dick had recently acquired a new nurse who – as in any classic psychoanalytic narrative – had caught him masturbating and threateningly prohibited this activity.

Dick arrived at Klein's clinic with what she called "a complete and apparently constitutional incapacity of the ego to tolerate anxiety" (Klein 1987: 101). Dick had withdrawn from his fantasy life, which was too saturated with pain and discomfort for his meagre resources to handle. He thus could not maintain connections with objects. Klein argued that Dick had become afraid of his own potential for destructiveness, as evidenced in his refusal to bite up his food. Deprived of any opportunity to enact a sadistic relation to the mother, he had never had the chance to develop control of his destructive impulses and to tolerate anxiety in the development and resolution of the schizoid phase. The task of his analysis, Klein accordingly argued, was to bring about the conditions in which Dick could become comfortable enough to express and come to terms with his aggression regarding the bad object, and to appropriate the good object. Such conditions would also serve to activate further development of his ego:

> In general I do not interpret the material until it has found expression in various representations. In this case, however, where the capacity to represent it was almost entirely lacking, I found myself obliged to make my interpretations on the basis of my general knowledge, the representations in Dick's behaviour being relatively vague. Finding access in this way to his unconscious, I succeeded in activating anxiety and other affects. (Klein 1987: 106)

The methods Klein employs to spur Dick's ego development have drawn the most criticism to her analysis of him. Central to her analysis is her evocative description of the frightening spectre (for the child) of adult sexual relations, concealed behind Dick's play with two trains. The "big train" was Daddy, Klein advises, the "little train" was Dick, and "the station is Mummy; Dick is going into Mummy" (*ibid.*: 102). Despite her own (and others') misgivings about clinical procedure, Klein was pleased with the results of Dick's analysis. She reports that subsequently Dick came to represent normal (sadistic) object relations through play, developing an appropriate affection for his mother and nurse, and adopting the normal Oedipal attitude toward his father. In short, he was able to engage with his surroundings and become a functioning member of his family.

Anxiety, symbol formation and the love of wisdom

As well as recounting Dick's fate, Klein's "The Importance of Symbol Formation in the Development of the Ego" also discloses her (albeit-nascent) theory about something also vital to Lacan's work: the psychological function of language and the symbol. Klein's thesis is that an affective relation to objects is a precondition for language acquisition.

This is because object relations themselves prefigure relations to symbols and to abstract thought, identifications with objects being for the child a mode of equation: of faeces with weapons, for instance, or the mother's nourishing breast with the good part of the self. By developing these elementary "equations", the child manages anxiety and frustration through its fantasy life, creating meaning through the manipulation of part objects. Fantasy thus represents a kind of symbolic, protolinguistic exchange of part objects for the real things. Language in turn is understood by Kleinians as merely a variety of shared fantasy life, wherein signs are standardized for more general consumption. To this extent, anxiety is what, psychologically or "genetically", keeps symbol formation and exchange in train. "A sufficient quantity of anxiety is the necessary basis for an abundance of symbol formation and of fantasy," Klein writes. However, "an adequate capacity on the part of the ego to tolerate anxiety is necessary if it is to be satisfactorily worked over" (Klein 1987: 98). For this reason, language and anxiety operate together as the psyche's dual currency at the level of the unconscious as well as conscious thought. More precisely, words serve as "mother substitutes", or sites of investment for the management of anxiety concerning the mother.

Just as Klein traces the origins of language to the rudimentary exchanges enacted through fantasy, she also locates the motivation for intellectual curiosity in these early object relations. As we saw in Chapter 2, Freud originally identified the "epistemophilic impulse" (which in ancient Greek means literally love of knowledge, while "philosophy" refers to love of wisdom) as the infant's early curiosity about sexual matters. For Klein it refers to the desire to explore the mother's body, and is connected also to sadism, the wish to control the mother and appropriate all that is good within her. According to Klein, this relation to the mother's body sets up the child's relation to the whole external world. Its intellectual curiosity is then either promoted or stifled, depending upon its early ability to deal with inevitable frustrations and fears in connection with the mother's body. Dick, for instance, was inhibited in his relation to the world, and remarkably incurious because his early experiences of aggression actually pushed his mother away, leading to his withdrawal from destructiveness, and from all object-cathexes. The kind of engagement with the world productive of philosophy requires an ability not only to withstand discomfort and anxiety, but also an adeptness in the manipulation of anxiety to one's own ends, through the kind of symbol formation characteristic of fantasy.

In this light, we might understand philosophers' preoccupations with the question of the role of imagination in thinking (particularly Aristotle's, Kant's or Castoriadis's (who was influenced by object relations)) in connection with the object relations conception of thinking. The imagination has a similarly basic or "constitutive" function for Kant as fantasy does in Klein. It is what forms a connection between the subject and its world. Likewise, the object relations account of the perilous relation to the mother's body is reminiscent of some philosophers' (especially Nietzsche's) descriptions of their own philosophical activity, as involving a kind of fearlessness and readiness to face "abysses". Might it not be the case, then, that the old intuition that the philosopher risks madness signals the heritage of thinking as a mode of defending oneself against destruction by the mother's body?

Art, reparation and creativity

Klein also had something to say on the question of why humans create visual works of art. Here as elsewhere, rather than reinterpret Freud on her own terms, Klein deviates substantially from Freudian orthodoxy. As we shall see in Chapter 7, the usual psychoanalytic explanation for the work of art is that it is a product of the "sublimation" of otherwise disruptive drives into activities, such as art, amenable to the peace and cultural development of civilization. The object relations account of creativity and art by contrast refers us back to the depressive position, and the need to make reparations with the damaged object (particularly the mother). Klein addresses this question in her short article, "Infantile Anxiety-Situations Reflected in a Work of Art and in the Creative Impulse" (1929). Here she discusses Ravel's opera *Das Zauberwort* ("The Magic Word"). Ravel's opera revolves around a childhood scene of frustration and compromise: a little boy would like to go out, play, and "eat up all the cakes in the world", but is told by his mother that he must finish his homework or she will give him tea without sugar, and dry bread. He consequently flies into a rage and tears up the things in the room. The destruction culminates in his attempt to stab a caged squirrel, which escapes from an open window. But next the objects in the room "come to life" and start to exact revenge upon the boy. The room starts to rip itself up, and, if that were not surreal enough, a little man appears from under a book cover to instruct the boy in maths. The boy faints, and then escapes to a nearby park, where animals proceed to attack him. Finally, a wounded squirrel falls beside him, and he bandages its paw with his scarf. The child utters the "magic word", "mamma", and, as Klein puts it, is "restored to the human world of helping, 'being good' " (Klein 1987: 211).

KEY POINT *Klein's interpretation of "The Magic Word"*

Klein reads Ravel's opera as an artistic representation of the Oedipus complex: the schizoid position, and its resolution with the depressive position.

- When the boy's wishes cannot be immediately satisfied, he lashes out against the mother's room (or "womb"), unleashing his destructive impulses against it/her.
- That the objects he attacks "come to life" means that they turn his aggression back on him.
- The room is rent apart. He is afraid he has damaged his mother's body, and that he has destroyed all that is good in the mother and in himself.
- The little man in the opera is the father, "about to call the child . . . to his reckoning for the damage he has done and the theft he had committed in the mother's body" (Klein 1987: 214).
- Finally, the child is moved to repair the damage he has done, represented by his attending to the squirrel's paw. He is restored to "mamma", who loves him for being a "good boy" after all.

For Klein, artistic creativity represents an attempt to make amends with the mother, through the act of reparation characteristic of the depressive position. With reference to a narrative concerning the motivations of artist Ruth Kjär, Klein argues that the creative impulse derives from a feeling of loss or emptiness that results from having driven away or destroyed the mother. The artist manages her anxiety regarding the object's revenge and the emptying of the ego by means of the reparative activity involved in the creation of the art-object. Klein ascribes particular significance to Kjär's work because she had begun painting her works (mostly of women) in response to her feelings of sadness, or emptiness, after her brother-in-law retrieved a piece from her home: "This left an empty space on the wall, which in some inexplicable way seemed to coincide with the empty space within her" (Klein 1987: 215). The principle Klein wishes to communicate with the aid of these examples is clear: art and creativity are the drive's attempt at object-reparation rather than indirect satisfaction (as per Freud's account of sublimation, see Chapter 7). This is not a mere question of emphasis – rather, Klein's difference from Freud here is fundamental. Art is not merely an attempt to release an accumulated "neuronal" tension that would otherwise build until breaking point. It is instead a redeployment of energy to the purpose of caring for the loved object, which is also intimately connected to the ego's own core, and with a fear of the mother. Or in more "poetic" terms, art is for Klein a loving acknowledgement of the mother's creativity, and so contains an ethical dimension missing from Freud's account.

Other object relations theorists

Winnicott, the "Good-enough mother" and the "transitional object"

As Klein's work became better known among British psychoanalysts, differences between her theories and those of "the Freuds" (her relationship with Anna Freud was particularly adversarial) came also to be more pronounced. In the 1930s, Klein and her advocates started to be referred to as "Klein and her school", and analysts began to identify themselves as followers of the object relations approach: most notably Joan Riviere, Wilfred Bion, Hanna Segal, Paula Heimann, Donald Winnicott, Harry Guntrip, Herbert Rosenfeld and W. R. D. Fairbairn. In this concluding section of this chapter, we shall address three of the most prominent object relations theorists – Winnicott, Bion, and Fairbairn – each of whom took this approach in a distinct direction.

As we have seen thus far, during the reparative or depressive position, the child's world "becomes whole", and the child more integrated, paradoxically, through the mourning of a loss. As Klein writes in "Notes on Some Schizoid Mechanisms",

> With the introjection of the complete object in about the second quarter of the first year marked steps in integration are made. This implies important changes in the relation to objects. The loved and hated aspects of the mother are no longer felt to be so widely separated, and the result is an increased fear of loss, states akin to mourning and a strong feeling of guilt, because the aggressive impulses are felt to be directed against the loved object.   (Klein 1987: 189)

The child's mourning signifies the fear of the loss of the mother at its own hands: that he may have destroyed all that it loved. Donald W. Winnicott refigures this discussion in terms more readily accessible to the experience of those concerned with the primary care of children: presenting a kind of everyday phenomenology of the parent–child relationship. For Winnicott, what the child mourns is its own sense of omnipotence embodied in consoling action of the mother; and what it must learn to make do with is the "good-enough mother", or a mother who is not a simple extension of the child's will, and who sometimes frustrates its desire for instant gratification. Specifically, for Winnicott the "good-enough mother" is "one who makes active adaptation to the infant's needs":

> The good-enough mother . . . starts off with an almost complete adaptation to her infant's needs, and as time proceeds she adapts less and less completely, gradually, according to the infant's growing ability to deal with her failure.
>
> (Winnicott 2005: 10)

While Winnicott articulates the concept of the "good-enough mother" in different terms to Klein's discussion of reparation, it refers to the same stage and the same phenomenon, wherein the child learns to tolerate the mother's failures at complete gratification. The key difference is that Winnicott places the child within the context of the home rather than the clinic. Winnicott also emphasizes the mother's active (rather than merely spectral) part in the exchange of unconscious material between herself and the child.

Alongside the good-enough mother, Winnicott theorizes the role of the "transitional object" as key to the child's development of autonomy, and reparation of the mother. A transitional object may be a doll, blanket or soft toy that comes to serve a comforting function for the child in their negotiation of the difference between "me" and "not-me". It is an object most typically encountered during weaning, where the ideal mother is also making the transition to the "good-enough mother". The transitional object is thus invested with a degree of cathexis proportionate to what the child feels is being withdrawn by its mother. Winnicott also designates as "transitional phenomena" activities such as babbling, idiosyncratic mannerisms, or the singing of familiar tunes in preparation for sleep. Both transitional objects and transitional phenomena refer, for Winnicott, to "an intermediate state between a baby's inability and his growing ability to recognize and accept reality" (Winnicott 2005: 3).

"1. The infant assumes rights over the object, and we agree to this assumption. Nevertheless, some abrogation of omnipotence is a feature from the start.

2. The object is affectionately cuddled as well as excitedly loved and mutilated.
[. . .]

4. It must survive instinctual loving, and also hating and, if it be a feature, pure aggression.

5. Yet it must seem to the infant to give warmth, or to move, or to have texture, or to do something that seems to show it has vitality or reality of its own.

6. It [does not come] from without . . . from the point of view of the baby. Neither does it come within; it is not a hallucination.

7. Its fate is to be gradually allowed to be decathected, so that in the course of years it becomes not so much forgotten as relegated to limbo . . . It is not forgotten and it is not mourned. It loses meaning . . ." (Winnicott 2005: 5).

The transitional object is thus a kind of quasi-animated object, which is both real and an extension of the child: invested with illusion, but not illusory. Like the toy within Klein's clinical play technique, the transitional object takes on a role within the child's fantasy life as an object on to which anxiety can be projected, and from which comfort is sought. However, Winnicott's idea of the object here is a significant development of Klein's understanding of the toy. The transitional object assists the child to come to terms with the reality principle – or the requirement that it defer immediate gratification – negotiating the fine line between absolute illusion, through which reality is disavowed (see Chapter 1), and the illusions required in order to develop relations with others at all. More precisely, the transitional object helps the child utilize illusion (or fantasy) in order to negotiate the processes in which the ideal mother becomes the "good-enough mother". The function of the transitional object is, however, perversely reflected in its "fate" (point 7 above): for it helps the child achieve its detachment from the primary object, the mother. Yet, once it has done this, it "loses its meaning", to be replaced by "the whole cultural field": all the art, religion and cultural pursuits that absorb us in adulthood.

Bion: a containment or modification of Klein's thought

Wilfred Bion extends object relations theory in a different, but related, trajectory. Bion develops Klein's account of the psycho-dynamics between mother and baby in terms of "containment" and "modification". In the best-case scenario, according to Bion, the mother receives and "contains" the child's projected anxiety, so she may return it to the child to be "reintrojected" in a "modified", more palatable, form.

> From the infant's point of view [the mother] should have taken into her, and thus experienced, the fear that the child was dying. It was this fear that the child could not contain. He strove to split it off together with the part of the personality in which it lay and project it into the mother. An understanding mother is able to experience the feeling of dread that this baby was striving to deal with by projective identification, and yet retain a balanced outlook. (Bion 1967: 104)

This is the paradigm of good communication, according to Bion, and provides a model for the role that the analyst performs for the analysand. Communication originates in what he calls "realistic pro-jective identification" (*ibid.*: 118), wherein the infant engages in a "behaviour reasonably calculated to arouse in the mother feelings of which the infant wishes to be rid" (*ibid.*: 114). A mother who, unlike Little Dick's, allows herself to feel, but is not overwhelmed by, the child's fear of self-annihilation is then able to reassure him that he is safe. Such exchange is deeply corporeal, as it is the mother's gaze, as well as her breast (a "thinking breast"), that plays this role of containing the child's anxiety:

> Normal development follows if the relationship between infant and breast permits the infant to project a feeling, say, that it is dying into the mother and to reintroject it after its sojourn in the breast has made it tolerable to the infant psyche. (Bion 1967: 116)

In this manner, Bion inflects the act of breastfeeding with an inter-subjective, ethical dimension.

On the other hand, where the intersubjective process (of contain-ment and modification) between mother and child fails to occur – in situations where a mother is despondent or a child especially anxious – the returned material appears to increase in volume and menace, such that the infant reintrojects "not a fear of dying made tolerable, but a nameless dread" (*ibid.*).

KEY POINT *"Containment" and symbol formation*

That Bion designates this dread as "nameless" indicates that it is in some sense beyond symbolization.

- The relation of "inside" and "outside" that the child masters by means of the mother's body is the basis of the binary opposition, and the first "system of difference" that the child recognizes as such. In it inheres the possibility of symbolization.
- Language finds material support in this first, bodily relation with the mother, and words eventually come to stand in for the mother's body, as "objects" that mediate the subject's relation to his own anxiety or death drive.
- When the system of exchange between the child and the mother breaks down, anxiety escapes the technique of management that this proto-symbolization represents (thus producing "nameless dread").

For Bion (*à la* Klein), then, thinking is nothing other than a mechanism for dealing with frustration brought about by the obstacle of reality when, for instance, the breast is found to be empty or unavailable. Thought, far from in essence "abstract", is the body's means of negotiating the demands and limitations placed upon it by other bodies, and by the self-regulation of the ego. Following Freud's contention in "Two Principles of Mental Functioning" (see Chapter 1), Bion states that a "capacity for tolerating frustration . . . enables the psyche to develop thought as a means by which the frustration that is tolerated is itself made more tolerable":

> I shall limit the term "thought" to the mating of a pre-conception with a frustration. The model I propose is that of an infant whose expectation of a breast is mated with a realization of no breast available for satisfaction . . . If the capacity for toleration of frustration is sufficient the "no-breast" inside becomes a thought and an apparatus for "thinking" it develops. (Bion 1967: 111–12)

W. R. D. Fairbairn: psychoanalysis between science and philosophy

W. R. D. Fairbairn studied philosophy as an undergraduate at the University of Edinburgh before turning to medicine, and his particular deployments of object relations theory – especially his objections to Freud – reflect this philosophical background. Fairbairn radicalizes a more general object relations objection to Freud: one more significant than the question of, for instance, when the onset and resolution of the Oedipus complex occurs. Like Ricoeur or Habermas (see Chapter 8), Fairbairn's position is that Freud's libido theory is potentially inconsistent: and in particular, that his commitment to an energetic model of the drive – derived from nineteenth-century neuroscience – is in conflict with the principle that it is the relation to objects (in Oedipus) that determines ego development. The former view, he argues, casts the drive as essentially aimless, dissipating itself by the most expedient means available (given any number of obstacles set in its path). By contrast, the latter, object relations, view of the drive is concerned with intentionality – and it is this intentionality towards an object that generates its "energy", rather than a reservoir, or quantum, of energy native to it. Fairbairn thus pitches a structuralist account of the libido against a vitalist account, and argues that anxiety issues from object relations rather than the reverse.

What, then, are we to make of Fairbairn's disagreement with Freud? Should we put it down to a mere quibble between members of a closed fraternity? In fact, something more is at stake, both philosophically and for psychoanalysis. First (for psychoanalysis), Fairbairn's claim concerns the undue influence of a particular (and perhaps limited) scientific model over the entire corpus of psychoanalytic theory and practice. Freud's commitment to the energetic model of the drive is a factor both of his desire to maintain scientific legitimacy for his discipline, and his own training in medicine. Yet, if this account is wrong, then it might have deleterious effects upon what psychoanalysis can do as a discipline. For Fairbairn, this model of the instincts not only stymied our understanding of the psyche and of human being. It also ignored what were in his own time the most recent advances in science – advances that, according to Fairbairn, emphasize structure over underlying substance: "atomic physics has revolutionized the scientific conception of the physical universe and has introduced the conception of dynamic structure" (Fairbairn 1994: 176). Secondly (and for philosophy), Fairbairn held that Freud's two-tiered (or internally incoherent) explanation of the drive – as on the one hand energetic, and on the other determined by its relations to objects – leads us back to the mind–body dualism that psychoanalysis would ostensibly seek to avoid. Fairbairn held that while the energetic account of the drive explains how materiality – cells, "neurones" – motivates psychological behaviour, when it comes to explaining more complex social and cultural phenomena, Freud shifts gear. Faced with these topics, Fairbairn argues, Freud recurs instead to what he calls a "structural" model of the self (organized in terms of the id, ego, superego; and catalysed by object relations, with reference to Oedipus). Is Freud's double concept of the drive, then, not equivalent to Descartes's pineal gland, as the intermediary between two incommensurate "substances", body and soul?

We might intervene at this point, however, that Fairbairn's exclusive "either/or" approach to the drive misses the evocatively dialectic register of Freud's theory. As we saw in Chapter 2, Freud's drive is not a simple impulse or instinct, but rather is both impulsional and sociolinguistic: it alters the body in relation to its environment. In response to Fairbairn, we might then ask, could not the drive be both object-oriented and pleasure-seeking? If we understand the structural and visceral elements of Freud's drive theory as working in tandem, rather than as opposed to one another, then perhaps we thereby find in Freud a solution to mind–body dualism instead of its reiteration. We shall return in Chapter 8 to consider the value of Freud's energetic account of the drive. The French psychoanalyst Jacques Lacan, whom we will address in Chapter 5, also read Freud's theory of drives in structural terms. It is to Lacan's contribution to understanding psychoanalysis that we now turn.

Summary

- Melanie Klein adapted Freud's clinical methodology of free association for children, using rudimentary toys rather than words as units of meaning. This approach she called the play technique.
- Drawing on Freud's later, "death drive" hypothesis, Klein's account of early mental life emphasizes the domination of sadistic impulses, conceived as defences against discomfort or pain.
- During the earliest, schizoid, position, the infant manages aggression and anxiety by projecting these into the fantasmatic "bad" underperforming breast, and bolsters itself by appropriating the "goodness" of the nourishing breast. The exchange of psychic

energy between the child and its objects in fantasy at this stage, whether defensive or appropriative, is characteristically violent.

- When the child realizes that the good and bad mother are one and the same "object" (the depressive position), guilt replaces aggression, and diverts instinctual energy to the task of repairing the loved object (and the parts of the self associated with it).
- The depressive position marks the resolution of the Oedipus complex, and the complete integration of the superego. It also signals the ability to tolerate anxiety and frustration rather than projecting it on to the object, and to feel ambivalence regarding the loved one. When the individual is intolerant of anxiety and loss (as in the case of Little Dick), difficulties in thinking and symbol formation arise.
- The Oedipus complex culminates far earlier according to Klein than other Freudians allow – in the first two years of life.
- Creativity and artistry involve, according to object relations theory, the attempt to recuperate the loved object to the self – it is thus a return to the depressive position, and an act of mourning.
- Donald W. Winnicott develops the concept of the "transitional object", which assists the child in negotiating the separation from the loved object (a role that is eventually played by culture in general). He also introduces the notion of the "good-enough mother": a mother who will lovingly apply to, yet sometimes frustrate, the child's desire for instant gratification – thus preparing it for independence.
- Wilfred Bion theorizes the manner in which the mother "contains" and "modifies" the infant's mortal fear, returning his projected material back to him in a more palatable form. This process lays the groundwork for communication in general.
- W. R. D. Fairbairn emphasizes the potential inconsistency of Freud's approaches, favouring the topographical (interpretive) over the dynamic (biological) account of the psyche. According to Fairbairn, the former approach is elaborated and developed by object relations theory. Furthermore, the object relations approach avoids mind–body dualism, whereas, Fairbairn claims, Freud's energetic account of the drive revisits it in psychoanalytical terms.

five

Jacques Lacan: rereading Freud to the letter

Introducing Lacan's return to the meaning of Freud

Few twentieth-century thinkers have exerted such far-reaching influence on intellectual life as Jacques Lacan (1901–81). Lacan's intervention changed the face of the psychoanalytic movement internationally. Lacan's seminars in the 1950s and 1960s were one of the formative environments of the poststructuralist ideas that dominated French intellectual life in subsequent decades. Yet Lacan's writings are notoriously difficult. As we shall see in Chapter 7 (when we look at Mulvey's reading of "the gaze"), many of the secondary presentations distort Lacan's ideas, or share the original's esoteric character. In this chapter, we shall provide as clear an understanding as we can of Lacan's central ideas. We take as our cue the way Lacan suggests we should read his work: as a "return to the meaning of Freud" (Lacan 2006: 415).

Three points need emphasizing from the start.

First, Lacan proposed a return to the meaning of Freud in the 1950s. Implicit in the idea that we should need to return to this meaning is Lacan's strong criticism of the way psychoanalysis had developed in the previous decades. Although Lacan's relationship with the object relations theorists (Chapter 4) is nuanced, he is uncompromisingly critical of the "ego psychology" of figures such as Hartmann and Loewenstein (who analysed Lacan), predominant in the United States by the 1950s. For reasons we shall see, Lacan is particularly critical of the ego psychologists' idea that psychoanalysis should strengthen analysands' egos, on the model of the ego of the psychoanalyst. One consequence of this reconception of psychoanalysis, Lacan argues, is that Freud's discovery of the unconscious has been repressed in the history of psychoanalysis. This means that psychoanalysis itself needs to be (re-)analysed.

Secondly, Lacan adopts Freud's aspiration that psychoanalysis should keep abreast of the most advanced sciences of the day. Lacan brings to his rereading of Freud resources taken from developments in the human sciences that took place after Freud was writing his ground-breaking psychoanalytic texts. Lacan's interpretation of Freud in the 1950s is centrally indebted to resources taken from the structuralist linguistics developed by Saussure and Jakobsen (especially "The Instance of the Letter in the Unconscious", Lacan 2006: 493–528; and "The Function and Field of Speech in Psychoanalysis", *ibid.*: 237–322), and its application in anthropology by Lacan's friend, Claude Lévi-Strauss. However, Lacan also draws on ideas from disciplines such as ethology, game theory and mathematics (especially "The Function and Field of Speech"), not to mention his debts to the philosophers Sartre, Kojève, Heidegger, Hegel, Kant, Aquinas, Augustine and Plato.

Thirdly, by bringing these resources to the "Freudian field", Lacan rereads Freud the way psychoanalysis suggests we ought to read all productions of the human psyche. According to Lacan, Freud thought beyond his means, never "catching up" theoretically to what he had stumbled upon in the clinic, and by dint of his speculative acumen. Lacan argues that it is only in the light of the subsequent developments in the human sciences that the resources have become available to "formalize" the field of investigation Freud opened up into the unconscious and its effects on human life (Lacan 2006: 267, 284–5).

This third point is vital to understanding Lacan's contribution to the history of psychoanalysis. Lacan's return to Freud's meaning is neither uncritical nor wholly apologetic. Lacan instead attempts to "work through" symptomatic enigmas in Freud's metapsychology, using structuralism and resources from the other disciplines mentioned above.

KEY POINT *Symptomatic points in Freud to which Lacan "returns"*

- Freud at different points in his text presents the ego as both the subjective agency of reason and sanity, and a narcissistic love-object. This later account of the ego as love-object sees the strengthening of the ego not as the key to mental health, as ego psychology was to maintain, but at the heart of psychotic megalomania.

- Freud argues that the human sexual drives are "de-centred" from the natural cycle of the seasons, or from any direct link to one type of object (Chapter 2). How is this possible?
- Freud tells us that, in the event of a psychical trauma, the representatives of repressed drives are "fixated", so the person develops a permanent tendency to repeat infantile forms of sexual activity in later life. How can the unconscious be a "timeless" memory system, given the nature of the "wetware" (the brain) it is housed in?
- How, most broadly of all, can we synthesize the biological account of the mind we saw in Chapter 1 and Freud's interpretive procedure of psychoanalysis, his case studies, and in *The Interpretation of Dreams*, *Jokes and Their Relations to the Unconscious*, and *The Psychopathology of Everyday Life*?

At the basis of Lacan's return to the meaning of Freud is an emphasis on how psychoanalysis is a talking cure: one whose efficacy concerns the "agency" of language on the human psyche. The pivotal breakthrough of Breuer and Freud, Lacan emphasized, is that the psychosomatic symptoms of neurotics are manifestations of desire which repeat in so far as they have not been "symbolized" by individuals. When analysands, through free association and analytic interpretations, do remember the cause of these symptoms, this linguistic recognition of the symptoms' causes affects the symptoms. More specifically, the desire "caught up" in the symptoms is evidently satisfied (Freud says "abreacted"). This elementary clinical datum, Lacan reasons – adapting Hegel's philosophical account of human desire as the desire for recognition – can mean only that the analysand's desire must have been shaped by their linguistic experiences, and their desire for recognition, from the start (e.g. Lacan 2006: 279).

What psychoanalysis reveals to us, Lacan contends, is that human beings are the "animals captured and tortured by language" (Lacan 1993: 243). The Freudian unconscious, he says, far from being a swirling chaos of primal drives, is structured like a language, "a chain of signifiers that repeats and insists somewhere" (Lacan 2006: 799). Remember from Chapter 3 how Freud, reflecting on parapraxes (such as his forgetting "Signorelli") and on dreams as distorted, censored "texts", developed his topographical account of the psyche. Lacan draws on structuralist linguistics to reformulate these ideas, arguing that the unconscious comprises *signifiers* (as we shall see, words, letters, also images) "at large" – or cut loose from their ordinary meanings. If certain traumatic things are permanently "remembered" in the unconscious, it is because they become "caught in the gullet of the signifier": maintained as symptomatic points in a larger system of linguistic *Vorstellungen* which a person carries with them from the time they learn their "mother tongue" to the grave. The unconscious, for Lacan, is what we might call a private language, had Wittgenstein not argued the impossibility of such a thing. Just as Freud's "Signorelli" case shows how the unconscious "files" the representatives of the drives in irrational ways inaccessible except by the individual's own free associations (including according to the coincidental sounds of words and personal associations), just so Lacan argues that the unconscious contains irrationally connected *Vorstellungen* whose insistence only ceases when they are symbolized before an other (the analyst) in the psychoanalytic clinic.

With these framing anticipations in place, we turn to Lacan's metapsychology in detail.

I is an other: from Freud to Lacan

The young Lacan was trained as a medical psychiatrist. Whereas Freud began his psychoanalytic career analysing hysterics, Lacan's early clinical and theoretical work was based on the clinic of the psychoses. Importantly, Freud's own confrontation with the psychoses after 1910 (the year of "The Schreber Case") was pivotal in his reconsideration of the nature of the ego, and eventually the later metapsychology of the superego and death drive. As Freud's essay "Some Neurotic Mechanisms in Jealousy, Paranoia and Homosexuality" (JPH) – which Lacan translated in the early 1930s – highlights, the reason concerns Freud's discovery through the clinic of the psychoses of the potentially regressive role of the ego and its identifications in cases of paranoia.

KEY POINT *Some mechanisms Freud sees involved in jealousy and paranoia*

Freud's "Some Neurotic Mechanisms in Jealousy, Paranoia and Homosexuality" analyses a series of progressively more severe forms of mental disturbance:

- *Normal jealousy*, the blow struck at a person's ego when they become aware, correctly, that their beloved can desire someone else.
- *Projected jealousy*, where a person accuses their partner of infidelity, whether fairly or falsely, in this way disavowing their own desire for

---

infidelity. Freud gives the example of a man who has an affair, and (lo and behold!) from this time starts suspecting his wife of infidelity at every turn. In such cases, Freud argues, the person's disavowed wish is projected on to their partner. In other words, I (the jealous one) identify with my partner and so "truly" see my desire operating in her – "*you* are unfaithful, *not I*!"

- *Delusional jealousy*: Freud argues that, in cases of pathological jealousy, what is at stake is an unconscious desire for homosexual infidelity. By way of projective identification with the other, this becomes: "*I* do not love him, *you* love him", matched by the same paranoid certainty that sees psychotics such as Judge Schreber (see below) "know" that God, the CIA, ASIO and so on are after him. The psychotic can be so certain that others love him (in the case of erotomania) or hate him (in paranoia) because the wishes in question truly do exist, but in the individual, not in the other with whom they identify.

Freud's account of the role of regressive identification in jealousy and paranoia confirms a finding he elsewhere talks of under the heading "hysterical identification" (ID: 149–51). This is the strange discovery that people seemingly structure who, what and how they desire by way of their identifications with others. In a famous case from *The Interpretation of Dreams*, for example, Freud claims to show how the apparently disappointing dream of a "witty butcher's wife" – about being unable to hold a dinner party (because she had only smoked salmon in her cupboard) – turns out to have been fulfilling her husband's wish not to get plump. Then there was her own, rather nasty wish that her slim friend (who loved smoked salmon) should not get any plumper. The rationale of this jealous wish again concerned the desire of her husband, since her husband (who always spoke well of this girlfriend) usually only desired plumper women (ID: 146–9).

In Lacan's early writings on "the imaginary", he considers how this strange phenomenon of "desiring through others" could be possible. Lacan's famous 1936/49 article "The Mirror Stage as Formative of the I" draws on observations on the behaviour of infants aged between 6 and 18 months. Before this time, as Freud and Klein agree, infants are unable psychologically to distinguish what is "inside" and "outside" their own bodies. Nor have they mastered their manifold "component drives". They are wholly dependent (for a length of time unique in the animal kingdom) on their first nurturers. In Lacan's formulation, their self-experience is rather like those "bodies in bits and pieces" pictured in Hieronymus Bosch's disturbing canvasses (Lacan 2006: 96–7, 105). Nevertheless, between 6 and 18 months, babies become able to recognize their own mirror image. Nor is this a dispassionate experience. It brings the child great pleasure, as their repeated, "experimental" movements in front of the mirror attest (*ibid.*: 93–4). For Lacan, we can only explain this "jubilation", (again) unusual in the entire animal kingdom, as testimony to how the child gains in front of the mirror its first "anticipation" of itself as a unified, separate "I" or ego (*ibid.*: 97, 112–13).

The implication, as Lacan examines it, is that we should not be surprised at Freud's accounts of "hysterical identification" or delusional jealousy. The human ego is an other, to invoke the poet Rimbaud, based on an "image-inary" mapping of the body. Lacan's account of the imaginary accordingly echoes Freud's second conception of the ego – intimated in Freud's recourse to Narcissus' mythical fascination with his mirrored image in the waters of the fountain. The formative role of a child's identification with the "images" it perceives in the mirror, and of the others among whom it grows up, is evident in the phenomena of "infantile transitivism", wherein one infant hit by another (for example) proclaims: "I hit him!", and vice versa (Lacan 2006: 112). It is evident also in our abiding superegoic capacity to think of ourselves in the second person, usually harshly – "What are you saying now? They'll never like you, if you act like that", and so on.

This imaginary make-up of our identity, Lacan argues, also underlies the irremovable component of jealousy and aggression in human behaviour. As we saw in Chapter 2, in *Three Essays on Sexuality*, Freud stressed the primordial ambivalence of children towards their love-objects: in the oral phase, to love is to devour; in the anal phase, it is to master; in the Oedipus complex, it is to hate the father one also loves. Lacan's theory of the imaginary reframes these Freudian insights on a more systematic basis. On the one hand, phenomena such as "following the fashion" reflect that human desire, framed in the imaginary, is the desire of the other from the ground up. We should not be surprised when for instance, children cease to desire something they ardently wished for at the same moment their sibling loses interest in it. It was their identification with this sibling that shaped their desire. On the other hand, and more enigmatically, Lacan's conception of the imaginary underlies his adaptation of Freud's later hypothesis of a primary masochism in human beings (EPM). Given that young infants shape their early identifications around fixed images of other(s), when the child's bodily drives subsequently change, this "ideal ego" will be rigidly unable to accommodate these new somatic demands. Instead, as we saw in Freud's account of repression (Chapter 1), such drives will be experienced as alien threats. This is what for Lacan explains the pre-eminence in dream imagery of the ego as a beleaguered camp or fortress (Lacan 2006: 97). It also explains children's invariant compensatory delight, noted by Klein, in the "mutilation, dismemberment, dislocation, evisceration, devouring, [and] bursting open" of their playthings (*ibid.*: 104).

"I'll be what she's having": rethinking Oedipus

Lacan's claim that the ego is an other constituted by the infant's imaginary identifications has remarkable implications for Freud's central doctrine of the Oedipus complex. Lacan's position is that, because of the unusually long period of infantile dependence on others, human beings' biological needs become inseparable from their demand to be recognized and loved by others. Events as apparently "natural" as toilet training are experienced by the child as episodes in the "history" of its relations with its parents – as expressive of its identification as a "good boy" or (say) revenge for some imaginary grievance (Lacan 2006: 261–2). Lacan agrees with Freud *contra* Klein that the Oedipus complex arises only in the fourth to sixth years of this developmental drama. However, given his account of the imaginary configuration of human desire, Lacan's understanding of the Oedipus complex rejects Freud's emphasis on the biological organ of the penis – an emphasis that famously compromised Freud's ability to ascertain what women want (see Chapter 6). Lacan talks instead of "the phallus". What "the phallus" names in Lacanian theory is what the child imagines its first provider and object of identification, the (m)other, desires (Lacan 2006: 690–93). Like Klein, that is, Lacan accepts the primary importance of the mother in the early development of the child. But for Lacan, it is primarily the desire of the mother as imagined by the child that is decisive, and that becomes the decisive stake in the child's Oedipal rivalry with its father.

KEY POINT *Lacan's rethinking of the Oedipus complex, around the desire of the (m)other*

- In their first years, Lacan contends, infants of either sex devote themselves to fathoming what the mother wants: *che voui?* The object of infants' first researches is not to discover where babies come from (Freud) or to make reparations to the mother (Klein). It is to try to make themselves the

---

- phallus for the mother. The child wants to be this singular, fully satisfying Thing or love-object.
- In the infant's fifth or sixth year, however, the father will normally intervene in a way that thwarts this aspiration. The Oedipal child perceives the father as its imaginary rival, on to whom it projects its hostile wishes. Lacan accordingly likens the father–child relation at this point (at least as it is perceived by the child) to the famous "struggle to the death for pure recognition" dramatized in Hegel's *Phenomenology of Spirit*.
- In this struggle for the desire of the mother, the child should cede to the father. The mother should cease to entertain the child's wish to be her Thing. (Lacan sometimes talks of this as the "castration of the mother".) The ensuing renunciation of the aspiration to be the phallic Thing for the mother, not any physical event or its imagined threat, is what Lacan more generally calls "castration".

On the basis of his critique of Freud's account of the Oedipus complex, Lacan at one point goes so far as to suggest that the Oedipus complex was Freud's "dream". What Lacan agrees with Freud about is that the child's acceptance of its "castration" marks the decisive moment in its libidinal education. Everything turns in this drama, Lacan adds, on how the child understands the "castration" of its infantile wish to be the phallus for the mother. The decisive issue is whether this renunciation is experienced as a violent, illegitimate humiliation by the imaginary father-rival or whether, as in Hegel's *Phenomenology*, its resolution involves the founding of a pact between the parties. If the castration complex is to normalize the child, Lacan argues, the child must "see" that what orders the desire of the mother is not any visible (imaginary) feature of the father – say, his obviously better endowments, ability to shout louder, beat the child and so on. The child must instead see that the "whims" of the mother are themselves ordered by a law that exceeds and tames them. Like Kleinian object relations, that is to say, Lacan's account of the imaginary underscores how the first years of life, wherein the infant's desire is nearly wholly dependent on the desire of the mother, are not any kind of paradise. Unsure of the boundaries between itself and the other, and of the destructive power of its aggressive wishes, if its infantile dependence on the mother is not "mediated" by the intervention of the law, the individual will remain subject to fantasies of the unpredictable omniscience of the devouring (m)other, therefore incapable of normal sexual desire (Lacan 2006: 814).

In order to clarify the stakes in the dissolution of the Oedipus complex, Lacan introduces a key distinction, not in Freud, between the imaginary, the real and the symbolic father:

- *The imaginary father* is the father as perceived by the Oedipal child. The child projects all his sexual jealousy on to the imaginary father, and imagines and fears the father feels such unchecked, castrating hostility toward him.
- *The "real father"* in Lacan's early seminars is the real individual who bears the freight of the child's imaginary hostility, and is asked to intervene as the symbolic father.
- *The symbolic father*, decisively, is the bearer of a "structural function" which may or may not come into being for the child. Everything depends on how the father's words are received by the mother. Problems will ensue if, when the father speaks, "he may as well be whistling", as Lacan puts things concerning the relations between Little Hans' mother and father. As in Hans' case, in the absence of the law-giving words of the father, nothing can check the child's aggressive imaginary fantasies about the real father (and the omniscience of the mother), and phobia (or worse) will ensue. The symbolic father acts through his words ("symbols"), which ideally "break open" the child's dyadic relation with the mother, carrying the force of the social law for her, and thereby for the child.

The law mediating the child's dyadic relation with the mother is what Lacan dubs the "name of the father", "the paternal function" or "metaphor". In French, *le nom du père* invokes a homonymy between *nom* (name) and the *non!* the symbolic father's intervention "says" to the child's incestuous wishes concerning the mother. When the father intervenes as the symbolic father, he does so less as a living, enjoying individual than as the delegate of a set of social conventions respected by the mother. The symbolic father is always a dead father, Lacan thus says (e.g. Lacan 2006: 812) – expanding on a motif in Freud's analysis of the Ratman (and Dostoevsky), and in Freud's "Totem and Taboo" (see Chapter 7). The body of social convention the father symbolically represents, Lacan in turn calls the "big Other" of the child's sociolinguistic community – to distinguish it from the "little-o others" with whom the subject is caught up in the aggressive *tête-à-têtes* of its imaginary identifications.

So the child's acceptance of the sovereignty of the impartial law borne by the father over the whims of the mother leads it out of its ambivalent attempts to be what Freud jokingly called "His Majesty the Baby" (ON: 91). All such incestuous wishes are henceforward repressed by force of social law. If things go well, as Lacan puts it in his unpublished "Seminar V", the child will go away with "title deeds in its pocket" that guarantee that, when the time comes (and if it plays by the rules), it can have a substitute for its first "lost" love-object. What occurs with the acceptance of one's symbolic castration, Lacan argues, is that the individual's imaginary identifications (or "ideal ego(s)") have been supplemented by an identification of an entirely different order: what Lacan calls a symbolic identification with an "ego ideal". This is an identification with something that cannot be seen, touched, devoured or mastered in the ways the child has hitherto deployed to impose itself on its world, namely, the words, norms and conventions of its society. Symbolic identification is always identification with a rule-governed way of organizing the social world, within which the subject can take on its various imaginary identifications and play out its rivalries. For example, the hysterical–vulnerable female identifies at a symbolic level with the patriarchal way of structuring social relations between sexes. Outside of this order, her imaginary identification as a "cute", vulnerable female in need of male protection makes no sense.

Opening the purloined letter: Lacan's sructuralist anthropology

With Lacanian psychoanalysis, the resolution of the Oedipus complex thus becomes a structural operation that should elevate the child's identifications to a different, symbolic level. In place of its incestuous desires, repressed by law, one identifies with a symbolic ideal and way of arranging social relations "in the name of which" one defers gratifications of one's wishes. In patronymic societies, the child at this point ceases to see himself as "little Johnnie", "Mommy's special little guy", and to understand that he is "John *Winston*". If Freud pointed to the singularity of sexuality among the human drives, and stressed how it needs to be educated in the earliest years of our lives, Lacan specifies that human sexuality is uniquely closely associated among the drives with the dimension of social law. One's surname does not after all usually have a say in what you can eat. What having a "surname" or "name of the father" means is that one can absolutely not have sexual relations with anyone sharing that surname no matter how attractive they might be, and so on – except in the statistically exceptional, and potentially psychologically fraught, case wherein one meets an unrelated person with the same surname. To evoke another of Freud's essays, the child has now passed beyond the "family romance" to become part of the wider, social system of kinship exchange. In this system, the family "Winston" is only one amidst many others, from among whom the person must choose the objects of its desire.

So since for Lacan human desire is the desire of the (m)other, which ought to be mediated by the law-bearing words of the "paternal func-tion", so for Lacan human beings' desire is caught up in the social imperatives borne by the "mother tongue" of their society. Lacan picks up on certain cues within Freud's essays (notably those on the "Psychology of Love" (STC; UTD)) to emphasize the "dialectical" con-stitution of human desire in relation to the prohibitions of law. We not only desire illicit things *despite* the law, Lacan agrees with Saint Paul. It is because the law prohibits them that they take on such a "fatal attrac-tion" for us (Lacan 1992: 83–4). In colloquial terms, there is always something "sexy" about transgression *per se* for human beings that haunts our unconscious fantasies. In "On Narcissism" and his essays on "The Psychology of Love" (see Chapter 2), Freud argued that with the resolution of the Oedipus complex, the affectionate "current" of the boy's love for his mother is "cut" from its incestuous–sexual current. Lacan rejoins that, from this point on, the incestuous–illicit current of the child's desire will be separated from its conscious demand for affection (Lacan 2006: 691). Unconscious desire (not "demand") will now insinuate itself "between the lines" of what is said in polite con-versation, in symptoms, slips and jokes, and the double entendres upon which these and dream condensations play.

KEY POINT/EXCURSUS Jouissance, *the Real, the* objet petit a, *and fantasy*

- The child's identification with the symbolic other "cuts" it from the object of its incestuous wishes. Lacan argues that, because this occurs, individuals are prey to fantasies about the things and acts we retrospect-ively suppose are prohibited by the symbolic law. Lacan calls the type of illicit enjoyment we suppose ourselves to have lost *jouissance* (see Chapter 2).

- The Lacanian "Real" involves the content of these fantasies concerning what is "before the law". The Real is what "cannot be symbolized", instead haunting and interrupting the sense the subject makes in symptoms, slips and other excursuses into ordered social discourse.
- The Lacanian formula for the fundamental structure of fantasy is $ (the subject) ◇ a. The "a" here is the famous "*objet petit a*" Lacan introduces after 1958. The *objet a* is no normal thing. It is that "X-factor" that causes a person to desire another. Lacan models it on the secret treasures (*agalmata*) the love-sick Alcibiades "sees" in Socrates in Plato's *Symposium* (see Chapter 8). The *objet a* is the principal exemplar of what Lacan calls the Real: an object "even better than the real things" we ordinarily encounter, because the subject sees in it the mnemic trace of its fantasized, lost *jouissance*.
- Unconscious fantasy has a compensatory function. It allows the subject to cope with its castration by sustaining the false idea that it once knew a fully satisfying relationship with another (the mother) that was taken from it, and so can be regained. Predominant in the obsessional's fantasy life, for instance, is the figure of the ferocious, "anal" father (modelled on the imaginary Oedipal father) who took its lost *jouissance*. Predominant in the fantasies of hysterics (like Alcibiades) is the fantasy of one real man who knows the truth of what women want, and – as such – the idea of a true woman capable of resolving the enigma of desire.
- Lacan's formula for the fantasy, $◇a, aligns the subject ($) with the *objet petit a*. The subject is "barred": there is a line through the "S" to indicate that the individual is subject to law, which "strikes out" its direct access to *jouissance*. That the "*a*" is aligned with the subject (◇) indicates that the Real object is something that is relative to each individual: it reflects the implication of their desire in the way they experience the world. The *objet a* that causes an individual's desire only becomes so esteemed for them because of the place it holds in their unconscious fantasy, cobbled together out of the history of their development.
- The fantasy is finally a lure that preserves the subject as the passive object of his fate, rather than a subject who takes on responsibility, Oedipus-like, for the contingent events that make up its history. In the Wolfman's primal fantasy, for example (see Chapter 3), the uncanny gaze of the wolves conceals from the Wolfman his own desire to actively see the primal thing.
- Fantasy conceals from us "the non-existence of the other": the fact that the symbolic order with which we have identified, and its authoritative others, are themselves finite. The other does not have the real thing we (fantasmatically) "lost". Love, neuroses and the guilt central to the subject's superego are hence for Lacanians different ways of preserving the other against this recognition.

So Lacan does not preach good news to the unconscious fantasy that "the grass is always greener" on the other side of the law. Oedipus, the man who satisfies all repressed human wishes, strikes out his eyes. Bringing his reframing of Freud's notion of the castration complex together with the structuralist anthropology of Lévi-Strauss, Lacan's principal emphasis is instead on how far-reaching the effects of the symbolic order of law and language are upon human experience. "Alienated" by our imaginary identifications with others, Lacan argues, we are irrevocably "separated" from the Real of *jouissance* when we take on a name in the symbolic order. Indeed, despite our abiding imaginary misrecognitions, Lacan argues that the place we occupy in the symbolic order determines how we stand towards (what people usually take to be) the most important or satisfying things (Lacan 2006: 258).

Lacan's reading of Edgar Allen Poe's story "The Purloined Letter" illustrates well this point concerning "separation". The story centres around a stolen letter, whose secret contents symbolize for Lacan the unconscious "letters" of our repressed wishes. There are two key scenes in the story, as Lacan reads it (Lacan 2006: 12). The first is in the queen's chambers. A conniving minister "purloins" (steals) a letter of the queen's from right before her eyes, hoping to use the threat of its disclosure as a way to bribe her. He can do this because, looking around in good imaginary fashion, he sees how the queen is very anxious that the king, also present, should not have his attention drawn to the letter. The second key scene takes place in the home of our minister, once the police have finished their vain and thorough search for the letter. Lacan's emphasis is on how the same symbolic matrix our minister so successfully exploited in the queen's chambers is repeated in this second scene – but now, decisively, he has a different place in the game (see Figure 5.1).

Nothing about the minister's visible or other imaginary qualities has changed between the first and second scenes. Moreover, he now has the illicit thing he is banking on. Yet, because he has it, he can do nothing to stop our hero Dupin, when he sees the letter "hidden" in plain sight above the fireplace, from taking it from him. Like the queen in the first scene, to make a fuss would be to alert the law (the police who are present), and in this way to confess his guilt. What the strange case of the purloined letter illustrates for Lacan in this way is that, whatever we might imagine about the spoils of social power (or illicit *jouissance*, embodied in the story by the stolen letter), it too is de-centred in the symbolic order – power and the ability to "win friends and influence

A. The law = power without knowledge (of the letter) (1) the king (2) the police	B. Possession of the letter = knowledge without power (to act to prevent the thief) (1) the queen (2) the minister
C. Knowledge and power (1) the minister (2) Dupin	D. The letter (content unknown)

Figure 5.1 The social structure of the "purloined letter" (see Lacan 2006: 15) Note: (1) is the scene in the queen's chambers and (2) is the scene in the minister's rooms.

people" in social situations are shaped by the places we hold in the social structures we inhabit.

To be castrated, for Lacan, means to be subject to a social structure which determines how one stands towards *jouissance*. In the symbolic order, in fact, to act violently to "get to the point" is generally a sign of weakness. It signifies to others that you had to use violence, and that your words have failed to resolve the issue. As animals who are "captured and tortured by language", the best things in human life indeed are not free, Lacan argues. We can attain them only indirectly, if at all, by playing by the rules of the phallic/symbolic order, "climbing up" what he calls "the inverse scale of the Law of desire" (Lacan 2006: 827). To be loved, for instance, one should not be too abject in one's demand for love. Equally, to be respected, one should not be too obviously interested in achieving exactly this end – instead, one must act as the symbolic representative of a cause, or produce works of culture "to make a name for oneself".

On negation: Lacan's "linguisterie"

Lacan's most apparent departure from Freud is the importance he accords to developing a psychoanalytic "philosophy of language" after 1953. This follows from his founding commitment to psychoanalysis as the clinical practice of the talking cure. Yet Lacan's conception of language is the result of his developing certain "currents" in Freud's texts in light of resources taken from structuralist linguistics, as founded by

Ferdinand de Saussure and developed by people such as Jakobsen and Benveniste.

KEY POINT *What is structuralist linguistics?*

For Saussure, every sign (words, or any material thing, such as letters, used to communicate) has two components, and a "referent" in the real world:

- The first is the "*signifier*", like the words of the English language. Our example can be the word "dog" as written here, or spoken.
- The second is the "*signified*": the concepts these signifiers "d-o-g" taken together invoke. Our word "dog" calls to mind the concept of what a dog is: say, "a canine, four-legged mammal known for its friendliness to humans".
- The referents of the signifier "dog" will be the real canine animals out there.

Why "structuralism"?

The elementary insight of structuralism is that there can never be just one signifier or one signified. One sign could not "make sense" or pick out anything specific in the external world. Each sign is instead part of a larger structure. The proof is that:

- Different languages have different "signifiers" for the same signified: "*Hund*" in German, "*chien*" in French, "dog" in English, and so on.
- Different cultures have concepts with different semantic "boundaries": the English-language concept of a river, for example, covers the extension of the French concepts of a *riviere* (a waterway that runs to the sea), and a *fleuve* (a waterway that does not). Structuralism emphasizes how signifiers hence signify only in contrast and combination with other signifiers in a linguistic system or "structure" (such as English or French). They do so on the basis of their differences from other signifiers in the structure ("d-o-g" is not "f-o-g" or "d-a-g" or "d-o-c", which signify different concepts). Equally, each of the individual "signifieds" that a culture develops to understand the world gets its "ostensive boundaries" through its differential relations to the culture's other signifieds.
- Our natural language's structure is something we learn from others early in our lives. Far from able to "mean whatever we choose", the meanings of our wishes are shaped and can only be expressed by way of this linguistic structure, which preceded us and will outlast us.

Individual signs, Saussure argued, are "unmotivated" by their referents in the natural world. The reality of this canine animal here does not demand that I call it either "*un chien*" or "a dog". Either will do in different places around the world, so long as everyone else in each society agrees on the word to use, and this signifier is not already in use in each language's structure to signify something else. Saussure's description of the sign as unmotivated by its referents is vital to the way Lacan brings Freudian psychoanalysis to bear upon structuralist linguistics. The key to why this is so can be shown by considering in Lacanian light Freud's remarkable short paper "On Negation" (see Lacan 1988a: 52–61, 289–98), which we saw Melanie Klein put to a different purpose in Chapter 4.

Freud argues in "On Negation" that the ability (which has puzzled philosophers since Parmenides) to speak about things that do not exist or are not this or that, is a development from earlier, more primitive ways of our rejecting things in the world. We recall that for Freud, the infant "introjects" what gives it pleasure, and "projects" what gives it pain. This primitive operation, Freud argues, must lie at the origins of linguistic judgements concerning the predicates or features of things, especially those concerning whether we think they are good or bad objects. Every satisfaction the infant achieves, we also recall, is for Freud modelled on the initial satisfactions that left a "good" mnemic trace in the baby's mind. On this basis, Freud argues that the infant's ability to use what philosophers call the "existential predicate" (to say of things that "it is the case") develops from the more primitive wish-fulfilling process of testing whether external things match its primal, good "mnem". The earliest wish motivating judgements of existence (such as what Lacan discerns beneath the structure of fantasy ($\$\diamond a$)) is thus to refind the first (lost) Thing. Our ability to make judgements of negation, by contrast to affirmative judgements, hence presupposes a capacity to withhold satisfaction, and an ability to sharply separate what we see externally from our wish-fulfilling "good memories":

> the performance of the function of the judgment is not made possible until the creation of the symbol of negation has endowed thinking with its first measure of freedom from the consequences of repression and, with it, the compulsion of the pleasure principle . . . (N: 239)

On such bases as Freud's "On Negation", Lacan can argue that the elementary "cut" of the linguistic sign from its referents – which structuralism's account of the differential nature of signs presupposes – is none other than the castrating *non!*, which "cuts" the individual from the Thing of its first wishes. Freud says in "On Negation" that the precondition of a child's ability to competently use the symbol of negation is "that objects shall have been lost which once brought real satisfaction" (N: 238). Lacan reads Freud as referring to the child's renunciation of its wish to be the phallus for the mother. All subsequent negations will be predicated, as we might say, on this first absolute *non!* All the child's subsequent experiences, also, will be shadowed by this first negation, and the consequent sense that *"Ce n'est pas Ca"* / "This is *not* It (the lost Thing)." It is in this gap between reality and the lost Thing, and the sense of lack it creates, indeed, that Lacan situates human desire in relation to language. Human desire is a "metonymy", Lacan says, evoking the figure of speech whereby the part(s) of an object (say, the crown) comes to stand for the whole (king, country). Each of the things we desire, Lacan means, will evoke some part of the lost Thing of our unconscious fantasies: this elusive "part object" or "x factor" being the *objet petit a* we encountered in our excursus on the Real.

So Lacan agrees with Saussure that each natural language is a system of differential signifiers. Lacan agrees with Saussure's idea that each natural language is "bigger than any one of us", since it is the product of a culture into which we are socialized by our first others. Yet Lacan extends this structuralist undermining of the modern idea that each of us is the sovereign master of his own meaning(s) by aligning it with Freud's "Copernican" discovery of the unconscious. Just as Freud said that sexuality is that drive that binds us to what is immortal in the species (Chapter 2), so Lacan argues that the unconscious is "the discourse of the Other" (SSD: 689–90/812): that part of our desire caught up in a linguistic system which, if not immortal, is the moving image of countless generations. When anyone forms a meaningful wish or intention, Lacan agrees with Saussure, they must do so in terms of the code of their natural language. As Wittgenstein noted, even Descartes had to say, in Latin, *cogito ergo sum.* Other people, equally, can only understand individuals' speech via this code of the "big Other". Only psychotics believe people's thoughts can be directly transmitted between their minds. When subjects speak, Lacan maintains, they are so far from being fully "in control" of their meanings that they receive their true message back from the (big) Other in an inverted form.

This in fact is where Lacan's Freudian-inspired criticisms of Saussure come into their own. For Saussure, despite his structuralism, still holds on to the (for Lacan, untenable) idea that the basic unit of sense is a single sign (see Figure 5.2). Lacan by contrast joins other influential twentieth-century philosophers of language in claiming that the most

Signifier	"tree"
Signified	(the concept of a self-standing arborescent growth with a trunk, branches, leaves, etc.)

Figure 5.2 Saussure's (sychronic) theory of signification

basic unit of sense is a sentence. The feature Lacan stresses is that the meanings of sentences, and of each of the signifiers comprising them, only becomes clear at the end of the sentence. This is why reading interminably long sentences is so profoundly frustrating. Conversely, if I cut my sentence short, saying, for example, "I went down . . ." – and find myself (for whatever reason) unable to remember what I meant to say – my hearers will be left in suspended semantic animation: "Where did you go down? What?" When any of us speaks a sentence, that is, our hearers anticipate our meaning as we go. Until we finish each of our speech acts, the signifiers we use each "float" or "slide". Far from signifying by themselves, as Saussure suggested, each waits to receive its signification until the subject arrives at its destination, the "last word". It is in this time between the formation of one's intention and its linguistic consummation at sentences' ends, Lacan contends, that the unconscious – trading on the differential nature of our signifiers ("duck" is close to "truck" but also . . .) – makes itself heard in the small distortions characteristic of slips, plays, puns, inhibitions or the forgetting of words (see Figure 5.3).

Only at such time that I complete any utterance (on the right-hand side) will my listeners be able to understand me. This is achieved by referring what I have said to the big Other of socially accepted rules and possibilities: "so he went down to the milk bar . . . the sports ground . . ." Lacan hence talks about the big Other as a "tribunal" to

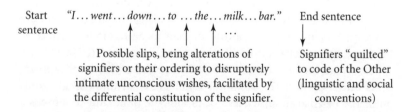

Start sentence "I . . . went . . . down . . . to . . . the . . . milk . . . bar."   End sentence

Possible slips, being alterations of signifiers or their ordering to disruptively intimate unconscious wishes, facilitated by the differential constitution of the signifier.

Signifiers "quilted" to code of the Other (linguistic and social conventions)

Figure 5.3 Lacan's (diachronic) theory of signification

which our linguistic utterances are referred – a tribunal based on the dimension of symbolic pacts into which our castration initiates us:

> As a rule everyone knows that others will remain, like himself, inaccessible to the constraints of reason, outside an acceptance in principle of a rule of debate that does not come into force without an explicit or implicit agreement as to what is called its basis, which is almost always tantamount to an anticipated agreement to what is at stake . . .   (Lacan 2006: 430–31)

Particularly important in this process of retrospectively tying signifiers to the Other are what Lacan calls "master signifiers" – words such as "freedom" in the United States today, or "the revolution" in the former Soviet countries. These are the types of signifiers in a culture whose meanings people tend to take for granted, because they carry with them the force of social law. Their (approving) use by a person identifies the speaker as belonging to the group, and "making sense" to others. The founding model of such master signifiers, Lacan claims, is at base the "paternal metaphor" or "name of the father": that signifier that "stands in" for the child's repressed desire of the mother at the re-solution of the Oedipus complex. Lacan's theory of language picks up, at a very foundational level, on the "promissory" component of the signification of the "paternal signifier" in the resolution of the Oedipal drama – since the child's identification with it signifies that it will with time be able to find a substitute for the renounced Thing. Similarly, Lacan argues that the master signifiers with which subjects identify "quilt" the subject's other signifiers, and guarantee that meaning will emerge from them, however incoherent or otherwise unconvincing their words have been.

Conclusion, on why Schreber had to become a woman . . .

With Lacan's central teachings concerning the imaginary, real and symbolic orders in place, we can appreciate that, for Lacan, mental ill-ness is not caused simply by conflict between the embattled ego, the superego and the id (see Chapter 1). What is decisive is how the subject bears up *vis-à-vis* the condition of being a castrated animal forced to pursue its desire on the "inverted scale" of the signifier, within the sym-bolic order of its society's big Other. The question to be asked, for Lacan, is: how fully has the subject acceded to its symbolic castration?

And, accordingly: how fully have they overcome the ambivalent transitivity and aggression characteristic of the earlier stages of their development? Lacan keeps Freud's tripartite diagnostic scheme of neurosis, perversion, psychosis. Yet here as elsewhere Lacan reframes Freud's scheme according to his structuralist refiguring of Freudian theory:

- *The neurotic* has submitted to castration, but with reservations. Her symptoms and slips stand testimony to her lasting resentment towards the agency of the big Other. As we commented above, underlying hysterics' and obsessionals' symptoms are fantasies concerning the possibility of fully satisfying, lost *jouissance*, little pieces of which their symptoms set out to restore to them.
- *The perverse subject* has only partly acceded to the law whose founding prohibition creates the lack constitutive of desire. In order to create such a lack, the pervert needs to enact (or have enacted) the agency of the law itself. This is why perversions invariably involve not simply aggression, but the enacting of quasi-punishments – "You have been a naughty girl", "You must chain me up", and so on.
- *The psychotic* has never acceded to castration and the agency of the law of the big Other. For him, the symbolic order in which people freely abide by the rules "because they are the rules" is experienced as a semblance – witness the common psychotic delusion that all others, except one's chosen persecutors ("them"), are robots or "hastily improvised men" (Schreber).

The power of Lacan's diagnostic refiguring of Freud around the parameters of the symbolic and the law becomes clear in his analysis of Freud's only great case study dealing with a psychotic, Judge Schreber.

KEY POINT *Freud on "The Schreber Case" (SC)*

The facts of the case

Daniel Paul Schreber was a gifted lawyer born in 1842. In 1884, he ran as the Liberal Party candidate for the Reichstag and, after losing, suffered his first nervous breakdown, undergoing extended treatment for "hypochondria" under the renowned neurophysiologist, Doctor Flechsig. After his release, Schreber worked as a district judge in Saxony for eight years, "marred only from time to time by the repeated disappointment of our hope of being blessed with children". In June 1893, Schreber was promoted to the position of *Senatspräsident* of the Supreme Court of Appeals, at which time he completely broke down.

What were Schreber's symptoms?

- Schreber claimed God was visiting painful physical "miracles" upon him: "[he] had lived for years without a stomach, without intestines, almost without lungs, with an oesophagus in shreds, with no bladder, with smashed rib bones, had sometimes eaten part of the larynx with his food, and so on . . ." (Doctor Samuel Weber).
- Schreber believed that God, in mysterious league with Doctor Flechsig, communicated with him in rays of light and the chatter of "miracled birds".
- Schreber suffered from a harrowing sense that the world was ending, that people around him were unreal, "hastily improvised men", and that Doctor Flechsig had committed "soul murder" upon him.
- Schreber became convinced that he was being "unmanned" (turned into a woman) by God, so that he might become His divine consort, and the progeny of their sexual union would repopulate a rejuvenated earth.

How did Freud understand the Schreber case? Well, as per Chapter 1, Freud argues that Schreber's delusions are his best attempts at a cure. They respond to a prior *Vorsagung*, and their contents reflect the nature of this libidinal "forsaking". Freud points out two key elements in Schreber's delusions. These elements point to one cause of Schreber's illness: foreclosed homosexual wishes. The first key element in Schreber's delusions is its theological content, and the central role played by God in the delusions. Freud interprets Schreber's heretical personal theology as re-presenting Schreber's father complex by delusional means (see Chapter 7). The second element, Freud argues, is the presence of homosexual wishes towards his father. These wishes are represented in disguised form in Schreber's delusions of being turned into God's female consort, and rationalized in terms of Schreber's messianic mission of saving the world.

The crux of Lacan's criticism of Freud developed in *Seminar III: The Psychoses* is the observation that Freud's notion of foreclosed homosexual wishes seems simply to be the wrong type of cause for Schreber's exotic theological delusions. These speak of a much more fundamental disturbance in his ability to signify or "make sense" of the world. Given Lacan's structuralist rereading of Freud, which places emphasis on the linguistic disturbances Schreber reports in his *Memoirs*, Lacan's interpretation is different. Like many psychotics, Schreber was subject to linguistic hallucinations: he heard voices inside his head that he took to have been put in there by a persecutory other (ultimately, God). Schreber's sense of these voices oscillated between two poles, Lacan notes. On the one hand, there were certain words charged with extraordinary meaning, like the "soul murder" he accused Flechsig of enacting upon him. On the other hand, for much of the time, the voices Schreber heard made little sense (Lacan 1993: 32–4). One feature of these "chattering" voices is that they would feature sentences that did not end, such as "lacking now is . . .".

As you can see, this last phenomenon in particular, passed over by Freud, seems made for Lacan to interpret. For Lacan, Schreber's entire sense of reality did not break down because of foreclosed, projected homosexuality – this was an effect, not the cause. What was "lacking now" for Schreber is what Lacan calls the "paternal function", the signifier "being a father" – that master signifier through which the order of the law, and of social trust, is instated, and which could tie psychotics' words and sentences to the Other (Lacan 1993: 196–205). This is why Schreber had to break down when he was called by the Other of his community to take on a law-giving, "paternal" role in the Court of Appeals in 1893. The big Other effectively said to him, "You will be a President in the Court of Appeals." But Schreber could draw only upon his imaginary identifications to understand this symbolic mandate. On the one hand, Schreber heard this invocation in the manner of a kind of sinister prediction – "How does the other know that I will become this paternal figure? How can he see into the bowels of my future?" His answer, of course, eventually took on the bizarre theological form of his delusions concerning his persecutory god, "not one hair on Schreber's head could move without Him knowing". On the other hand, Schreber's homosexual delusions take on sense for Lacan as his best attempt, using the tools of his imaginary identifications, to make up for the lacking signifier "being a father":

> This is why he had to make a mistake, become confused, to the point of thinking and acting like a woman. He had to imagine himself a woman and bring about in pregnancy the second part of the path that, when the two were added together, was necessary for the function of *being a father* to be realized.
>
> (Lacan 1993: 293)

Summary

- Lacan's return to the meaning of Freud attempts to "formalize" Freud in the light of resources from philosophy and the most advanced human sciences of his day (principally structuralism).

- According to Lacan, the infant gets its first, anticipatory sense of being an "I" by identifying with its mirror image, and the visible images of its first other(s) – this is the imaginary register in human subjectivity.

- Lacan agrees with Klein about the primacy of the child's relations to the mother in its first years, arguing that the decisive stake in the Oedipus complex is the Real thing the child imagines the mother desires. The child perceives the father as a rival for this "phallus".

- The Oedipus complex can be satisfactorily resolved only if the father intervenes in the name of social law or "the symbolic", impressing upon the child that the desire of the mother, too, is subject to impartial, social law.

- The unconscious is that part of us which resists this "castration". Its nucleus is found in fantasies concerning the thing or *jouissance* "lost" to us at this time – what Lacan calls "the Real".

- Lacan's account of the symbolic order brings together insights from structuralist anthropology and linguistics, arguing that "castration" opens up the space for the differentially constituted linguistic signs we are each bound to use to form and express our wishes.

- When we speak, we "get back our message from the Other in an inverted form", Lacan claims: our words "make sense" in so far as they are "quilted" to the "big Other" of our society's norms and conventions.

- Particularly important in this process are "master signifiers", modelled on the original *nom/non!* of the father (to the incestuous wishes of the child). As the Schreber case exemplifies, in the absence of such signifiers, individuals will be unable to stabilize their sense of linguistic meaning, sexual difference, and their place in their society's kinship system.

six

What does woman want? Feminism and psychoanalysis

The relationship between feminism and psychoanalysis has been intimate, if troubled, since its very beginnings. The question of "what woman wants" was central to the inception of psychoanalytic thought, even before Freud entered the scene, as we saw in our Introduction, via the case of Anna O. Yet, depending on which feminist analysis one reads, this "woman question" has been either totally manhandled by psychoanalysis, or treated in a most ground-breaking way. We might say feminists' disagreements over psychoanalysis mirror contentions at the heart of feminism in general. Are women's social disadvantages engendered by their biological differences from men? Or is culture paramount over nature, and the body? Is there a distinction between sex and gender, or was Freud right that "anatomy is destiny"? Can bodies simply be set aside in order to attend to social disparities? Or are there already more primary inequalities perceived at the level of anatomy?

Psychoanalysis has unwittingly become one battleground where such larger disagreements between feminists have been played out, not least because of certain, rather inflammatory, claims made by Freud – centrally the idea that girls experience "penis-envy" as a key part of their maturation. As we shall see, feminist contentions about psycho-analysis turn particularly on whether Freud's account of femininity described a particular, predominantly social, circumstance for women – and is thus a measure of how ideology affects the way the body is lived and interpreted – or if this account was prescriptive of how women's lives should be lived, due to fixed, anatomical factors. As we shall see, the question of whether Freud's account of "woman" was descriptive or prescriptive cannot be definitively answered, even through the kind of close reading of his texts offered by feminists such as Sarah Kofman, Luce Irigaray or Juliet Mitchell. Freud's own vacillations and ambivalences about "the woman question" ensure that his conclusions about femininity remain obscure and contested. Yet the answer to this question is crucial to how feminists are able to situate themselves in relation to psychoanalysis. For instance, what are we to make of the centrality of the penis to Freud's, or the "phallus" to Lacan's, accounts of childhood development? How should we evaluate Freud's implied equation of all women with the maternal, as either "mother" or "mother substitute"? And is it acceptable, in the final analysis, that "woman" can be reduced to the one who lacks, or has no sex, because her path to sexual maturation diverges from that of "man"?

Prescriptive or descriptive? Freud on femininity

Given feminism's fraught relation to psychoanalysis, it is perhaps surprising that many of the early adherents and practitioners of psychoanalysis were women. Women were the first objects of study for psychoanalysis – Lacan once called Anna O, Dora and the other women the young Freud analysed the "patron saints" of psychoanalysis. And the question "what does woman want?" was an enduring and seemingly insoluble problem throughout Freud's lectures and writings. Indeed, early psychoanalysis was primarily concerned with a condition (hysteria) arguably brought about by the excessive sociopolitical repression of women, over and above that required of men. Because women were socially designated as "passive", and because such passivity was supposed to characterize every arena of their lives – intellectual, emotional, physical and sexual – women at that time were subjected from infancy to the most throughgoing repression of their natural and cultural potentials.

Unsurprisingly, then, it was from the very social context Freud's early case studies, such as those of Anna O or Elizabeth von R, that the beginnings of a new feminism emerged, concerned with universal suffrage and the improvement of conditions for women within marriage, and regarding property rights. In connection with this burgeoning movement, many women were drawn to psychoanalysis because of the tools it promised to theorize, in Freud's own words, "how [a woman] comes into being, how a woman develops out of a child with a bisexual disposition" (F: 116).

The "question of woman" haunts Freud's entire *oeuvre*. As Sarah Kofman has convincingly argued (see later in this chapter), Freud's ambivalence about femininity can surely be understood in relation to his own anxieties about his masculinity, and also his relations to his mother. Freud's early suggestion was that feminine identity and sexuality develop in a symmetrical manner to masculinity. Taking the Oedipus complex as the central apparatus for explaining the beginnings of sexuality, Freud first understood the little girl's primary love-object to be her father, in an exactly equivalent manner to the boy's attachment to the mother. This would explain not only the heterosexual imperative that appears to shape desire, but also the evident conflict that women in his clinic repeatedly avowed, in one way or another, towards their mothers. Just as at the height of his Oedipus complex, the boy's attachment to his mother had led him to want to do away with his father, at the time of writing *The Interpretation of Dreams* Freud hypothesized an equivalent rivalry between the little girl and her mother:

> We learn from [dreams of the death of parents] that a child's sexual wishes – if in their embryonic stage they deserve to be so described – awaken very early, and that a girl's first affection is for her father and a boy's first childish desires are for his mother. Accordingly, the father becomes a disturbing rival to the boy and the mother to the girl; and I have already shown . . . how easily such feelings can lead to a death wish.
>
> (ID: 257)

By the time Freud's theory reaches its later maturity, however, he revises this thesis in ways that have profound consequences for how we might understand the relation between the sexes, and the relation between socialization and desire. In "Female Sexuality" (1931) and his lecture on "Femininity" (1932), Freud argues that, in contrast to his earlier ideas, girls' first love-object is also the mother, and the later attachment to the father is a screen for this early, repressed wish for the mother. According to this scenario, girls start out life just like little boys, but must be socialized to renounce their primordial love for the mother, before being able to achieve femininity. The key points of Freud's later position on femininity can thus be summarized.

- The little girl at first sees herself as a "little man", with a "little penis", the clitoris.
- Upon seeing the boy's penis, the little girl inevitably develops a deep-seated feeling of inferiority. She recognizes her own lack in relation to the boy – the little girl's "castration complex" thus in fact pre-dates her Oedipal phase, rather than dissolving it, as with Freud's boys.
- This feeling of inferiority gives rise to "penis-envy", and generates in her an ambivalence towards her mother, whom she blames for her own lack, but also identifies with.
- The girl seeks social value by attempting to acquire the "phallus" either through "masculine" projects or, if she is to achieve normalcy, by repressing her active desires and replacing them with more passive satisfactions – particularly vaginal pleasure instead of clitoral, and pregnancy (wherein the baby stands in for the phallus).

Accordingly, whilst for the little boy, the Oedipus complex and rivalry with the father resolves itself with the castration complex, for the little girl this is where her problems begin. Her "recognition" of her lack of a penis gives rise to "penis-envy", given which she understands herself as inherently inferior. From here on, she will be driven by the need to create social value, approximating the penis with its symbolic substitutes (for instance, babies).

Understandably, this schema has divided feminists. It is time now to examine their responses directly.

Female psychoanalysts, and the desire of the mother

One common feature in the differing responses to Freud developed by figures such as Lou Andreas-Salomé, Helene Deutsch, Karen Horney, as well as Anna Freud and Melanie Klein, is the central place they allot to the mother instead of to the father. However, there are significant differences between their theories, which are reflected in how feminists have evaluated them in the later part of the twentieth century. Particularly Deutsch and Horney have received attention from feminist readers of psychoanalysis. Deutsch tends to be read as a "stooge" for Freud's particular articulation of patriarchal ideology, while Horney is taken up as a voice of resistance against it.

Ambivalence about the feminine: Helene Deutsch

Helene Deutsch's theoretical position is subtler than her detractors suggest. But it is true that, like Freud, she emphasized "passivity" and "narcissism" as characteristically feminine traits, and saw motherhood as the pinnacle of female experience. Deutsch's emphasis upon motherhood and passivity certainly raises questions similar to those posed to Freud's own account of femininity. For instance, what are we to make of women with no desire to have babies, and who pursue "active" goals, such as intellectual, artistic or sporting endeavours? Do these proclivities necessarily render such women "masculine", and thus deviant? And what is the task of analysis in this context? Is it simply to "normalize" women, so they desire gender-appropriate goals that complement, rather than emulate, "masculinity"?

Deutsch does not question Freud's characterization of woman as passive and narcissistic, and declares no allegiance to feminism (through which, she holds, women depart from their "nature"). However, Deutsch does challenge Freud's explanation of feminine passivity in an interesting manner – particularly with regard to the nature/nurture debate central to feminist thought. The orthodox psychoanalytic view had been that women become passive, and then narcissistic, to compensate for a perceived genital mutilation ameliorated only by pregnancy and motherhood. Deutsch argues, on the contrary, that feminine narcissism is invoked as a defence against passivity; and she redefines passivity as an instance of masochism, whereby active instincts are turned inwards to attack the ego. In this manner, feminine narcissism becomes an active response for Deutsch to a situation in which a limit has been placed upon women's powers – in other words, as an environmentally conditioned response – rather than as indicative of innate passivity or weakness. And, as you can see, this presents a potential advance for feminism, in that the restrictive sociopolitical situation that produces feminine masochism might conceivably be altered.

Deutsch's own account of how women's active instincts come to be inverted, however, is subject to some confusion between what she considers as natural or essential to woman, and what may be attributed to social conditioning. On one hand, Deutsch holds that, just like the little boy, the little girl identifies with her father rather than her mother. The father represents the outside world – the "environment" or "culture" – and thus a turn away from the mother and the inner life of simple nourishment. The trouble begins when the father discourages this identification, thus inhibiting her active drives and forcing the little girl to divert them inward. Deutsch seems, with this argument, to suggest that the impetus for what ultimately is to become feminine narcissism is cultural or social. Yet on the other hand, she admixes the social and biological in this account, writing that the function of the father is to provide "an inhibiting influence on the woman's activity and drive her back into her *constitutionally predetermined* passive role" (Deutsch 1944: 252, emphasis added). Deutsch thus regards the social pressure that the father provides as a mere trigger to a more primary, biologically determined situation.

Likewise, Deutsch's focus upon motherhood can be read as simultaneously advancing and working against the interests of feminism. On the one hand, her account of motherhood repudiates Freud's emphasis upon penis-envy, or feminine lack. She emphasizes a positive connection to one's own mother as galvanizing the desire for motherhood. For Deutsch, a woman's strong identification with her mother in fantasy can never entirely be broken, and corresponds to a wish to bring forth one's essence through "motherliness". Freud's stress upon feminine passivity and lack as catalysts for woman's desire for a child is in this sense moderated by Deutsch's account, in the importance she gives to women's identification with the image of the active mother of early childhood. On the other hand, Deutsch characterizes motherliness as a narcissistic activity, wherein love for the self as object is diverted to the baby, conceived as only a piece of the self. In this context, Deutsch's contention that woman's greater purpose lies in "motherhood" loses any feminist edge it might have had were motherhood conceived less ambiguously, as promoting a positive identification between generations of women.

In general, feminists have good reason for discomfort concerning Deutsch's emphasis upon the biological register of motherhood and gender: for instance, her suggestion that motherhood behaviours are instinctual remnants of our primeval past. Like the great French philosopher Jean-Jacques Rousseau, Deutsch suggests that problems encountered in mothering (and female sexuality) arise primarily because women come to be alienated from their nature by culture. Likewise, feminism itself falls within the scope of this criticism, as an unnatural deviation from woman's biological destiny. Yet other elements of Deutsch's naturalization of female sexuality might just as easily be turned towards, rather than against, feminism. For instance, she sexualizes her account of motherhood, in counterpoint to Freud's sexualization of infancy, and thus shifts the balance of subjectivity from the little boy of Freud's account to the mother. In this way, the mother becomes an active participant in her own sexuality, with a libido and fantasy life distinct from that of men. With her various case studies of nurses, childcare workers, prostitutes and women found in literature, Deutsch was able to trace a connection between sexuality and a woman's relation to her feelings about motherhood and her own mother, rather than to the father. Such a focus paved the way for later feminist approaches to understanding female psychology in terms of women's intergenerational relations to one another, or maternal lineages rather than the patrilineage that has tended to dominate Freudian psychoanalysis.

Karen Horney: a holistic approach to feminine sexuality

Karen Horney was far more open in her opposition to Freud's perceived sexism than Deutsch, and so has been easier for later feminists to embrace as a precursor and example. Horney adopted what might be called a "holistic" attitude to the study of female sexuality, explicitly rejecting the biological focus championed by Deutsch and other Freudians, instead unambiguously emphasizing environmental and social influences. Horney criticized Freud's scientific methodology, arguing that Freud was too general in applying his findings to all women, given the clinical setting in which his observations were made (since all the women he analysed were neurotic). For Horney, psychoanalysis's "truths" are shaped primarily by the observer's gender, rather than the true nature of what Freud and other male psychoanalysts observed. Horney highlights this charge of masculine bias in psychoanalytic theory by directly and compellingly comparing the infantile theories of little boys about little girls to mature psychoanalytic theory's observations about femininity. For instance, the little boy's "naïve assumption that girls as well as boys possess a penis" is mirrored by the psychoanalyst's belief that "for both sexes it is only the male genital which plays any part" (Horney 1967: 57).

Horney argued that what Freud had called "penis-envy" is truly a specific form of a more general envy evident in boys as well as girls. Particularly, she set penis-envy against a backdrop of the envy the little boy exhibits in relation to the mother, and those activities associated with motherhood: childbirth, the suckling of babies, and pregnancy. Boys' "breast-envy" and "womb-envy" is not only as psychologically significant for boys as penis-envy is for girls. It also explains men's investment in the denigration of female experience. That women's creative and nurturing bodies are so clearly enviable, according to Horney, gives rise to a "reaction formation" in men. Their envy of the female body is repressed, emerging instead as disgust and a conviction in their own biological superiority. In this vein, Horney issues a challenge to Freud's account of the origins of culture in "Civilization and Its Discontents" (wherein culture is the effect of the sublimation of sexual energy; see Chapter 7). Horney argues that culture and civilization emerge as a means for men to compensate themselves for being unable to create life, and thus for their own lack in relation to the female body. This critique of masculine culture prefigures other feminist attempts to construct alternative myths about the origins of civilization, such as those found in Irigaray's "Women, the Sacred, and Money" (1986).

"Second-wave" feminism, and the sins of psychoanalysis

Simone de Beauvoir, her progeny, and Dora

A second wave of feminist responses to psychoanalysis was precipitated by Simone de Beauvoir in 1953, with the translation into English of *The Second Sex*. In this text, de Beauvoir addressed to the philosophers her own question: "Why is woman the *Other*?" Or: why is man so widely considered the prototype of humanity, while woman is reduced to her sex? Psychoanalysis figures as one object of criticism for de Beauvoir's programme, because – as Horney emphasized – Freud's model of human sexuality took the little boy to occupy the "normal" position, from which the little girl must deviate in order to become a woman. By defining woman precisely as she who lacks man's essential organ, psychoanalysis became exemplary of the masculine position, which relegated woman to its Other, the sole purpose of whom is to reflect back to man his subjectivity and transcendence. Thus, while *The Second Sex* attempts to describe the lived experience of being a woman, in relation to the different registers through which femininity is evaluated (social and biological, as well as age, economy, race and class), Freud describes womanhood as the experience of not being a man. In doing so, moreover, Freud makes reference to a biological model of femininity that, arguably, is already inflected with these other registers.

De Beauvoir's refrain "one is not born, but rather becomes, a woman" (de Beauvoir 1972: 296) set feminism alight in the 1960s and 1970s. Feminists' primary concern became to separate one's socially prescribed identity (or "gender") from a perceived given essence (or "sex"). Many also uncritically adopted de Beauvoir's negative assessment of psychoanalysis, presenting it as one more central pillar of patriarchal ideology. These feminists (including such luminaries as Betty Friedan, Kate Millett, Germaine Greer, Shulamith Firestone and Eva Figes) emphasized the repressive and sexist times to which Freud belonged, and his complicity in the subjugation of women in "Victorian" Vienna. This contention might be best highlighted by examining another of Freud's great case studies – his first, and arguably least convincing – the case of Dora, frequently cited by feminists as an allegory for the failure of Freud's theory to understand femininity.

KEY POINT *Freud's "Dora" case study*

The facts of the case

- Freud analysed the eighteen-year-old "Dora" for three months in 1899, after which she ended the analysis, unsatisfied with Freud's treatment of her.
- Dora suffered from a *"petite hystérie"*. Her symptoms included a persistent, unexplainable cough, a phantom appendicitis, a sore and paralysed ankle, and, recurrently, aphonia or the complete loss of her voice. She had also had what Freud regarded as a history of hysteria since childhood.
- The particular crisis that prompted the analysis concerned her avoidance of her family's friends Herr and Frau K, the former of whom Dora accused of trying to seduce her, and the latter of having an affair with her father.

Freud's interpretation

Freud's conclusion is drawn from the analysis of Dora's symptoms, her own narration of the events, and his interpretation of two dreams she brings to him. Freud suggested that:

- Dora was attracted to Herr K, but wants him to prove to her that his intentions are honourable: thus she deflects his advances – obscuring this attraction even from herself – such that he will be pushed to take her more seriously than if she were only a maid or governess.
- Freud speculates that Dora identifies Herr K with her father, and admonishes himself in a "postscript" for failing to notice during the analysis the "transference" of her affections for Herr K and her father on to himself (see Chapter 8).

Freud's Dora case is particularly instructive about the sexual politics of late-nineteenth-century Vienna – the relations between bourgeois men, their wives and female servants – and the difficulty for a young woman to negotiate her way in this social world. Interestingly, from a psychoanalytic perspective, Freud's text shows signs of an awareness of its own "failure" – or that alternative interpretations of the situation were possible – especially in what might be called the "unconscious" of the text.

- In the footnotes to Freud's case study, Freud entertains an alternative interpretation of Dora's case, in which her homosexual love for Frau K emerges based on an inherent bisexual tendency in hysterics, as well as Dora's possible identification with her father rather than her mother.
- Moreover, Freud momentarily acknowledges Dora's own, quite plausible, interpretation of the situation, which she states in economic terms: that her father had turned a blind eye to Herr K's advances toward her, in exchange for Herr K's tolerance of the father's affair with his wife.

From a feminist perspective, then, Dora's hysteria can be understood less as a wholly irrational mental illness than as a curious manner of "protest" against her part in the commerce of women tolerated within Victorian society, the best manner available then to a girl of her age.

Following de Beauvoir, Friedan *et al.* criticize Freud's biological determinism to explain what are in fact socially decided phenomena, like Dora's terrible social plight. Moreover, they stress the effects of Freudianism upon contemporary women who, coming across psychoanalysis in the course of their studies, might take to heart his recommendations regarding normal femininity. They feared psychoanalysis's potential to return women to the home and to patriarchal dependence. Arguably the most thorough representative of this particular response to Freudian psychoanalysis is Kate Millett.

Kate Millett: forget Freud's feminine fantasy!

Like de Beauvoir, Millett sets out to show that Freud consistently misrecognized the effects of social conditioning and disparity, entrenched only through their historical repetition, for predetermined and necessary biological differences. By insisting that anatomical difference bears an intrinsic cultural significance, Freud naturalizes (and thereby justifies) the prejudice he pretends only to describe. Freud represents for Millett a chief protagonist in what she calls the "counterrevolution" against the "sexual revolution" – which Millett dates from 1830 to 1930 (Millett 1971: 63) – contributing to a general reaction against the success of the early women's rights movement, and a reassertion of patriarchal ideology. In this light, according to Millett's analysis, the primary purpose of Freud's account of femininity was to return women to a position of sexual subordination to men: "the effect of Freud's work ... was to rationalize the invidious relationship between the sexes, to ratify traditional roles, and to validate temperamental differences" (*ibid.*: 178).

Notably, Millett brings to her analysis of Freud a very rigid understanding of the relations between the body and culture, sex and gender, where the former represents that which is fixed and inevitable, and the latter is conceived as mutable, or subject to change through a conscious alteration of behavioural patterns. In doing this, Millett arguably fails to grasp the subtler nuances of the psychoanalytic account of femininity, and what it has to say about a body that is already cultural, viewed subjectively by the child, through the veils of fantasy. The incompatibility between Millett's understanding of the relation of the body to society and Freud's can be brought out within her analysis of penis-envy, where she states as an aside:

> (It is interesting that Freud should imagine the young female's fears centre about castration rather than rape – a phenomenon which girls are in fact, and with reason, in dread of, since it happens to them and castration does not.)
> (Millett 1971: 184)

We can see here that for Millett what is significant is the world of actual things and events. Accordingly, the little girl's "fantasy life" can only plausibly pertain to what realistically can occur, not to cultural prejudice. The distinction between body (unchangeable fact) and culture (imaginary and arbitrary) is crudely maintained, in comparison with a figure such as Melanie Klein, for example. It is inconceivable for Millett that a little girl might fear the loss of an organ she never had in the first place. For Freud, as for Klein, though, the "real" body apart from its social significance had no role in his explanation of feminine subjectivity – however otherwise contentious their accounts. The little girl's experience of her own body is already mediated by culture, through fantasy: neither purely bodily nor simply social, but rather the nexus of their intertwining.

Feminist recuperations of psychoanalysis

The Anglo-American reconnaissance: Juliet Mitchell

Within the Anglo-American feminist movement, there are some who have understood Freud's account of sexuality and gender identity differently from the feminists we have looked at so far. For them, Freud's account of sexuality is not primarily another biological description of how a girl "inevitably" becomes a woman. It is also an account of how the body comes to be invested with social significance through fantasy. For instance, within her own reinterpretation of Freud for feminism, *Psychoanalysis and Feminism*, Juliet Mitchell objects to Millett's criticisms of Freud on grounds similar to those outlined above. According to Mitchell, whilst Millett presents a more rigorous analysis of psychoanalysis than Friedan, Firestone or Figes, her position still exemplifies the kind of error that follows when Freud's work on femininity is read in isolation from his broader psychoanalytic theory. Mitchell contends that although ostensibly these feminists each object to what Freud had to say about women, what actually offends them is his theory of infantile sexuality and the unconscious. This is perhaps partly due to the influence of de Beauvoir's existentialism – particularly her existentialist objection to psychoanalysis from a concern to preserve free choice from past determinations. According to Mitchell, Millett's and her contemporaries' political project also informs their discomfort about the existence of irrational influences – such as unconscious fantasy. The reason is that these threaten to obscure and complicate the separation between nature and culture they believe must remain clear if feminist social reform is to be successfully advocated. There is no room for the unconscious if one wants only rational feminist agents, ready to transcend their bodily immutability to enact social change. For Mitchell, by contrast, "Freud was trying to explain what feminine 'fantasy' did with social facts and cultural demands, and how a child reasoned" (Mitchell 1975: 354): a process that it is incumbent upon feminists to understand, if social change is to be possible at all.

For Mitchell, the status Freud accords the body is not as unequivocal as earlier feminists had suggested. Mitchell correctly understood that Freud had already effectively posed de Beauvoir's dictum, "one is not born, but rather becomes a woman", albeit through the rubric of psychoanalytic theory, rather than existentialism. By means of an amalgamation of Freud and the anthropological structuralism of Lévi-Strauss (reminiscent of Lacan's reworking of Freud through Saussure, Jakobsen and Lévi-Strauss (see Chapter 5)), Mitchell sees the Oedipus complex less as a biological mandate than as the culturally genetic element of a more or less universal social repression of femininity. For Mitchell, Oedipus represents at a mythic level the kinship relations that enable society to operate as such. More precisely, the Oedipus complex dramatizes within "fantasy" the social imperative to exchange women, and the equally necessary injunction against incest. Drawing upon Lévi-Strauss, Mitchell clarifies that the incest taboo is not grounded in biology – for instance, the avoidance of congenital weakness – but rather is a purely social measure to ensure the growth of society through marriage alliances.

Likewise, for Mitchell, the fact that it is women who have been circulated between kinship groups, rather than men, in most societies is not biologically determined. Instead it is explicable in terms of a "phylogenetic" (or prehistoric) heritage relayed to each of us through the cultural imagination or fantasy. This cultural memory, represented by the Oedipal complex, provides the impetus for children to make their way into social roles accorded to them through a bodily elaboration of social meaning. Mitchell is careful to state, against the sex/gender distinction, that bodies are never "simply" bodies: that from the beginning biology is already "transformed" by the structures into which individual girls and boys are born (Mitchell 1975: 407). Freud declares Oedipus to be "universal", she argues, but not in the same sense that the body is thought to be universal by the sociological feminists. Rather, Oedipus is a fantasy structure remnant of generations of accretion of social practices, which can then take any number of concrete cultural–historical manifestations. And for Mitchell this is the *coup de grâce* against those feminist critics that her interpretation of Freud counters. For the Oedipus complex – and its corollaries of penis-envy and feminine narcissism – are not only applicable to the specific situation of "Victorian" Vienna. It is recapitulated even in the contemporary Western, late-capitalist context, where "fathers" ("patriarchy" being the rule of fathers, not "men" *per se*) still have power in so far as they represent the law in terms of which each individual's social and sexual identities are organized. "Mothers", at the same level, represent the underside or repressed of that law: that is, the "natural" family, which, somewhat paradoxically, the law allocates the place of its own excess (Mitchell 1975: 405).

Perhaps most interesting in Mitchell's account is her analysis of the role of Oedipus and the nuclear family within late-capitalist societies. Employing a logic influenced by Hegel and Marx, she locates the family as the point of inner contradiction through which capitalism comes into its own. The family keeps the desultory tendencies of capitalism in check. Yet capitalism places the family under great strain by alienating all labour equally. Furthermore, under capitalism there is no longer a need for the exchange of women, as capitalist society is supported instead by the exchange of commodities and capital. In fact, Oedipus becomes most visible and pertinent in Freud's Vienna precisely at a time when it verged upon social redundancy. As an example of this irrelevance of the family, Mitchell cites Britain during World War II, where women were expediently sent into the workplace, men into combat, and children into the countryside, away from their families in London. Yet at the same time, at either extreme of the debate, the capitalists and socialists each expressed concern for the demise of the "traditional" nuclear family. This is because, according to Mitchell, the family recapitulates those very internal contradictions that Marx had hoped might blow capitalism apart: "[t]he ban on incest and the demand for exogamy howl so loudly in the contemporary Oedipus complex because they are reinforced precisely when they are no longer needed" (Mitchell 1975: 410). In this sense, the family itself has become a "fetish", standing in for a presumed unity (or "big Other") that the system now lacks: "Capitalist society establishes the family in the context of its redundancy" (*ibid.*: 411).

Mitchell's hope for feminism is that the current of contradictions within patriarchal capitalism will catalyse the unravelling of Oedipus: or a "cultural revolution" of a different, but related, kind to that envisaged by Marx. "Femininity", as described by Freud, designates the psychology of repression through which women live the ideology of patriarchy. Thus, according to Mitchell, the transformation of this ideology, as well as the material conditions of women, depends upon such analysis. From this point of view, social change is not only a matter of altering gender roles and the partition of work, as was argued by Millett *et al.* It also depends upon the transformation of psychology and ideology (or cultural memory), and through these even our biology. Mitchell presses for radical change through a thorough reconception of the sex/gender relation, arguing that psychoanalysis offers the best tools to enact such change.

The French resistance to psychoanalysis

Psychoanalysis has been critical to informing the development of theoretical feminism even more in France than in Britain or America.

Resistance to psychoanalytic assumptions of patriarchy has shaped the French articulation of feminism, so French feminist thought emerges through a conflicted engagement with Freud and Lacan. In this respect, theorists such as Kristeva, Irigaray, Cixous and Kofman have developed an ambivalent, yet integral, relation to psychoanalytic theory. Perhaps reflecting a wider "cultural difference", English-speaking feminists have accused them of various crimes against feminism: from "biological essentialism" (Irigaray; Cixous); to an over-reliance on the "word" of Herr Professor Freud (Kofman); to outright prejudice against their own sex (Kristeva). Here we shall look at but three proponents of this rich seam of thought within feminism: Luce Irigaray, Julia Kristeva and Sarah Kofman.

Julia Kristeva: powers of horror and desire in language

Given that she has distanced herself from the feminist movement (Oliver 1993), Julia Kristeva might seem an unlikely inclusion here. However, a current of feminism runs through her philosophy, quite inseparable from her concern for psychoanalysis. Kristeva is best known for her work on "abjection", contained in her book *Powers of Horror* (1982). Influenced by Klein, Mary Douglas and perhaps also Lou Andreas-Salomé (Markotic 2001), Kristeva engages with the question of how the ego is formed, arguing that the infant must be able to draw a boundary between itself and its waste products before being capable of recognizing itself as a separate entity. Such waste products comprise the "abject": neither "subject" nor "object", but demarcating the limit between them. The abject provides the self its connection to the object (through the piece of the self that is relinquished to the world), but also threatens to destroy this connection and the integrity of the self, precisely because it is what Kristeva calls "the jettisoned object": it is "radically excluded and draws me toward the place where meaning collapses" (Kristeva 1982: 2). For this reason, the abject elicits an uncanny feeling of dread and fascination in the subject, which can be summarized in the encounter with a dead body: the discarded self *par excellence*.

> The corpse, seen without God and outside of science [i.e., outside of a culturally mediated context], is the utmost of abjection. It is death infecting life. Abject. It is something rejected from which one does not part, from which one does

not protect oneself as from an object. Imaginary uncanniness and real threat, it beckons to us and ends up engulfing us.

(Ibid.: 4)

However, for Kristeva, abjection also characterizes the relation to the mother, from whom one must separate in order to individuate oneself, and (following Lacan) before one can become a speaking subject (*ibid.*: 13). Especially in the case of the boy, because the child and mother are but one merged entity before ego formation, he must relinquish this identification with her to make way for an identification with the "father" (or his equivalent), and the paternal law (language). Interestingly, for Kristeva the father merely represents some third term whose function is to interrupt the unity between mother and child. This function may just as easily be served by her friends, female lover or work, as by the male head of a nuclear family. Thus her theoretical apparatus does not necessitate patriarchy, although the meaning of abjection – particularly as it concerns the abjection of the mother – suggests a mechanism for the reproduction of misogyny.

Kristeva's work in linguistics – influenced by Lacan, as well as Saussure and C. S. Peirce – also gestures towards a concern for the cultural significance of femininity. According to Kristeva, there are two registers of language: the symbolic and the semiotic. The former is far less broadly encompassing than Lacan's use of the term, referring only to structural elements of language rather than culture in general: grammar, the extant or conscious dimension, and that which brings to language its stability and form. The semiotic, on the other hand, refers to the unconscious register of language: its mobile, motivating force (or "drive", in the Freudian sense of libidinal energy). The semiotic, then, comprises the material element of language, its rhythms and timbres, which, without the symbolic, would consist of nothing but inarticulate noise. Language as it is lived, in speech and in writing, requires each of these registers if it is to be meaningful: for, while the symbolic organizes meaning, from the semiotic issues language's "material conditions" – understood not merely in terms of biology, but as its historical and social significance. For Kristeva, this semiotic register, like the abject, simultaneously provides language with its ground, and threatens to upset meaning. It is the "feminine" – repressed, misunderstood, volatile, unconscious – quality of language, which both supports, and looms as a potential destroyer of, the boundaries of the symbolic through which language is structured, but which do not (*contra* structuralism) amount to its totality. In this respect, the "feminine" represents a revolutionary force of language and meaning, manifest in poetry and art, among other social practices.

Luce Irigaray: the speculum of the other woman

Luce Irigaray addresses psychoanalysis more directly as an antagonist of feminism. Yet, influenced by the deconstructive philosophy or interpretive practices of Jacques Derrida (as well as Freud and Lacan), she does so by situating her thought within its concepts, as its "unconscious" underside. Irigaray's aim is to enact a kind of "self-examination" of psychoanalysis against itself (Irigaray 1985a: 63). This involves an intimate reading of the theorist whom she addresses, sometimes at the level of a line-by-line analysis, from the viewpoint of the repressed. Like Derrida, Irigaray speaks from and for the very position within Western males' discourses that must remain silent, if the integrity of the author's position is to remain intact. However, Irigaray's point is directly political, concerning what she sees as a repression of femininity for the purpose of supporting the masculine subject's self-identity, at work in Western philosophy and culture in general. Feminist concerns can only be addressed, according to Irigaray, once the West's ontological reliance upon the subjugation of the feminine is reworked and relinquished.

Irigaray's technique for dismantling this "ontology" is to figuratively occupy this unvoiced position within the text, and push it out (speculum-like) until philosophers' unacknowledged debt to the feminine is fully revealed. In psychoanalytic parlance, Irigaray enacts a return of the repressed of the dominant discourse. Such an acting out invariably draws upon the very stereotypes of femininity that it hopes to abolish: like the hysteric or the *femme fatale*, who toys with the philosopher but refuses to bring him to climax. But such a mimicry of traditional female positions does not represent an uncritical com-plicity. It is about revealing what is at stake in Western philosophers' masculine self-understandings: what they take for granted, in order to function smoothly. In this manner, in *Speculum of the Other Woman* (a reference to de Beauvoir, as well as to gynaecology), Irigaray responds to Freud by "inhabiting" his lecture on "Femininity" as its own Other, interpolating within it objections to each statement Freud makes about the "truth" of woman's sex.

Reflecting her debt to deconstruction, Irigaray interrogates not only Freud's positive theories, but also the rhetoric with which he presents them. These stylistic nuances, Irigaray argues, far from being merely incidental, already reflect the masculine "imaginary" that conditions how the "question of woman" may be addressed. The force of Irigaray's argument against Freud, then, is that the "question" of woman is only a question because women's voices are excluded from representations of human enquiry. And it is this very "lack" of women's perspectives (and correlatively, of woman's sex) that ensures the smooth functioning of masculine identity and desire.

Irigaray's relation to Lacan is also oppositional – perhaps especially so after she was expelled from the École Freudienne, and her position at the University of Vincennes, upon publication of *Speculum*. However, the psychoanalysis with (and against) which Irigaray works is Lacanian rather than Freudian, in that it deals with structures and linguistics instead of drives. From Lacan she takes a focus upon the "symbolic" as the place in which gender is assigned, as well as the concept of the "imaginary" – albeit an imaginary that is retroactively gendered "masculine", and against which a "feminine" imaginary must reassert itself. Yet she criticizes Lacan for continuing to define "woman" in terms of penis-envy, even if elaborated in terms of structural linguistics, rather than Freud's "biologism". What Irigaray does with Lacanian theory is try to demonstrate what a female sexuality unhinged from masculine desire might look like. What are the corollaries we might invent for such a femininity in the fields of language and poetry, as well as in social relations between the sexes, and – most significantly – between women (whether mothers and daughters, lovers, colleagues, or friends)? The essay "This Sex Which Is Not One", for instance, develops a conception of the female body not as lacking (nor as complete, as masculinity represents itself), but rather as plural: as self-embracing, proliferating and contiguous to itself. Likewise, in "When Our Lips Speak Together", of the same volume, Irigaray depicts a feminine body and pleasure that is self-sufficient, drawing upon and enlarging (through mimicry) the image of narcissistic woman that Freud entertains in "On Narcissism" and elsewhere.

"And the One Doesn't Stir without the Other", on the other hand, emphasizes intergenerational relationships between women: a relation that is poisoned by the patriarchal culture that psychoanalysis summarizes, being mediated by the separating function of "the father". In this piece Irigaray plays the part of the daughter, imploring her mother to attend to their relation. Employing the metaphor of lactation, she contends that the relation between them should allow each to grow rather than devour one another. In this piece, Irigaray refers to the Lacanian indictment that, to an extent, girls must always stay trapped within the imaginary, by reappropriating the reflective function that each plays for the other as a mode of exchange between mother and daughter: "You/I exchanging selves endlessly and each staying herself. Living mirrors" (Irigaray 1981: 61). In this manner, Irigaray re-evaluates the identification between mother and daughter, and recommends that this relation be developed rather than discouraged. In so far as the mother is able to short-circuit a sexual economy in which she is defined as lacking, she will not resent the daughter for failing to provide her with the coveted phallus. In turn, the mother will avoid inflicting her own sense of lack upon her daughter. Thus, at this stage of her work, Irigaray emphasizes a self-sufficiency of women among themselves, challenging the status allotted to them as commodities of exchange enabling men's relations to each other. In some of her later works, by contrast, the question of "sexual difference", and relations between men and women, eclipses that of relations between women. And here the psychoanalytic Oedipal narrative remains central for her, as exemplifying the masculine imaginary to which her feminism responds.

Sarah Kofman: the enigma of woman

Sarah Kofman reads psychoanalytic theory as far more equivocal and subtle than Irigaray allows. Indeed, Kofman's book on Freud and femininity, *The Enigma of Woman*, in part serves as a vehicle to accuse Irigaray – parenthetically and in footnotes – of relying upon distortions and exaggerations of Freud's position (Kofman 1985: 12, 104, 109n, 122, 115, 116, 117, 118n, 120n, 126, 132, 132n). Kofman presents a very close, scholarly and sympathetic reading of Freud, who (with Nietzsche) was a formative influence on her work. However, *Enigma* is also a critical examination of Freud from a feminist perspective. Kofman's primary objective is to demonstrate how Freud's writings on femininity dramatize the underside of his own masculinity: or in other words, his investment in representing woman in the manner he does. One of her methods for doing this is to place Freud's various contradictions about "woman" alongside one another. For instance, she indicates the incompatibility between saying that woman lacks – constructing her botched desire by fabricating a relation to the penis – and the claim that woman is characteristically narcissistic, which would suggest an enviable self-sufficiency with regard to desire (Kofman 1985: 52). Other contradictions in Freud's representation of woman include his conflicting accounts of her "modesty" as cultural, and then as natural (*ibid.*: 49–50); his claims that woman is inscrutable to the male point of view, *and* that her truth is accessible only by means of the most scientific (i.e. psychoanalytic) methods (*ibid.*: 39–42); and that woman is a "great criminal" – self-sufficient and in possession of her own secret – whilst also being ignorant of herself, and thus requiring the expertise of the analyst (*ibid.*: 66).

Kofman's hypothesis is that these equivocations reveal Freud's fear of "woman". Woman for Freud is both an uncanny birthplace, and (correlatively) the enigmatic cipher of his own mortality. In this vein Kofman argues that penis-envy is a projection of men's fears regarding castration, and so does not reflect women's desires so much as what men *require* of woman's desire (Kofman 1985: 85). Through the notion of penis-envy, Kofman argues that Freud transfers to the father, as the bearer of the phallus, the omnipotence that the child originally accorded the mother (*ibid.*: 72). She argues that Freud's desire to be scientific and objective about woman is a means of mediating and controlling his discomfort respecting his own disavowed femininity and narcissism, as well as Oedipal desire for his mother and anxieties about death. Thus Freud domesticates the threatening and enigmatic "grand criminal" woman (who withholds her truth and so captivates men) into his own accomplice: the little hysteric, the meaning of whose "speech" the psychoanalyst alone is able to restore (*ibid.*: 67).

Arguably, Kofman's work represents the most worked-through and integral encounter between feminism and psychoanalysis. Other of her works, however, are haunted by her "unresolved" relation to both feminism and psychoanalysis, particularly her autobiography, *Rue Ordener, Rue Labat*, which documents her childhood in exile as a Parisian Jew during World War II, the loss of her father in Auschwitz, and her subsequent "abjection" (Kristeva), or pathological rejection of her mother. To this extent, Kofman might have had something to learn from other feminists about the mother–daughter relation. And for this reason, Kofman is an appropriate conclusion to this chapter. For as we have seen, the relation between psychoanalysis and feminism is precarious precisely because, through its engagement with psychoanalysis, issues central for feminism have been enabled to bubble to the theoretical surface – whether the question of how girls become women, of the relation between women, or the relation between the sexes. Contestation about the uses and disadvantages of psychoanalysis for feminism provides a very good way into the conflicts between feminisms. It also furnishes a privileged site for the ongoing negotiation of feminist futures.

Summary

- The question of femininity is one about which Freud equivocates throughout his career. His final position is that women's sexuality and identity are organized according to a masculine framework (i.e. the Oedipus complex), and are characterized by envy of the penis.
- Some of Freud's most significant followers and interlocutors have been women, from the earliest reception of his work: Helene Deutsch and Karen Horney, as well as Lou Andreas-Salomé, Melanie Klein, Marie Bonaparte and Freud's daughter, Anna.
- Helene Deutsch's focus was the influence upon a woman's sexuality of her mother. In her work, sexuality becomes a woman's means of exploring her relation to her mother, as well as her own "motherly" potential. Like Klein, Deutsch renders the mother more active than in Freud's accounts. Yet she also emphasizes what she (with Freud) identifies as women's passivity and narcissism, and has thus often been represented by feminists as regressive.
- Karen Horney was openly and scathingly critical of Freud's sexism. She is best known for her comparison of the psychoanalyst's attitude towards women and the little boy's attitude to the little girl. Horney rereads penis-envy in the context of other kinds of envy, such as womb-envy, challenging its primacy in Freud.
- Second-wave feminism (after de Beauvoir) identified Freudian psychoanalysis with patriarchy. Figures such as Kate Millett, Betty Friedan, Shulamith Firestone, Eva Figes and Germaine Greer argue that psychoanalysis served to naturalize cultural and social inequalities between men and women.
- Some Anglo-American feminists – notably Juliet Mitchell, Nancy Chodorow, Laura Mulvey, Jane Gallop and Joan Copjek – have since attempted to reappropriate psychoanalysis to feminism, by demonstrating how psychoanalytic theory provides insight into the social construction of gender and sex, family and patriarchy.
- French feminists, responding often principally to Lacanian theory, have attempted to negotiate a position between advocacy and criticism of psychoanalysis: particularly Luce Irigaray, Julia Kristeva and Sarah Kofman.

part III

Psychoanalysis and its discontented

seven

Freud as philosopher? Civilization, art and religion

In Part I, we examined Freud's ground-breaking theoretical work. In Part II, we looked at subsequent developments in psychoanalytic thought, in object relations, Lacanian, and feminist (readings of) psychoanalysis. Part III continues the process, begun in Chapter 6, of understanding how psychoanalysis has influenced and been challenged by thinkers in other disciplines, and in particular by twentieth-century philosophers. We shall begin in this chapter by looking at what psychoanalysis has said on three topics traditionally reserved for philosophers or theologians: questions concerning the nature of civilization, art and religion.

Psychoanalysis, civilization and Marxism

(The) Freudian ethics? Bearing civilization and its discontents

Freud's magisterial 1930 "Civilization and Its Discontents" (CD) is arguably his most philosophical text, in the several senses of that term. No sooner has it begun than Freud has posed the most perplexing philosophical question of all, concerning the meaning of human life. Like Aristotle, whose *Nicomachean Ethics* Freud's text darkly doubles, Freud agrees that whatever we pose as this question's solution, the pursuit of happiness must have a central place. Yet different people seek happiness in different ways: from the quests for love, sensuality or intoxication, to the cultivation of the arts, piety or ascetic withdrawal.

And unlike Aristotle, Freud's diagnosis for the prospects of human happiness is singularly grim. Human happiness, Freud sagely remarks, does not seem to have been written into the plan of Creation. Reprising the ancient philosophers' low estimation of sensual pleasure, Freud even notes that our very bodily constitution seems more suited to suffering than enjoyment – since physical pleasure is the result of (preferably sudden) releases of built-up, painful energy (CD: 76; see Chapter 1). Human beings are beset by three types of suffering which, Freud argues, make life "too hard for us, it brings us too many pains, disappointments, and impossible tasks" (*ibid*.: 75). The first is our bodies' frailty and ultimate mortality. The second is the overwhelming might of nature. Freud's third proposed source of our suffering, and the main focus of the essay, is the most controversial. This is the suffering occasioned by living with others in civilized societies (*ibid*.: 76, 86).

Now "civilization", Freud concedes, is the very name for all those devices human beings have contrived together to alleviate their natural and bodily sufferings. Freud acknowledges the great technological advances of the modern world in this regard. He credits the benefits accruing to all from societies' law and order, hygiene, the arts, sciences and religion. Nevertheless, Freud proposes that at least three points in European history, a widespread wish has made itself evident to reject civilization altogether. The first, as Freud controversially contends, was the conversion of the warlike Romans to other-worldly Christianity. The second (Freud is perhaps thinking here of Rousseau and Romanticism) was Europeans' encounters with the apparently more noble "primitives" of the New World. The third, however, is Freud's own time of world war, and growing numbers of neurotics – whom psychoanalysis shows to be living testimony to the inability of many to attain even "ordinary unhappiness" in modern societies (CD: 86–8).

Freud's "Civilization and Its Discontents" in this way comes to pose *the* animating question of modern social theory: why, despite all the comforts of modern societies, do many people remain unhappy – perhaps more unhappy than our forebears? Freud's answer draws upon his psychoanalytic account of the drives and their vicissitudes (Chapters 1, 2 and 4). He reprises an idea present in Hobbes and earlier political thought: that for individuals to move from barbarism to civilization, each must give up the unlimited liberty to pursue their every whim. Justice and the laws, Freud notes, establish the common interest over that of the individual. But they do so at a cost: the sacrifice of our untamed libidinal drives. The civilizing process, in this way, Freud argues, mirrors the education of each human infant, but this means also that it brings with it "changes . . . in the familiar instinctual dispositions of human beings" (CD: 96). The incest taboo, Freud says, represents "the most drastic mutilation which humans' erotic life has in all time experienced" (*ibid.*: 104 [Chapters 2 and 5]). And herein lies the rub of Freud's argument. If the "sacrifice of the drives [civilization demands] is not compensated for economically," Freud warns, "one can be certain that serious disorders will ensue" (*ibid.*: 97).

Civilization deploys a number of means to compensate subjects for their founding sacrifice of liberty and enjoyment. Principal among these are material benefits, the security of law and order, our libidinal identification with ideals, leaders and our fellows, and the beneficent "illusions" of religion and the arts (see below). Moreover, for all the libidinal sacrifices civilization exerts, Freud argues that it also has a powerful instinctual ally: *Eros*, our sexual drive. Freud places *Eros*, alongside the benefits of common work, at the basis of civilization. Men's desire to secure regular access to sexual gratification with women, Freud hypothesizes, must have lain at the basis of the most basic social institutions: families or kinship groups. This is not to deny sexual desire can itself cause social discontents, given the proverbial blindness of Cupid to established social norms. Echoing (nearly literally) Hegel's account of women as "the eternal irony of the community", Freud notes how the love between family members can stand against men giving themselves over to the common good. Nevertheless, Freud argues that, this all granted, it still seems plausible to imagine a society of contented sexual couples with their families, bound together by common interests and shared labour. In such a world, Freud implies, we might even entertain Christianity's idealistic precept to "love our neighbour as ourselves" – at least with an aim-inhibited, generalized love (*agape*). However, each time Freud approaches such a "contented" possibility in "Civilization and Its Discontents", he halts.

Freud does so initially on near-Aristotelian grounds. Our love is a sign that we give preference to the beloved, and take especial care about all that affects her happiness – the well-being of her family, children and so on. To love everyone, it follows, is to devalue our love, and by implication, those upon whom we have conferred it (IV: 102, 109). Freud's second reason for saying "No thanks!" to Christianity's "love thy neighbour . . ." (cf. Žižek 1997: ch. 2), however, projects him squarely into the Presocratic orbit of the tragedians. It rests on his later account of the death drive in light of which, as Freud writes in a series of darkly magnificent passages:

Not merely is this stranger in general unworthy of my love; I must honestly confess that he has more claim to my hostility and hatred . . . men are not gentle creatures who want to be loved . . . they are, on the contrary, creatures among whose instinctual endowments is to be reckoned a powerful share of aggression. As a result, their neighbor is for them not only a potential helper or sexual object, but also someone who tempts them to satisfy their aggressiveness on him, to exploit his capacity for work without compensation, to use him sexually without his consent, to seize his possessions, to humiliate him, to cause him pain, to torture and to kill him. *Homo homini lupus.* (CD: 110, 111)

"Civilization and Its Discontents" thus joins "Beyond the Pleasure Principle" (see Chapter 4) as a principal statement of Freud's later theory of the drives. This theory ultimately pictures not only civilization, but the entire universe, as the battleground between *Eros* – which strives to bind things and people together – and *Thanatos* – which strives to render them asunder. Psychoanalysis always acknowledged a component of aggressiveness in human sexuality, principally in the perversions (Chapter 2). Yet Freud now berates himself for having not seen earlier the evidence for a human drive towards non-erotic aggression, tied to the ego's primitive wish for omnipotence. Such a drive, Freud argues, "constitutes the greatest impediment to civilization" (CD: 122), guaranteeing "there are difficulties attaching to civilization *which will not yield to any attempt at reform*" (*ibid.*: 115).

If civilizations persist, Freud bleakly suggests, they can only do so by finding ways (like scapegoating outgroups: Jews, Muslims, illegal immigrants and the like) to pacify individuals' innate, asocial aggressiveness. Freud closes "Civilization and Its Discontents" by focusing on one such measure whose mysterious ways he argues only psychoanalysis has managed to unravel: the turning around of the death drive upon individuals' own egos. Animated by fear of losing its carers' love and protection, we have seen how the child represses socially illicit drives, in their place identifying with its first others. The culmination of this process is the formation of the superego, an internalized agency of social law that monitors not only the subject's external behaviours, but its every wish (see Chapter 1). Freud, however, stresses in "Civilization and Its Discontents" that the superego, far from being (only) the pacifying psychical bearer of social law, typically "torments the sinful ego with . . . anxiety and is on the watch for opportunities of getting it punished by the external world" (CD: 125). Why is it the most virtuous people who are most wracked by guilt about their moral conduct?, Freud asks, pointing to a fact exemplified *in extremis* by obsessional neurotics. The only way to explain this, Freud argues, is to posit that "every piece of aggression . . . the subject gives up *is taken over by the superego and increases the latter's aggressiveness (against the ego)*" (CD: 129).

And with this argument in place, you can see, Freud has his answer to why advances in civilization have not delivered us from discontents. *Au contraire*, "the price we pay for our advance in civilization is a loss of happiness through the heightening of the sense of guilt . . ." (*ibid.*: 134).

Dialectics of disenchantment: psychoanalysis and critical Marxism

One of Freud's targets in "Civilization and Its Discontents" is Marxism. Freud rightly associates Marxism with the fundamentally optimistic view that human aggression is the product of social conditions, not ahistorical human nature. Freud does not deny that there are and have been unjust social arrangements. He chastises socialism for its "youthful" wish of unveiling a wholly peaceable human nature through social change alone:

> If we do away with personal rights over material wealth, there still remains prerogative in the field of sexual relationships, which is bound to become the source of the . . . most violent hostility among men who in other respects are on an equal footing. If we were to . . . allow complete freedom of sexual life . . . we cannot . . . easily foresee what new paths civilization might take, but . . . this indestructible feature of human nature [aggression] will follow it there . . .   (CD: 113–14)

Given "Civilization and Its Discontents", then, it seems surprising that Western or "critical" Marxism has been one of the philosophical movements most interested in psychoanalysis. In a famous essay, Max Horkheimer dismisses Freud's theory of the death drive as the latest exemplar of a long lineage of "dark", "bourgeois" philosophical anthropology dating from Machiavelli and Luther (Horkheimer 1995: 104–8). This lineage, Horkheimer argues, theoretically repackages the antisocial egoism unleashed by modern market societies as if it were timeless human nature, and "there is no alternative" (Margaret Thatcher). Yet the critical Marxists in non-Soviet countries after 1920 faced an urgent dilemma. This was the dilemma of how to explain the "no-show" of the worldwide revolution that earlier Marxisms had predicted, and the profoundly repressive features of the "really existing" Marxist–Leninist states. Thinkers like those in the Frankfurt School of Social Research (principally, Fromm, Marcuse and Adorno) turned to psychoanalysis in this context to explain the lasting unwillingness of the workers of the West to unite under socialism, and the failures of Marxist states to deliver the promised, better world.

Psychoanalysis's influence, for example, is clearly present in *The Dialectic of Enlightenment*, written by Adorno and Horkheimer in exile during World War II. *The Dialectic of Enlightenment* challenges the optimistic idea that modern, enlightened societies have overcome "primitive", mythical modes of thinking. The seeds of the modern world's global strife, it suggests, were sown as far back as Homeric Greece. Homer's Odysseus in *The Odyssey*, the *Dialectic* argues, was already a kind of proto-modern entrepreneur, winning his release from the mythic powers he encounters (the Cyclops, the goddesses and so on) by his strategic wits alone. Yet, as Adorno and Horkheimer reprise Freud, Odysseus could do this only by sacrificing his own libidinal nature. For Adorno and Horkheimer, *The Odyssey*'s vignette of Odysseus and the sirens condenses *in nuce* the discontents of Western civilization *per se*. In order to hear the sirens' mesmeric music (a sublime symbol of lost *jouissance*), Odysseus has first to plug the ears of his oarsmen – who continue to labour silently below decks, deaf to the siren's strains. Simultaneously, Odysseus must tie himself to the mast, thereby suppressing his own wishes, in order to attain even a small part of the satisfactions lost to him in his enlightened pursuit of self-mastery (Adorno and Horkheimer 1979: 43–80).

The greatest trauma of the last century for the critical Marxists was the working classes' widespread embrace of the fascist regimes in interwar Europe. Marcuse's and Adorno's writings on this topic, and on the "authoritarian personality", arguably represent the most enduring legacy of "Freudo-Marxism" (and are especially resonant in today's period of widespread political reaction across the first world). The advent of fascism, they argued, showed the historical limitations of Freud's account of civilization and its discontents. For what demarcated fascist regimes from earlier authoritarian forms of government, they observed, was how the fascists employed populist, aesthetic means (such as art, rallies, public spectacles and so on) to encourage individuals to act out their *Eros* by way of collective identification with the leader, and prosecute their aggressiveness against designated enemies. Yet this "desublimation" of their drives into more primitive outlets did not deliver fascist subjects greater freedom or happiness, as Freud's pitting of the repression of the drives against their direct satisfaction(s) suggests. On the contrary, the fascists' call for subjects to act out their aggression through identification with the leader was highly politically repressive. It steered Spain, Italy and Germany towards waging the most barbaric war in recorded history (Adorno *et al.* 1950; Adorno 1982).

Marcuse and Adorno, each in his own way, brought insights developed in understanding European fascism to their analyses, as émigrés, of postwar America and its developing "culture industry" (Adorno 1991). Postwar capitalist America, they argued, engendered conformity in subjects not by the repressive operations of executive prerogative, but by "repressive desublimation": the systemic encouraging of people to entertain their sexualized wishes in ways targeted by marketers to animate the next rounds of "consumer demand" (Marcuse 1972: 57–77). Notably, since 1989, philosopher and cultural critic Slavoj Žižek has written a series of important analyses of the malaises of contemporary capitalist subjectivity that adapt this explanatory framework by drawing on Lacan's work (see Chapter 5). For Žižek, the much-remarked cynicism of contemporary liberal subjects (and much poststructuralist theory) about traditional forms of authority is a lure. What it conceals, in Žižek's Lacanian re-theorization of the "repressive desublimation" motif, is subjects' abiding identification with the status quo: an identification sustained by the quasi-transgressive *jouissance* (played to by marketers) of subjects' thinking themselves singular or different, able to "see through" the operations of power and so on (esp. Žižek 1989; 1994; 1997).

Psychoanalysis and aesthetics

Freud on sublimation, creative writing and the uncanny

One way human beings search for happiness, "Civilization and Its Discontents" observes, is through the sublimation of the drives in art and culture. Sublimation is raised in "Drives and Their Vicissitudes" but not pursued (see Chapter 2). In "On Narcissism", Freud specified that sublimation (as against idealization, which changes the object) is a vicissitude that involves diverting the aim of one's "base" drives so they are satisfied in activities conducive to the development of civilization and culture. The romantic poet, unhappy in love, produces sublime words to describe his lost object. In this way, a "finer and higher", indeed non-repressive, satisfaction is achieved (CD: 88). Yet, Freud reflects, "the weak point of this method [of sublimation through art] is that it is . . . accessible to only a few people. It presupposes the possession of special dispositions and gifts . . . far from being common to any practical degree" (*ibid.*: 88).

Psychoanalysis has been shadowed from its beginnings by the "finer and higher" achievements of the arts. Freud's notion of the Oedipus complex is indebted to Sophocles, and Shakespeare's *Hamlet*. Freud scarcely writes an essay in which he does not cite his heroes, Schiller and Goethe; and he wrote essays on da Vinci, Michelangelo, Dostoevsky, other artists and artistic themes. Yet, in "Civilization and Its Discontents" as elsewhere, Freud underscores that psychoanalysis must fall silent before the beauty and power of artists' works, and the question of why only certain individuals develop such extraordinary aesthetic gifts.

There is one "bridge" between we ordinary mortals and the minds of artistic geniuses about which psychoanalysis can and has spoken at length, Freud's "Creative Writing and Daydreaming" contends: child's play (*Spiel*). In their play, Freud argues, children imaginatively create substitute worlds, complete with rules that must be followed with the greatest seriousness (see Chapter 4). As we grow up, we each largely give up our innocent pleasure in play, and temper the wishful productions of our imagination against the reality principle. Yet psychoanalysis, as we know, maintains that we never wholly renounce our earlier modes of satisfaction. They abide in unconscious fantasy and our nightly dreams. "Creative Writing and Daydreaming" in fact contains one of Freud's most important accounts of the temporal structure of fantasy (see Figure 7.1).

Recall from Chapter 3, how in dreams, the dream wish hails from our infancy to reshape the present day's "residues". The manifest content stages the fulfilment of the past wish in the "text" taken from our present concerns (the "day's residues"), collapsing the wish's "optative modality", which points to a possible future – "I wish that . . ." – into the declarative: "It *is* so . . .". The same structure, Freud argues, explains

Past (origin of [repressed] wish) ←→ Present (time of fantasizing) → Future (setting for wish-fulfilment)

Figure 7.1   The temporal structure of fantasy in "Creative Writing and Daydreaming" (CWD)

the fairytale wishes of orphan girls to marry a prince, escaping through fantasy the drudgery of their present by adapting their ancient wish for an all-protecting father, thereby projecting a much brighter future as if it were so.

Creative writers, Freud contends, are people who dream in broad daylight, on the page or canvas, reproducing the same kinds of structures as private fantasies in their works. Yet people's most intimate fantasies are usually repulsive to others, contravening law and propriety. How, then, can artists "get away with" publicly staging their own fantasies, often to great acclaim? It is here that Freud places the mysterious *ars poetica* (the art of poetry). The artist is able to soften and disguise the personal content of their fantasies by re-presenting them through their characters, plots, and in the artistic play of words, stone, paint and so on. The techniques the artist uses, Freud suggests, are indeed a kind of libidinal bribe. They allow us the audience to indulge our repressed fantasies "without self-reproach or shame", as a kind of "incentive bonus" "so as to make possible the release of still greater pleasure arising from deeper psychical sources" (CWD: 153).

Note then how this psychoanalytic model for the understanding of artworks tends towards psychologizing them as "only" the expressions of their author's particular fantasy lives. Such a model can itself then become the stalking horse for the most ignoble wish-fulfilment – the desire to relativize or "lower" many of the greatest achievements of art and civilization (see "Pscyhoanalysis and religion" below). It is worth remarking, then, that in essays such as Freud's analysis of "Michelangelo's Moses", Freud himself does not succumb to this model. In his intriguing essay on "The Uncanny", Freud also moves towards a more compelling psychoanalytic account of the *ars poetica* – and of why some artistic presentations have such powerful effects on their audiences, whatever their author's motivations.

Freud on the uncanny

The "uncanny" is that feeling, somewhere between terror, *déjà vu* and jubilation, that people describe "as if someone walked over my grave". It is this affect that draws people to read and watch the most eerie suspense or terrifying horror stories. How does Freud explain it?

- The "uncanny" (in German *unheimlich*) condenses two senses of *heimlich* (home-like): both what is most familiar *and* most hidden. Paraphrasing the philosopher Schelling, Freud writes that "everything is *unheimlich* that ought to have remained secret and hidden but has come to light" (U: 225).
- In line with "On Negation", the privative *un*, Freud argues, is a token that repression is involved in the affect.

For Freud, the uncanny involves the return of the repressed – what is at once most intimate and alien to us, like the picture of Dorian Gray (Oscar Wilde). Uncanny art-objects, Freud argues, contravene a series of oppositions constitutive of our adult sense of reality, in this way evoking ways of thinking familiar, but forgotten, from our childhood:

- *Between reality and our wishes*: as in nearly-universal stories about the "evil eye", wherein our projected hostility towards others returns as something "objective" in the world (see below).
- *Between reality and our purposive thoughts*: as in "meaningful coincidences".
- *Between life and death*: as in ghosts and spirits, sure signs that a subject's "time is out of joint".
- *Between animate and inanimate things*, such as dolls or machines that give body to our drives' mindless "compulsion to repeat".
- *Between me and not-me*, as in the double, sure harbinger that the individual's time is up.

Lacan, the gaze, and the ambivalences of film theory

Freud's account of the uncanny explains how certain types of artwork exert an emotional and disorienting influence upon the viewer: that the uncanny experience speaks of an unsettling proximity to what ought to remain hidden – the unconscious. In Lacanian terms (Chapter 5), we could say that uncanny objects intimate a rupture in subjects' symbolic order – and accordingly, the identity of the viewer. While Freud's concept of sublimation attempts to understand what motivates the artist to create, Lacan's thoughts on aesthetics follow Freud's account of the uncanny into a focus on the viewer's experience of the artwork.

It is for this reason that Lacanian psychoanalytic theory has enjoyed a prominence in cinema studies, particularly since the publication of

Laura Mulvey's landmark piece, *Visual and Other Pleasures*. Mulvey and others are concerned to understand the powerful fascination that the moving images on our movie screens exert upon us, transfixing us without need of the chains that bind the citizens of Plato's cave in the *Republic*. Lacanian theory proposes that our fascination with films reflects how filmic images do not simply mimic reality, as Plato's most famous criticism of art in the *Republic* suggests. Rather, Lacanians emphasize how the viewer's desire – or, more precisely, the fantasies that provide the unconscious frame for their self-understanding(s) – is "caught up" and affected by cinematic representations. A "sublime" art-object (Lacan indeed redefined sublimation "beyond" Freud) is one that becomes raised, by the *ars poetica*, to the dignity of the unconscious, lost Thing (Lacan 1992: 112).

A key basis for Lacan's influence in cinema studies is his concept of "the gaze", one of the four examples of *object petit a* Lacan raises in his eleventh seminar, *The Four Fundamental Concepts of Psychoanalysis* (alongside the voice, faeces and breast). As it has been taken up by film theory after Mulvey, the gaze is supposed to reflect a hierarchy of power relations, whereby the one who "gazes" objectifies and subordinates the one(s) seen. For Mulvey, what we see in films is gendered female, whereas we, invisible onlookers, are situated as male. The task for a psychoanalytically informed criticism is then to problematize this alleged, intrinsic sexism of filmic enjoyment, by interrupting our pleasure of looking. As Mulvey puts it: "It is said that analysing pleasure, or beauty, destroys it. That is the intention of [my argument]" (Mulvey 1989: 16).

Yet Žižek (2001) and others have pointed out that Mulvey and her film-theoretic successors arguably misread Lacan's notion of the gaze as *objet petit a*. (For this reason, Žižek has called for a "return to Lacan" in cinema studies.) So what *is* the gaze for Lacan, and how does it affect this aesthetic debate? *Contra* Mulvey, Lacan's account of the gaze reflects his wider psychoanalytic position that any attempt at conscious, egoic self-representation involves a fundamental act of misrecognition. As we saw in Chapter 5, for Lacan, our egoic sense of identity is constructed by the alienation of the self in its identification with images of others, and its own inverted image in the mirror. This imaginary representation of the self tends both to conceal the constitutive role of the symbolic order (language and law) in shaping who we are, and to actively thrust out whatever cannot be represented by the self's "official" image or "ideal ego". The *objet petit a*, for Lacan, is a little piece of the Real that is in this way repressed or excluded from the ego's imaginary unity and symbolic identifications: Freud's *Es* or "id".

When Lacan raises the gaze as *objet petit a* in *Seminar XI*, then, it is to underline this "split" nature of our subjectivity. The gaze, Lacan says, represents in the visual field the *unheimlich* embodiment of that piece of the self that we repressed and projected outside, which now is returning to haunt us in the Real we confront. Like the anatomical "blind-spot" or the "evil eye" of superstition, we typically do not see, or want to see, anything about the object-gaze. As Žižek puts this idea, "When I am looking at an object, the object is always already gazing at me, and from a point at which I *cannot* see it" (Žižek 1991: 35). Yet, Lacanians stress, without such a point where "the object is already gazing at me", there could be no subjectively experienced, coherent field of vision (Lacan 1978: 95–7, 105–6).

Lacan uses art to illustrate this difficult idea of the gaze. Particularly, his interest falls on artists' use of perspective. Lacan connects the invention of perspective by early modern painters such as Leonardo da Vinci and Albrecht Dürer to philosophy's landmark moment at that time: Descartes's *cogito* ("I think, therefore I am"). Descartes's "first philosophy" sets up the modern subject as "a sort of geometral point" that founds all other objects of experience, not to mention Cartesian geometry (Lacan 1978: 85). Similarly, Dürer's "Lucinda" was a device devised by that artist to plot a three-dimensional field (including objects at various distances) to a two-dimensional plane. Where Descartes's mapping of flat space rendered spatiality neutral, uninhabitable ("the view from nowhere"), though, Dürer *et al.*'s artistic invention of perspective reflected the investment of the self in the object world (*ibid.*: 87). Through the *ars poetica* of perspective, we are drawn to share the artist's particular, spatially located point of view when we look at the canvas, as if we were there ourselves.

Where then does the "gaze" appear in all of this? Lacan draws our attention to how certain artworks that – very soon after Dürer – came to utilize devices such as shadow, draped fabric, as well as "vanitas" to remind viewers of the partiality of their "perspective" on the world. Lacan singles out *"anamorphosis"*, the name for artists' deliberate concealment of images by means of the calculated distortion of perspective. The example Lacan uses is Hans Holbein's famous *Ambassadors* of 1533. The painting at first appears to be a typical portrait of two young ambassadors, emissaries of the modern world, pictured with all the trappings of their worldly accomplishments: navigation and musical instruments, books and other symbols of secular learning. Yet in the foreground of the painting there floats an obscure (strangely phallic) oblong shape. This object catches the eye, but is curiously unrecognizable. However, if one takes up another perspective – or "looks awry" at it, in Žižek's memorable phrase (Žižek 1991) – *the unheimlich* Thing reveals itself as a leering skull: a *memento mori* highlighting the *vanitas* of all the ambassadors' modern culture (*ibid*.: 79–90, 92).

This uncanny object, according to Lacan, is the object-gaze unsettling Holbein's *Ambassadors*. It is not pleasurable, in the simple sense of "pleasure" indicated by Mulvey *et al.* Like Holbein's skull, it instead evokes the death drive: the destructive potential, which, for Freud, underlies and threatens reason and civilization (see "Psychoanalysis, civilization, Marxism", above). Nor is the gaze what organizes the field of vision from outside it, with all the power relations that this implies. As against the gaze in Sartre's *Being and Nothingness*, Lacan's gaze is rather what upsets our external "look" from within the frame, reminding us that we are not fully in control of what we see, and that our fears and desires structure even this.

The Lacanian gaze in film theory, we might accordingly say, represents film theory's own "blind-spot" with respect to what makes viewing, and theorizing about viewing, possible. It is as if film theory ironically affirmed the very mastery it set out to critique when it failed to recognize the critical potential of its principal Lacanian inheritance.

Psychoanalysis and religion

Freud's ambivalence towards God (as) "the father"

It is only forcing things a little to say that, alongside women, God was the single topic that most confounded Freud throughout his theoretical career. Of all the means civilization has at its disposal to sublimate the drives, and to console us for the discontents fate visits upon us, religion is the most powerful and universal. Freud was certainly aware of the powerful effects religious representations and rituals have upon the human soul. "Civilization and Its Discontents" opens by considering a religious critic (Romain Rolland) who asserted that psychoanalysis could say nothing concerning the "oceanic" feeling at the base of religious experience. Freud published four separate writings devoted to religion, whose writing spans all his mature life.

Yet, as his impulse to repeatedly return to religion indicates, Freud was never satisfied with his conclusions on this issue. For exegetical purposes, Freud's texts on religion can be divided into two currents of thought.

The "Materialist" account

The approach to religion in "The Future of an Illusion" (1927) situates Freud in a long philosophical tradition: that of philosophical materialism. This doctrine suggests that religion is a kind of illusion premised on ignorance of nature. For the ancient philosophers Epicurus, Democritus and Lucretius, one should undertake philosophy to overcome such fear. The impulse to religious beliefs, they argued, results from the confrontation of pre-philosophic minds with the sublime, terrifying and unexpected events "mother nature" visits upon us. Faced with such events, people reach for anthropomorphic (humanizing) explanations. They attribute these events to quasi-human deities: for instance, the lightning bolts of Zeus, the anger of YHWH and so on. Anticipating Freud's account of the timelessness of the unconscious, the Roman materialist Lucretius even argued that departed loved ones' "second life" in mourners' dreams form the real basis for human beings' (seemingly universal) propensity to posit an afterlife.

In "The Future of an Illusion", Freud agrees that the origins of religion lie in human beings' powerlessness before external nature and *Ananke* (natural necessity). But, prefiguring "Civilization and Its Discontents", Freud adds to the ancient materialists' list of belief-promoting natural facts the evil of our fellow human beings. Like the ancient materialists, Freud stresses that the "god-making impulse" (Nietzsche) arises from anthropomorphizing what would otherwise remain wholly beyond human control. If what we fear above all else is an invisible god, we can at least (fantasmatically) enter into relations of exchange with him: offering prayer and sacrifices to beseech his blessings, and explaining the harshness of fate as justified punishment for insufficient piety. Freud, however, gives the ancient materialist critique a distinctly psychoanalytic spin. The belief in anthropomorphic gods, Freud famously assessed, is "patently *infantile*" (CD: 86). The way believers respond to their powerlessness before natural necessity and human evil has as its prototype the powerlessness of the child in the first years of its life. Just as children look to their fathers to shield them from a world they can neither understand nor control, so the religions posit deities modelled, ultimately, on the protective figures of our fathers. In the monotheistic formula of "God the Father", Freud suggests, the non-religious source of religious beliefs is unwittingly confessed for everyone with the ears to hear.

The second Freudian account

In "Totem and Taboo" (TT [1913]), however, Freud developed a more original, and arguably more compelling, psychoanalytic account of religion. This account understands religion not according to a dialectic of fear and consolation, but of guilt and repetition. "Totem and Taboo" draws on ethnological ideas in Robertson Smith and Charles Darwin to propose a "phylogenetic" ground to religion. In Chapter 2, we saw how Freud elevates the Oedipus complex to the pivotal civilizing event in every child's life. In the resolution of the Oedipus complex, the father acts as a pacifying figure: the ultimate object of the (boy-)child's identification, who responds to the child's imagined violence against him by "laying down the law". According to "Totem and Taboo", by contrast, a real parricide lies at the origin of religion and civilization *per se*. "Totem and Taboo", moreover, introduces a different version of the father into Freud's theoretical vocabulary: the father of a "primal horde" that allegedly preceded human civilization as we know it. This father, far from being the pacifying agent of social law, was an obscene figure enjoying unlimited sexual access to all the women of the horde – like the leader of a pride of lions. The primal parricide occurred when, somehow, the sons banded together against him in a violent attempt to bring his social and sexual tyranny to an end.

KEY POINT *Totems, taboos, and the "truth" in their suspensions*

In "Totem and Taboo", Freud places not infantile fear, but an originary, history-making crime at the origin of religion.

- Freud's contention is that this crime, the "truth in religion", engendered a guilt between the sons and its perpetrators. It was this guilt, not the *Eros* or common labours of "Civilization and Its Discontents", that "Totem and Taboo" places at the origin of social laws regulating sexual and kinship relations – in a kind of psychoanalytic rewriting of the monotheistic notion of original sin.
- The compelling nature of the human religious impulse is thereby traced back to the ongoing need of the sons (and, by inheritance, us all) to make reparation for this primal guilt. (Freud also pointed towards such a guilt-based conception of religion in "Obsessive Actions and Religious Practices" [OA, 1907]).
- According to the same "primitive" thought process at work in Little Hans' phobia of horses (Chapter 1), the totem animals of early religions were the culturally sanctioned representatives of the primal father. The taboos surrounding how people could treat these animals represented "reaction formations" against the primal crime, and its now-repressed parricidal wish.
- Yet totem meals – sacred feasts at which tribal members could eat the totem animals – represented ritually circumscribed, exceptional repetitions of the primal crime; or returns of the repressed, true origins of religion.
- Freud suggests that this model of "totem and taboo" is not restricted to earlier religions. Christianity gives a uniquely direct form to the repressed historical truth of religion, in its central account of the murder of the God-man (re-enacted symbolically in the Eucharist) which gives rise to the "holy spirit" of Christian communities (TT: 146–55).

Written in the last years of Freud's life (1934–38), the three essays of "Moses and Monotheism" (MM) are presented as a particular exemplification (Judaism) of the general theory of religion in "Totem and Taboo". Yet closer analysis shows that this is not quite so. The alleged historical murder of a founding father by his people remains – one scandal surrounding this book comes from Freud's hypothesis that the historical Jews murdered Moses. Yet Freud pictures the murdered father in "Moses and Monotheism" as an eminently rational, law-founding figure, unlike the anomic father of the primal horde in "Totem and Taboo". According to Freud, moreover, the original Moses was an Egyptian – the second cause of the often-bitter recriminations against Freud's text.

This Egyptian Moses led the Israelites from exile, Freud hypothesizes, when he was himself ostracized from his native country because – no less – of his heretical, monotheistic faith in a single God *Aten*, threatening to Egypt's ruling priestly caste. After this Egyptian Moses had led his adopted Hebrews from exile, however, Freud's account follows the scriptural exegesis of Ernst Sellin to contend that the Hebrews turned upon and killed Moses, rejecting the highly spiritual demands of his Egyptian monotheism. How, then, does Freud argue that Judaism as we know it emerged, and why does it present such a different account of its foundations? Some generations later, Freud argues, there emerged among the Hebrews a second "Moses", a Midianite who worshipped a jealous, volcano deity, YHWH: the god who says, at Exodus 3:14, "I am *that* I am." Spurred by inherited guilt for the murder of the Egyptian Moses, Freud argues, Judaism emerged out of an uneasy synthesis of the highly rational monotheism of the first Moses (reprised in the thought of the great prophets) and this Midianite worship of YHWH. The fateful conflation of the two very different religious sources, Freud contends, was ultimately facilitated (as in a dream condensation) by the linguistic coincidence between the names of the two "Moses". The memory of the murder of the first Moses, together with his Egyptian identity, was meanwhile "repressed" from all scripture, with the exception of certain enigmatic passages in Hosea (see esp. Reinhard 1999).

If this much of the content of "Moses and Monotheism" is clear, debated more fiercely are Freud's intentions in penning this tenuously grounded historical case for the ignoble, foreign and particularistic roots of Judaism as almost his last theoretical will and testament – and at the same time as the Nazi Shoah was taking shape in Europe.

The returns of the religious

The inescapable importance psychoanalysis's confrontation with religion had for the new movement of thought is underscored by its most traumatic early moment. This was Freud's break, between 1910 and 1914, with his designated psychoanalytic successor Carl Jung, in part because Jung believed that psychoanalysis's discovery of the unconscious might provide the basis for a new religiosity. Living in the Europe of the turn of the twentieth century (still a widely religious society), Freud could not avoid considering psychoanalysis's relations with religion. Several of the early analysts, such as his friend Pfister – whose imagined objections structure "The Future of an Illusion" – were deeply religious. Analysands' religious convictions loom large in the Schreber, Wolfman and several other of Freud's case studies (Little Hans asked his father whether Doctor Freud knew God!). Was psychoanalysis's role to deliver people from their religious beliefs, ignore them, or substitute for them?

Psychoanalysis's confrontation with religion in its way condenses the wider philosophical and socio-theoretical issues raised in this chapter, and the challenges psychoanalysis poses to accepted modes of thought. On one side, psychoanalysis's account(s) of religion – particularly the second account, focusing on guilt and reparation – unearths a rationality to religious ideas and practices. In Lacan's work in particular, and that of figures such as René Girard, religious texts take on a renewed dignity and interest in the light of psychoanalysis, as reflections of the structuring parameters of human desire (e.g. Lacan 1990: 82–95; 1992; Girard 1977). As in its challenge to the hubris of the modern, Cartesian account of subjectivity, psychoanalysis's account of the religions in this way overturns earlier, more facile modernist dismissals, thus pointing towards a dialogue between modern–secular and theistic understandings.

On the other hand, Freud's religious critics were quick to point out how his framing conception of religions as collective neuroses – especially in "The Future of An Illusion" – seem profoundly reductive. As Freud underlines in "Civilization and Its Discontents", religion *per se* is for him a phenomenon of "mass psychology". He does not countenance the manifold developments of Christian theology, or the Jewish and Islamic philosophies of law. The implication is that they could amount to no more than so many sophisticated rationalizations of religion's "patently infantile" core. It is true that, in "Moses and Monotheism", Freud defends the cultural advance represented by (particularly Jewish) monotheism, with its prohibition of orgiastic rituals and graven images. Freud reads these, with marked pride, as the reflections of a higher level of the civilizing sublimation and repression of primal drives (Gay 1987; Yerushalmi 1991; Strauss 1997: 285–90). Nevertheless, as critics have repeated, Freud's wider position seemingly ignores "the noblest utterances of religion" which would point towards "a higher conception of human nature, which certainly does not arise from lower instinctual demands, but . . . from an idealistic realism that can be achieved only with severe difficulties . . ." (Pfister, in Meng & Freud 1963: 158–9).

Probably the most fundamental philosophical questions raised by Freud's encounter with religion concern the type of account of religion Freud presents. This account, as we have seen, traces human beings' beliefs in transcendent or sublime deities back to their "all-too-human" libidinal sources, and alleged historical origins. Religious beliefs are discredited by Freud in so far as they reflect the strength of our earliest wishes. Yet, as the political philosopher Leo Strauss has pointed out, this type of psychological critique of the motivations for belief in no way counts for or against the truth of the contents of the beliefs in question. That people turn to God out of "adult" strength or infantile weakness does not affect whether He exists. The infinite transcendence of the monotheistic God means that human beings, as finite, can strictly never decide this question (Strauss 1997: 301). Equally, the meaning of (say) the laws of physics has nothing to do with their "genesis": how or when they were discovered, or what Newton, Einstein, Bohr and the like might psychologically have "got out of" formulating them. The psychoanalytic account of religion, that is, seems to flirt perilously – like Freud's account of art (see above) – with what philosophers call the "genetic fallacy": erroneously reducing questions about the truth or meaning of religious things to their origins.

Arguably the most profound philosophical reflection on psychoanalysis and religion is that of Paul Ricoeur. Ricoeur brings together criticisms of Freud with a profound appreciation of psychoanalysis. For Ricoeur, as for Freud's friend Pfister, there is truth in Freud's critiques of religion. At the very least "analysis can reveal to the religious man his caricature", and so renew and deepen his quest for truth (Ricoeur 1970: 533). Yet Ricoeur joins other critics in noting that Freud's texts on the religions are among his most "fragile" or contentious. Tasked with understanding the psychological power of religion, Ricoeur notes, Freud evidently felt compelled to revive "a conception he was forced to abandon in his conception of the neuroses" – namely, the idea that the repressed "truth of religion" was a historical trauma. "We recall that the true interpretation of the Oedipus complex was achieved in opposition to the erroneous theory of the real seduction of the child by an adult", Ricoeur reflects. Yet in Freud's texts on religion:

> The individual Oedipus complex is too brief and too indistinct to engender the gods; without an ancestral crime as part of our

> phylogenetic past, the [religious] longing for the father is
> unintelligible . . .   (Ricoeur 1970: 537)

The price for trying to defend such an "archaeological" claim, as other critics agree, is that Freud accepts the most questionable ethnographic hypotheses (in "Totem and Taboo") and practises the most forced scriptural exegesis in "Moses and Monotheism".

Why, Ricoeur asks, was Freud drawn to these tenuous straits? In the force of religion, Ricoeur proposes, Freud confronted an enigma finally "inaccessible to us along psychoanalytic lines" – like, we note, the genius of artists (see above). Freud's attempt to reduce religious beliefs to these "lines" accordingly forced him, regressively, to "turn his back on the demythologizing interpretations which . . . deprive [religious] myths of any etiological [causal] function" (Ricoeur 1970: 537), as well as on what his own clinical work had indicated. Instead, Freud's position in "Totem and Taboo" and "Moses and Monotheism" ironically mimics those earlier peoples whom moderns suppose believed in the "aetiological", historical truth of their myths of origin.

What Freud's account of religion misses, Ricoeur charges, is two, interrelated things. First, as we have said, Freud denies the possibility – and thereby the importance – of the progressive transformation or "epigeneses" in religious traditions over time. But, asks Ricoeur (and we think again of the genetic fallacy):

> What have I understood when I have discovered . . . that the
> father figure is the representation of the deity? . . . *I do not
> know what the father means* . . . I did not know what the father
> was *until his image had engendered the whole series of his
> derivatives* . . .   (Ricoeur 1970: 541–2, emphasis added)

As Freud argued in his clinical treatments of analysands' "primal scene" fantasies, that is, so Ricoeur argues that we simply need not maintain that the psychological force of religious stories depends primarily on the historical truth they allegedly report or distort. What is decisive is the meaning subjects attribute to these stories: a meaning that will be mediated by the "derivative" retellings of the traditions in which they live, and will reflect and speak to their present existential concerns.

When we pose the question of the meaning of religious symbols, Ricoeur claims, we must say that Freud's psychoanalytic account of religion occludes their decisive "mythopoetic" or "creative" dimension. Freud may well show us how religious stories can and do, truly, give repetitive form to repressed "archaisms" and fearful "idols". But this "archaeological" truth for Ricoeur in no way prevents these symbols at the same time from having another, forward-looking or "prophetic" dimension: one in which these archaic origins are "denied and overcome" at the same time as they are repeated. Religious symbols, as religious, for Ricoeur, intimate that there is more to human experience than is dreamt of in philosophy, psychoanalysis, let alone Freud's pale ethnography. Whatever we might say concerning where religious symbols came from,

> The force of a religious symbol lies in the fact that it . . . transforms [a primal scene fantasy] into an instrument of discovery . . . it is in and through certain primal scene fantasies that man "forms", "interprets", "intends" meanings of another order, meanings capable of becoming the signs of the sacred . . . (Ricoeur 1970: 540)

At base, then, confronting Freud's critiques of religions returns us to our beginning in this chapter, with "Civilization and Its Discontents" and its questions concerning the meaning of human existence, whether there is anything irreducibly enigmatic about our condition, or whether, as Freud typically proposed (see Chapter 8), a scientific culture informed by psychoanalysis could be sufficient for a good life and society.

Summary

- Freud's "Civilization and Its Discontents" contends that, while living together in law-bound societies yields unquestionable benefits, civilization itself is a source of ineradicable "discontents". For the later Freud, there will always be a quota of non-erotic aggression (the death drive) that resists taming by civilization.
- The guilt particularly evident in obsessional neuroses shows how the psychological costs of living peaceably with others is the redirection of the death drive against the ego – this is why the superego, especially of the most moral individuals, always has a snarling, excessive core.
- The sublimation of the drives, which redirects their aims into culturally sanctioned practices such as art, is one of the principal instruments of civilization.

- Artists for Freud dream or "play out" their own – and indirectly all our – personal fantasies in their art, using the *ars poetica* to disguise the personal, offensive content of these wishes.
- Film theory has used psychoanalysis, and particularly Lacan's notion of the gaze, to explain audiences' enjoyment of films. Nevertheless, Lacan's "gaze" arguably upsets this programme, for it names a strictly uncanny object that confronts audiences with the return of the repressed, and reminds them of the finitude or partiality of their perspectives – something that implicates them in *jouissance*, rather than masterful self-satisfaction.
- Freud's encounter with religion is central to psychoanalysis, yet deeply ambivalent. Freud argues both that religions console us for the fears that attend our finite condition, and that the compelling character of religious beliefs and ritual attests to their origins in guilt for a primal, phylogenetic crime – the murder of the father of the primal horde.
- For Freud, monotheism represents the truth of religion, in our infantile ambivalence towards the father, in a "purer" form – indeed, in Christianity, the repressed phylogentic murder of the father is represented in the crucifixion.
- Religious critics such as Pfister, Strauss and Ricoeur have suggested that Freud's attempt to psychoanalytically discredit religions falls prey to the genetic fallacy, cannot "disprove" the truth of religious propositions, and flattens the meaning of these propositions, by seeking out their causal, historical and psychological explanations. In place of the "future of an illusion", they propose, Freud erects the ambivalent prospect of an "illusion of the future", a wholly rationalized, secular society.

eight

Where psychoanalysis has come to be: philosophy, science, society and ethics

Understanding psychoanalysis at the turn of the centuries

Freud withheld publication of *The Interpretation of Dreams* until 1900. His aim was to signal his ambition that psychoanalysis should play a decisive role in the new century. From its tenuous beginnings in an elite *Männerbund* (or inner circle) of analysts around Freud in Vienna, Berlin and London, by the time Freud died in 1939, psychoanalysis had become a global movement. Even before the inauguration of the International Psychoanalytic Association (IPA) in 1910, psychoanalysis's founding postulate of the unconscious had begun capturing the imaginations of film-makers, ad-men and the avant-garde. The embrace of Freudian ideas by the avant-garde in the first decades of the last century inaugurated a wider process that would see psychoanalytic motifs saturate popular culture by the 1950s. Despite repression at the hands of both Soviets and Nazis in the 1920s and 1930s, clinical psychoanalysis was practised between the wars in the United States, Italy, Holland, France, Turkey, Palestine, Argentina, India and Japan. In the United States, psychoanalysis was from the 1920s closely integrated into the medical establishment. So entrenched a facet of the post-New Deal state did it become that by 1941, when the United States entered World War II, the Surgeon General's Office required every military doctor to know its basic principles. In the 1950s, more than half of the university chairs in psychiatry in the new world were held by analysts (Kirsner 2004: 345). By 1976, as Lacanian psychoanalysis flourished in France and South America, the American Psychoanalytic Association boasted 27,000 psychoanalysts (Zaretsky 2004: 281).

Yet at the turn of the twenty-first century, the psychoanalytic movement is in widespread decline. The 1980s and 1990s saw a host of popular attacks on Freud (so-called "Freud bashing"), and considerations of whether Freud might finally be "dead" (Masson 1984; Crews 1995; Webster 1995). A 2003 *Time Magazine* article reported that there were only around 5,000 analysands in the United States, roughly only two per analyst, and that the mean age of the analysts was 62 (in the UK, 66). Psychoanalysis (principally Lacanian) has continued to flourish only in France and South America (particularly Argentina) (Kirsner 2004: 339–44; 2000).

Eli Zaretsky, in his *Secrets of the Soul* (2004), presents an intriguing hypothesis to explain the rise and decline of psychoanalysis in the century since *The Interpretation of Dreams*. Psychoanalysis's "golden age" until the 1960s corresponded to the "second industrial revolution". This revolution, associated with the advent of mass, "Fordist", production and consumer culture, led to a decisive separation of people's work lives from home and family. In this context, Freud's discovery of a "personal" (versus collective) unconscious spoke to a widespread "lived sense of disjuncture between the public and the private, the outer and the inner, the socio-cultural and the personal" (Zarestky 2004: 6). Its more recent decline, by contrast, reflects a third "industrial revolution". This revolution dates from the 1960s and the emergence of new social movements, such as second-wave feminism and identity politics movements. These movements' politicizations of the private sphere (for instance gender roles, see Chapter 6) reflected a debt to psychoanalysis – perhaps one reason why "Freud bashing" is such a part of today's "culture wars", particularly in the United States. Yet these new social movements also challenged the psychoanalytic focus on the personal unconscious. They shifted the focus of public debate and intellectual enquiry on to groups, culture and institutions. From around the same period, meanwhile, breakthroughs in neuroscience, cognitive behavioural psychology and psychiatric drugs have seen the advent of shorter, cheaper treatments for mental illness. The psychiatric treatments associated with these changes have been much more successful than psychoanalysis in retaining public funding, despite the worldwide rolling back of the welfare states since 1980.

As we commented in our Introduction, psychoanalysis promised, uniquely, to bring together three components. These components span the sanctified boundaries in the modern West's intellectual division of labour: psychoanalysis's materialist-biological philosophy of mind (Chapters 1, 2); its hermeneutic–interpretive understanding of culture (Chapters 3, 7); and its clinical embodiment as an ethical practice in self-discovery (see the section "The ends of psychoanalysis", below). As a result of the cultural and pharmacological revolutions of recent decades, Zaretsky observes that these three components have been torn asunder. Psychoanalytic practice has declined, and we shall see presently how even many of its friends now question its sufficiency. Psychoanalytic theory, meanwhile, has largely migrated into the film and cultural studies departments in universities (Chapter 7). Here, stripped of its clinical clothing, it competes with other philosophical and interpretive theories of "discourse" or "representation". In this context, an understanding of the philosophical and other criticisms of psychoanalysis becomes particularly salient. It behoves us to evaluate whether this decline should be celebrated or rejected *tout court*, or what should be salvaged from psychoanalysis's fall.

Mais qu'est-ce que c'est? Psychoanalysis and science

Popper et al.: psychoanalysis is not a science

Freud's writings on religion (see Chapter 7) underscore his lifelong commitment to the modern scientific *Weltanschauung*, and what he ironically called "our God *Logos*". Freud recognized that psychoanalysis, which takes as its objects dreams and the symptoms of the mad, steps boldly into territory traditionally reserved for the religious or superstitious. Yet from the start, Freud was at pains to distance the talking cure from its "one might say, mystical" origins – in Breuer's method of hypnotic suggestion (see Introduction). In Chapter 1 of "The Unconscious", Freud underscores how psychoanalysis's founding theoretical postulation of the unconscious is anything but the result of a taste for esoterica. When faced with symptoms, slips and dreams, we can give up on explaining them, assigning them instead to chance or the gods. Or we can argue that these irrational phenomena are rationally explicable as the products of the human psyche. If we take this second, more scientific, option, Freud's proposal is that we have no choice but to postulate the existence of the unconscious (Ucs: 167). To be sure, we cannot directly see the unconscious. But then, neither can physicists unaided see the atoms (subatomic particles, quarks, strings and so on) they postulate as the building blocks of nature. Neurotic symptoms and dreams, Freud's claim is, represent "*indirect* proofs of the most cogent kind" for the unconscious (NU: 262). More directly, for Freud the validity of psychoanalytic metapsychology can be attested by the clinical testimony of analysands, and the curative efficacy of clinical psychoanalysis (Ucs: 167).

Arguably the most important philosophical criticisms of psychoanalysis challenge its would-be scientific status. While not questioning Freud's scientific intentions, analytic philosophers such as Nagel, Scriven, Skinner and Popper dispute whether psychoanalysis proceeds scientifically in gathering and understanding its evidences, direct or indirect. Ernest Nagel's "Methodological Issues in Psychoanalytic Theory" (1959) exemplifies this type of criticism. Nagel, like Freud, was deeply committed to the belief that the modern sciences afford us a privileged (if not the only) way to truly know the world. For Nagel, what singles out genuinely scientific theories such as those of physics or chemistry is that their hypotheses make empirically testable predictions about the way things behave in the natural world. The theory's predictions can be verified by any number of independent observers, in controlled experimental conditions. By contrast, Nagel observes that clinical psychoanalysis meets none of these conditions. The "data" the psychoanalytic clinic produce are irreducibly embedded in the singular transferential relationship between each analyst and her analysands. A particular analysand's psychoanalysis cannot, by its nature, be repeated or verified with just anyone. However ethically or otherwise defensible such a procedure might be, Nagel suggests, clinical psychoanalysis has no just claim to a scientific status (Nagel 1959).

The types of criticisms Nagel raised against psychoanalysis were, however, most famously developed by Karl Popper. Popper's intriguing philosophy of science maintains that true scientific theories do not seek out only confirmations of their predictions. In fact, the epistemological problem with religious and superstitious worldviews is that believers see everything that occurs as so many confirmations of their beliefs. Their belief systems are flexible enough to "explain" whatever transpires – from good harvests, proofs of the gods' favour, to bad harvests, equally compelling proofs of their wrath. What distinguishes scientific theories, Popper argued, is their openness to "falsification". A true science is a "risky business". It makes hypotheses about events that might not occur, and that could be proven wrong. Popper gives the example of Einstein's hypothesis about the effects of the force of gravity on the behaviour of light. Initially the technologies did not exist to test

Einstein's theory. But the theory was exacting enough to make predictions that subsequent photographic developments could have "falsified" – had Einstein's theory not been right (Popper 1962).

Popper's critique of psychoanalysis is, then, not that it claims to explain too little; his concern is that psychoanalytic metapsychology, like theologians' metaphysical systems, claims such power that it allows practitioners to "predict" any human behaviour. Consider, for example, Freud's famous notion of "resistance" to psychoanalysis, which lies at the heart of his "Papers on Technique" (see "The ends of psychoanalysis", below). According to this idea, analysands can be expected to resist their analyst's disclosures of the content of these wishes, because their unconscious wishes are repressed. Instead, analysands will repeat earlier ways of behaviour towards the analyst, "transferring" on to her/him their ancient loves or hatreds, based on the "stereotype plates" of their childhood relations with parents, siblings, carers (DT: 99–100; RRW). But, asks the Popperian, what happens when a given analysand rejects their analyst's interpretation of some symptom? Does not the notion of resistance license the analyst to see this "resistance" as confirmation of the interpretation, so that the analyst is really playing a kind of "heads I win, tails you lose" game with analysands? As Freud's "On Negation" concludes:

> There is no stronger evidence that we have been successful in our effort to uncover the unconscious than when the patient reacts to it with words "I didn't think that", or "I didn't (ever) think of that". (N: 239)

We will return to these concerns at the conclusion of this chapter.

Ricoeur: psychoanalysis is, indeed, not a natural science

One of the "splinters" into which psychoanalysis has today divided is a hermeneutic or interpretive one. Following Freud's psychoanalytic interpretations of civilization, religion and art (Chapter 7) into the promised land of the humanities and social sciences, academics have embraced psychoanalysis as a theory of culture. Paul Ricoeur's 1965 *Freud and Philosophy: An Essay on Interpretation* provides the most sophisticated defence of this interpretive repackaging of psychoanalysis.

Philosophical hermeneutics emerged out of Protestant attempts to reclaim the true meaning of the "book of books" (*sola scriptura*) from beneath centuries of Catholic dogma. In the nineteenth century, however, thinkers such as Schleiermacher and Dilthey argued that a hermeneutic approach should become the basis for those modern "human sciences", for example history or sociology, for these human sciences aim to interpret the products of intentional human actions, as well as causally explaining historical events. In *Freud and Philosophy*, as Ricoeur's criticisms of Freud on religion reflect (Chapter 7), Ricoeur agrees with Popper, Nagel *et al.* that psychoanalysis is not a natural science. Ricoeur contests that this is the standard against which psychoanalysis should be judged. Psychoanalysis is based upon the spoken, subjective testimony of analysands, Ricoeur stresses – not any experimental facts. Both the "past dramas" analysands recount, and the analytic process itself, are intersubjective. They involve multiple people, whose actions are shaped by the others' responses – as we stressed in looking at Klein and Lacan (Chapters 4 and 5). But this is a different type of practice from that of conducting physical experiments, where the scientist is faced by objects that do not "answer back". Analysands' words and actions, Ricoeur contends, should for these reasons be understood as "signifiers for the history of [their] desire" (Ricoeur 1970: 369). They convey the meanings analysands give to their experiences, true or imagined. Analysis is not forensics, police work or criminology, as people who lament Freud's 1897 sidelining of the "seduction theory" of the neuroses reflect (Masson 1984). Just as one might read a book looking for its meanings, Ricoeur echoes Lacan, so the testimony of analysands is a type of "text" the analyst is called upon to interpret (see Chapter 3):

> [A]nalytic experience unfolds in the field of speech and . . . within this field, what comes to light is another language, dissociated from common language, and which presents itself to be deciphered through its meaningful effects – symptoms, dreams, various formulations, etc.   (Ricoeur 1970: 366–7)

How then does Ricoeur account for Freud's continual framing of psychoanalysis in the biological language of "drives", "cathexes" and "abreaction"? In Habermas's concurring words (see below), Ricoeur proposes that Freud was the victim of a "scientistic self-misunderstanding" (Habermas 1978: 246). Clinical psychoanalysts, Ricoeur notes, never encounter such "energetic" phenomena as the "drives" except through their "instinctual representatives" in the speech, slips, dreams and neuroses of analysands. (And we think here of Freud's "frontier" definition of the drives; see Chapter 2). Freud's ideas, to which "energy" is attached or "cathected", Ricoeur contends,

> operate at the level of the instinctual representatives and are accessible to analysis only in the distortion of meaning . . . as soon as the economics [of the drives] is separated from its rhetorical manifestations [in symptoms, slips, dreams], the metapsychology no longer systematises what occurs in the analytic dialogue; it engenders a fanciful demonology, if not an absurd hydraulics.   (Ricoeur 1970: 370–71)

Neuropsychoanalysis: a new synthesis?

In the last decade, a third approach – "neuropsychoanalysis" – has emerged concerning psychoanalysis's relationship to the sciences. This approach is led by a group of neuroscientists including Antonio Damasio, Mark Solms and Nobel Laureate Eric Kandel, in the International Neuropsychoanalytic Society (NPSA). The neuropsychoanalysts' argument is that our continuing inability to scientifically test Freud's metapsychological hypotheses about the workings of the mind does not forever discredit these hypotheses. It potentially reflects how far ahead of his times Freud was. Freud always granted his metapsychological ideas a provisional status – as ideas that "will presumably one day be based on an organic substructure" (ON: 77–9). Perhaps, the NPSAs website suggests, that day has now come:

> Freud, in his 1895 "Project for a Scientific Psychology," attempted to join the emerging discipline of neuroscience of his time. But that was a hundred years ago, when the neuron had only just been described . . . We have had to wait many decades before the sort of data Freud needed finally became available. Now . . . contemporary neuroscience allows for the resumption of the search for correlation between the two disciples.   (Arnold Pfeffer, at http://www.neuro-psa.org.uk)

Notably, the starting position of the advocates of the "neuropsychoanalytic turn" is a rejection of all attempts, like Ricoeur's, to hermeneutically reground psychoanalysis. Eric Kandel asserts that this move "has hindered psychoanalysis from continuing to grow intellectually" in the last three decades (Kandel 1999: 508); for Mark Solms, it has "insulated" psychoanalysis from continuing scientific progress and kudos

(Solms 1996: 701). Kandel concurs with Nagel that "although psycho-analysis has historically been scientific in its aims, it has rarely been so in its methods: it has failed over the years to submit its assumptions to testable experimentation" (Kandel 1999: 507; 1998: 468–9). Unlike both Nagel and Popper, however, Kandel and other neuropsycho-analysts believe that psychoanalytic hypotheses can and should be sub-mitted to natural-scientific testing. "The failure of psychoanalysis to provide objective evidence that it is effective as a therapy can no longer be accepted" (Kandel 1999: 523). What then do the neuropsycho-analysts propose for psychoanalysis, to reverse its institutional decline?

Recall how Klein and Lacan's developments of psychoanalytic theory were based on the most advanced scientific observations of infants' behaviour, ethology and the social sciences (see Chapters 4 and 5). Kandel's position is that psychoanalysis, in this vein, should shed its present pretences to disciplinary autonomy. It should recognize that "if it is to have a future, it lies in the context of empirical psychology, abetted by imaging techniques, neuroanatomical methods, and human genetics" (Kandel 1998: 468), that is, the most advanced scientific tech-niques available at the start of the twenty-first century. As Kandel sees things, this will involve psychoanalysis in a two-way exchange with empirical biology and psychology. On one hand, the key metapsycho-logical notions should each be tested, and where necessary revised, against the data furnished by today's experimental sciences. As the neuropsychoanalyst–philosopher Jim Hopkins concurs:

> [I]f psychoanalytic claims about motivation are correct we should be able to relate them to those of other disciplines, such as social psychology, developmental psychology, evolutionary psychology, and neuroscience.   (Hopkins 2004: 1)

On the other hand, neuropsychoanalysts are aware that, for all the recent advances in psychopharmacology, these practical advances have forged far ahead of the current theoretical bases of neuroscience. Psychoanalysis, Kandel argues, still provides by far "the most coherent and intellectually satisfying view of the mind" (Kandel 1999: 505), one whose very scope as a theory of personality and mental illness far exceeds other materialist philosophies of mind. For this reason, he suggests, psychoanalysis can play an important role in the future of neuroscientific research, possibly one "equivalent to the one played by Darwin's theory of evolution in relation to molecular genetics", as Mark Solms concurs – namely, as "a [theoretical] template on which emerging [neuroscientific] details can be coherently arranged" (Solms 2004: 85). In several works, Solms has indeed sought to corroborate several of Freud's metapsychological hypotheses using neuroscientific techniques. In his *Neuropsychology of Dreams*, for instance, Solms shows that Freud's hypothesis concerning dreams' function to preserve sleep is consistent with the known data concerning the disturbed sleeping patterns of patients with brain lesions that prevent their dreaming (Solms 1997). Alongside Karen Kaplan-Solms, Solms has also used neurological mapping to corroborate what Freud could only anticipate: a material basis for the functional agencies (ego, superego, id) his later metapsychology postulated:

> Recent neurological mapping generally correlates to Freud's conception. The core brain-stem and limbic system – responsible for instincts and drives – roughly correspond to Freud's id. The central frontal region, which controls selective inhibition, the dorsal frontal region, which controls self-conscious thought, and the posterior cortex, which represents the outside world, amount to the ego and the superego.
>
> (Solms 2004: 85)

Freud's pharmacy: his sociocultural critics

Freud's academic refuge during the latter half of the twentieth century, the humanities, has its own sizeable contingent of "Freud bashers" – or at least those who take a critical stance towards psychoanalysis. From post-Marxist French philosophers (Foucault, Derrida, Deleuze and Guattari) to conservative critics (Carroll, Rieff and Lasch), psychoanalysis has, broadly speaking, been received in the humanities as kind of a *pharmakon* of modern civilization: both poison and panacea, and one that has left a sour aftertaste in the mouths of many.

The French poststructuralists

The philosopher Jacques Derrida's relationship to psychoanalysis is complex and ambivalent – perhaps even "Oedipal". Derrida differentiates his own "deconstructive" methodology from psychoanalysis, which he sees remaining too "dialectical" and "metaphysical": a discourse in which the unconscious truth is always to be returned to its "rightful place" *après coup* (or *Nachträglichkeit*), at the end of the analysis. In *The Margins of Philosophy*, however, Derrida acknowledges his debt to Freud's concept of the unconscious (Derrida 1982: 18), and elsewhere doffs his cap to Freud and Lacan's legacy to deconstruction.

Derrida's debt to Freud is clear in his early work, *Dissemination*. Derrida draws here on Freud's elaboration of a "kettle logic" (from *The Interpretation of Dreams*) to unravel the logics whereby philosophers defend some of their central notions. "Kettle logic" describes the mutually contradictory excuses a man Freud cites uses to clear his name from returning broken a kettle he had borrowed: he never borrowed it, it was already broken when he did, and besides, it was returned intact. The "kettle-logic" metaphor is a key element of Derrida's famous critique of Plato, Rousseau and Saussure's privileging of speech over writing, as closer to the full presence of meaning to the philosophical subject's living intentionality:

> Analogously: 1. Writing is rigorously exterior and inferior to living memory and speech, which are therefore undamaged by it. 2. Writing is harmful to them because it puts them to sleep and infects their very life which would otherwise remain intact. 3. Anyway, if one has resorted to hypomnesia and writing . . . , it is not for their intrinsic value, but because living memory is finite, it already has holes in it before writing ever comes to leave its traces. Writing has no effect on memory.
>
> (Derrida 1981: 111)

Derrida's best-known *contretemps* with psychoanalysis is "The Purveyor of Truth" (*The Post Card*), written in response to Lacan's seminar on Poe's "Purloined Letter". At first glance, there would seem to be ample basis for Derrida to agree with Lacan. We saw in Chapter 5 how Lacan's commentary on Poe's short story emphasizes the role of the signifier, and its location in an intersubjective network of social relations, in determining the subject's identity. "Purloined", Lacan stresses, means "displaced" [*in suffrance*] – rather than simply "stolen" [*volée*] (Lacan 2006: 29). For Lacan, as for Derrida, meaning is produced through a movement of continual displacement and deferral in relation to differences within a linguistic, social structure – a movement Derrida calls *différance* (with an "a").

However, in "The Purveyor of Truth" Derrida is mockingly critical of Lacan. He targets psychoanalysis's alleged "imperialism": the tendency to find itself wherever psychoanalysis looks. Derrida objects to Lacan's allegedly "Hegelian" tendency to neutralize dyadic ("imaginary") tension and ambiguities into a third ("symbolic") term. For example, Derrida challenges the legitimacy of Lacan's resolution of the conflicting duos (the queen and the minister; the minister and Dupin) in the story's key scenes into a "symbolic" trio, wherein the "purloined letter" – like the castrating operation of language more widely – is the "third" term that interrupts individuals' imaginary identifications (since, as we recall from Chapter 5, the letter, a symbol of power, disempowers its possessor). A second and related instance of "Hegelianism" Derrida decries is Lacan's alleged substantialization of the "lack", embodied by the unopened letter, as originary cause of desire. According to Derrida, this "substantive" lack comes to illegitimately order (and stifle) the play of absence and presence which, he argues, produces linguistic meaning:

[I]t will suffice to change a letter, perhaps even less than a letter, in the expression "*manque à sa place*" [missing from its place], perhaps it will suffice to introduce into this expression . . . an *a* without an accent mark, in order to make apparent that if the lack has its place [*manque a sa place*] in this atomistic topology of the signifier . . . then the existing order will not have been upset: the letter will always refind its proper place, a circumvented lack . . . the letter will be where it always will have been, always should have been, intangible and indestructible via the detour of a *proper*, and properly circular, itinerary.   (Derrida 1987: 425)

Derrida's critique culminates with his reading of the final line of Lacan's Poe seminar. "Thus, it is that what the 'purloined letter', nay, the 'letter in sufferance', means is that a letter always arrives at its destination" (Lacan 2006: 46/61). Derrida interprets the letter's eventual return to its "destination" here as indicating its teleological predisposition, as theorized by Lacan. For Derrida, the displacement of the letter/signifier that Lacan had previously emphasized is thus ironically nullified by this final statement. Emphasizing the extent to which the word is always in excess of the subject who speaks/writes it, Derrida ponders: if the letter is truly displaced, then could it not also miss its destination? Both Barbara Johnson (1988: 248) and Slavoj Žižek (1992: 10) argue, to the contrary, that, by juxtaposing "displacement" and "destination" in the final sentence of the Poe seminar, Lacan simply indicates the transference (see below). Accordingly, that the letter always reaches its destination means only that the subject misrecognizes itself in the other. "I" receive myself from the other in reversed form – much like the Queen's letter, which the minister conceals by simply turning its envelope inside out. In this context, Lacan conceives of the letter's "destination" not as a fixed position to which it must ultimately be delivered, but rather as the (subject) position determined by its reception.

Michel Foucault, and Gilles Deleuze and Félix Guattari, pose objections to psychoanalysis concerned more with the question of desire than of meaning. Foucault, like Derrida, both affirms and criticizes psychoanalysis. In *The Order of Things* (1966) Foucault accords a privileged position to psychoanalysis (alongside ethnology) among the human sciences. Despite Freud's scientistic ambitions, Foucault sees Freud as a tireless questioner of the role of science in human affairs, and of the possibility of a truly exhaustive science of humanity. Psychoanalysis, Foucault says, serves a much-needed "critical function" respecting the human sciences:

> [B]y following the same path as the human sciences, but with its gaze turned the other way, psychoanalysis moves towards the moment . . . at which the contents of consciousness articulate themselves, or rather stand gaping, upon man's finitude. (Foucault 1970: 374)

For Foucault, psychoanalysis is distinct from the other human sciences (sociology, criminology, economics and so on) because of its encounter with human finitude. The concept of the unconscious radically decentres human subjectivity, Foucault stresses, such that the modern "subject" is less a foundation than an effect of discourses, power and knowledges.

While this understanding of psychoanalysis arguably still haunts the first volume of Foucault's famous *History of Sexuality* (*La Volonté de savoir* – literally "the will to knowledge"), *La Volonté* also critiques psychoanalysis. Foucault sets out a two-pronged attack. First, he contends that there has been a proliferation of discourses addressing sexuality since the eighteenth century, during which sexuality has taken on culturally unprecedented importance as the secret truth of subjects' inner selves. Secondly, Foucault challenges the idea, expressed pre-eminently by Freud, that sexuality has been socially "repressed", so that in speaking the truth of our sexuality, we speak *for* freedom *against* power.

According to the Foucault of *La Volonté*, the Freudian "talking cure" bears a significant resemblance to the confessional of the eighteenth and nineteenth centuries, many of whose features it adapts. Psychoanalysis in this way both exemplifies and conceals the subtle ways in which modern medical, social and juridical institutions – far from simply saying "no!" to subjects' sexuality – actively incite subjects to speak concerning their most intimate lives, and documents their testimony for its own purposes. Indeed, by arguing that all human drives are ultimately both sexual and unconscious, and then clinically prescribing that analysands speak their mind to release it, psychoanalysis represents for Foucault a wider cultural shift – wherein modern subjects have been encouraged by scientific culture to think of themselves as living, desiring animals (versus political subjects or citizens), whose private lives and drives are of governmental concern for managing the population, diseases, birth rates, productivity, GDPs and so on.

In Foucault's *La Volonté de savoir*, the Oedipus complex is seen as a process through which the family comes to be a conduit of sexualized repression and governmental control. Gilles Deleuze and Félix Guattari's contemporaneous work, *Anti-Oedipus*, similarly emphasizes the role of "Oedipus" in normalizing desire and subjectivity. Deleuze and Guattari draw upon the psychoanalytic battery of concepts in order to produce their own philosophy of desire – given that Félix Guattari was trained and analysed by Lacan, this is hardly surprising. However, their reference to psychoanalytic concepts is marked by a displacement of these concepts: where the aim is to reinvest psychoanalysis with a different, Nietzschean, "force". As Philip Goodchild writes, this "attack on psychoanalysis can be regarded as an attempt to reform and redirect it from within" (Goodchild 1996: 122).

KEY POINT *"Desire" in* Anti-Oedipus *and in psychoanalysis*

- For both Deleuze and Guattari, and for Freud, desire is a sexual or corporeal energy that permeates and produces all relations, whether political, social or psychological (*ibid.*).
- But where Freudian desire suggests a kind of deprivation or "lack" (summarized by castration, the *"non"*, and the pleasure principle), for Deleuze and Guattari desire is affirmative, productive and even wasteful: creating from superabundance rather than need (Deleuze & Guattari 2004: 28). Deleuze and Guattari identify "lack" as an effect (or "countereffect", implying reactivity) of desire that psychoanalytic theory then retroactively posits as its cause.

- For Deleuze and Guattari, desire is, rather, heterogeneous and positive:

> Desire does not lack anything; it does not lack its object. It is, rather, the *subject* that is missing in desire, or desire that lacks a fixed subject; there is no fixed subject unless there is repression. Desire and its object are one and the same thing . . . Desire is a machine, and the object of desire is another machine connected to it . . . Lack is a countereffect of desire . . .   (*Ibid.*: 28)

In *Anti-Oedipus*, desire is characterized by two movements of production (synthesis) and creative "anti-production" (dissolution). Deleuze and Guattari call these, respectively, "desiring production" and the "body-without-organs" – loosely aligned with Freud's later division of the drives into "libido" (or *Eros*) and the "death drive" (*Thanatos*) (see Chapter 4). Desiring production, like libido, is industrious. It connects and assembles, creating new forms and occupying more and more space. Capitalism is the paradigm of what they call the "desiring machine", as its chief capacity is to incorporate and co-opt other forces and bodies, in search of ever-renewed profits. The "body-without-organs", on the other hand, tends towards disintegration – providing a limit for desiring production (and capitalism). It is a point of stasis and overfullness, wherein new connections are refused and the body begins to devolve to its constituent parts. Deleuze and Guattari, however, repudiate the strong metaphysical dualism of Freud's theory of *Eros* and *Thanatos*. For them production and anti-production are only different "moments" within one and the same process, expressing implicit tendencies of desire, understood as what they call a "plane of immanence".

Deleuze and Guattari's claim that desire is a "plane of immanence" means that the field of desire comprises all bodies and their relations to one another – there is no transcendent "outside". Desire creates "reality" (corporeal, social, psychological) and not only representations (fantasies) and signifiers. Here, however, Deleuze and Guattari arguably oversimplify the part of fantasy within psychoanalytic theory: as Žižek points out, for Lacan the virtual – fantasy and the symbolic – provides the means by which reality can appear for us, phenomenologically. Fantasy is *how* desire gives shape to reality, as well as a specific kind of subjectivity (Žižek 2004: 3–9, 94–101). Deleuze and Guattari's critique of the subject is another case in point, The subject of psychoanalysis is represented as a "fixed" subject, rather than the fragile, "split" subject of Freud, Klein or Lacan. While for Lacan the assumption of a subject position inaugurates desire, for Deleuze and Guattari the subject stifles and represses desire. Drawing on Nietzsche and Pierre Klossowski, Deleuze and Guattari envisage subjectivity as a will-to-disintegration, or delirium, rather than a neurotic attachment to ideality and wholeness (Deleuze & Guattari 2004: 4). Klein's notion of "part objects" is revaluated in this connection, although Klein is duly rebuked for misunderstanding the "logic" of partial objects. For Deleuze and Guattari, the relation between the drive and its object does not inevitably lead to the integration of the object into a "whole" (*ibid.*: 47). Deleuze and Guattari shift the partial object from the realm of fantasy to reality, a move whose libertarian radicality is indicated by their elevation of Judge Schreber, the psychotic *par excellence* (see Chapter 5) to a kind of poster-boy for the *modus vivendi* they valorize.

Anti-Oedipus renders Schreber as enacting the fecundity and risk that Deleuze and Guattari prioritize in desire, but which, they contend, psychoanalysis attempts to circumvent. Judge Schreber creates connections and realities, and offers himself up to the productions of other "desiring machines" (e.g. God). Through his delirium, Schreber decomposes (or decodes) himself, rendering his diverse components ready for new compositions. Freud, Klein and Lacan are ill equipped to interpret psychosis in such a positive light, Deleuze and Guattari argue, because of their commitment to the Oedipal triangle (*ibid.*: 16). The "schizo" represents, for Deleuze and Guattari, a social and subjective possibility engendered by its relation to desiring production. It is thus irreducible to the clinically designated paranoid schizophrenic whom the psychoanalysts attempted to treat. The "schizo" of *Anti-Oedipus* is rather elevated to a romantic site of resistance to capitalism: "decoding and recoding" (or displacing) the "socius", as its "surplus product" (*ibid.*: 38). The Freudian clinic in turn participates in the codification of capitalist subjects by reinforcing and reproducing its Oedipal mandate: the neurotic mode of consumption and production amenable to capitalist society.

Therapeutic culture and the decline of the West: Rieff, Carroll, Lasch

Where the French poststructuralists emphasize the complicity of the psychoanalytic project with later capitalism, Freud's conservative critics are concerned with a different cultural crisis: what Nietzsche signalled as Western nihilism, arising from the growth of the "value-free" sciences and the diminishing role of religion in Western societies.

For these theorists, the twentieth century has seen the decline of Western "culture" – understood as a symbolic (or extra-empirical) system that directs the self outward, towards a higher purpose and a community of others. For these theorists, psychoanalysis plays a critical role in this shift, offering insight about, but also contributing to, the demise of culture.

In *Freud: The Mind of the Moralist*, Philip Rieff famously characterizes contemporary humanity as "psychological man" – arising at the end of a progression from "political man" of ancient times, through "religious man" of Judaeo-Christianity, and the relatively impoverished "economic man" of the Enlightenment. Psychological man adheres closely to Nietzsche's designation of the "last man", concerned solely with his own comfort. Freud's studies of neurosis offer valuable insights into the present crisis in culture because, according to Rieff, human beings without a transcendent purpose become trapped in their own narcissism. Freud's own part in humanity's "devolution" was then to legitimate "self-concern as the highest science" (Rieff 1979: 355). Furthermore, with his generalizing account of neurosis, Freud for Rieff succeeded in levelling out or "democratizing" human existence.

KEY POINT *The democratization of the human soul, according to Rieff*

1. Freud levels humanity by positing the thesis that so-called "normal" people are already "abnormal", in that coping involves becoming neurotic.

2. In order to illustrate this thesis, Freud takes a noble and tragic myth (of Oedipus) from the Greeks and renders it ordinary:

   > [T]he unique crime of the tragic hero becomes an intention in every heart, and in the most ordinary of plots, the history of every family ... The aristocratic bias of the "heroic" myth is replaced, in Freud, by the democratic bias of the "scientific" myth. (Rieff 1979: 354)

3. By means of the psychoanalytic ethic, whereby "everyone must be a confessant, everyone must aspire to be a confessor" (*ibid.*: 355), Freud levels differences in the hierarchy between doctor and patient. The clinic is thus democratized.

As Freudianism becomes more ubiquitous in contemporary culture, the clinic can be seen, Rieff argues, as a microcosm of society in general:

"the hospital is succeeding the Church and the parliament as the archetypal institution of Western culture" (*ibid.*). Rieff's *The Triumph of the Therapeutic* (1966) argues that the primary value of culture is now to administer "therapy" to an animal that constitutes itself as sick and suffering.

Lasch and Carroll (a student of Rieff's) continue Rieff's critique of culture. For Lasch, the "crisis" facing contemporary American culture is a crisis of confidence: a malaise confronting it after the 1960s and military defeat in Vietnam. A culture of narcissism and self-improvement has succeeded a Republican culture of political involvement, Lasch laments. In late-twentieth-century America, people feel disempowered and exhausted. In this context, psychoanalytic analyses afford unique insight into American society. In particular, Freud's clinical account of narcissism constitutes a "storehouse of ideas" (Lasch 1979: 34) that can inform strategies for diagnosing and treating cultural malaise.

John Carroll is more critical than Lasch of Freud's part in the perceived decline of Western culture – especially in Freud's account of religion as a projection of the "father" into the metaphysical sphere (see Chapter 7). This exemplifies, according to Carroll, a self-annihilating tendency in all humanisms, which can find nothing of value outside of the human ("all-too-human"). For Carroll, humanism is ultimately unable to respond to questions traditionally dealt with by religion: principally, questions of the meaning and value of human existence. Having rejected any notion of transcendence, humanist modes of enquiry must then ultimately trivialize their own object of investigation. Humanity is belittled by its privileging of reason over faith, and – as in Rieff – a concomitant turn from the public sphere to the private self. For Carroll, after Freud's account of civilization in terms of the Oedipus complex, we can find "no difference between Napoleon and Christ" as "both were 'father figures'" (Carroll 2004: 216); and God has been replaced by "the unconscious" (*ibid.*: 217), so we all carry a piece of the divine within us. Humanism has set humanity adrift in a relativistic sea of conflicting values – or, more dangerously, no value – according to Carroll; and we need to recognize that Freud, an "influential prophet of nihilism", has played his own unconscious part in this "colossal wreck" (*ibid.*: 1).

The ends of psychoanalysis: psychoanalysis and ethics

Habermas's reframing of psychoanalysis – as a practice

We mentioned Zaretsky's idea that psychoanalysis as a movement of modern thought uniquely promises to unite a materialistic account of mind, an interpretive understanding of culture, with an ethical practice of self-transformation. Throughout *Understanding Psychoanalysis*, we have stressed the clinical origin and end of psychoanalytic theory. Everything turns on the remarkable prospect of a talking cure for the neuroses. Freud's *oeuvre* accordingly contains not only his meta-psychological papers, and the intriguing writings on civilization, religion and art that we examined in Chapter 7. It also includes the case studies (Hans, the Ratman, Dora and others). At the same time Freud was developing his vital metapsychological papers (1911–15), moreover, he wrote a series of important "Papers on Technique", in which he reflects theoretically on what transpires between analysts and analysands in clinical sessions.

Given this "primacy of the therapeutical" to psychoanalysis, it is remarkable that so many of the criticisms of psychoanalysis we have examined do not engage more extensively with psychoanalytic practice. Or, if they do, they do so only to gauge its comparability to some other type of activity: whether a natural-scientific experiment, reading a text, or going to confession. Reflecting this tendency, even friends to psychoanalysis's cause such as Eric Kandel have proposed that psychoanalysis should forego its basis in clinical practice if it is to rejoin the scientific *Weltanschauung* (Kandel 1999: 506). In this context, Frankfurt School theorist Jürgen Habermas's critique of psychoanalysis in his *Knowledge and Human Interests* is particularly interesting. For Habermas, psychoanalysis is above all a type of practice – less something one knows, than something one does.

Working in a tradition of "Freudo-Marxism" more recently continued by Žižek (see Chapter 7), Habermas's *Knowledge and Human Interests* (1978) compares clinical psychoanalysis's activity of uncovering analysands' repressed wishes with Marxist ideology critique, with its aim to uncover political systems' "repressed" truth(s) (cf. Žižek 1989). Like Ricoeur, Habermas rejects Freud's attempts to explain what occurs in the psychoanalytic clinic through his biological account of energies "cathected" to repressed ideas; and "abreacted" when truly interpreted. If this were all that was in play, Habermas notes, a true hypnotic anamnesis would be sufficient for a cure, and Freud need never have invented psychoanalysis. By rejecting hypnosis for the talking cure, Habermas stresses that Freud was embracing a practice in which what is therapeutically decisive is not the "objective" truth of an interpretation alone, but the analysand's own, "conscious appropriation" of this truth (Habermas 1978: 247–51).

In line with Ricoeur and Lacan, Habermas understands analysands' symptoms as "split-off symbols . . . [whose] connection with public language . . . has gone underground" (ibid.: 257). Why do these "split-off" symbols repeat? According to Habermas's Hegelian formulation, what psychoanalysis posits is that, when a subject's wishes are repressed into the id, they take on a quasi-natural, causal status, like "the causality of fate" expressed in the oracle that pronounced Oedipus' doom in Sophocles' Oedipus Tyrannis (ibid.: 271). For this reason, Habermas stresses that the psychoanalyst ethically must not approach the analysand like a natural scientist approaches his objects, aiming only to enumerate, objectively, their unconscious thoughts. Such a scientific approach can only enforce the subject's sense that their repressed drives are an alien It. The analyst must instead adapt the "general interpretations" of Freudian metapsychology – the theories of the drives, Oedipus complex, symptom formation and so on – to the particular language of each analysand. For if the analysand is to overcome her self-alienation, she must actively reconceive her symptoms as a "hermeneutically understandable meaning structure", rather than the fatal incomprehensible "destinings" of an overpowering, malign Other (Habermas 1972: 272). If an analysis is to work, that is, the analysand must literally come to "make sense", for herself, out of her previously senseless symptoms. Psychoanalytic interpretations, Habermas contends, are "interpretive suggestions for a story the patient cannot [yet] tell" (ibid.: 260), rather than predictions of their behaviour. Their aim is to bring the analysand to the point where she can, as a subject, avow her repressed wishes as her own. And this, suggests Habermas's account, is where a Popperian criticism of psychoanalytic interpretations falls short (see above). For even if an analysand does resist and say "no!" to an interpretation, the falsifying standard is the effect this interpretation has upon her, and whether it facilitates her expanded self-comprehension. Sometimes an analysand's "no" to an interpretation means that it has truly missed the mark. Yet often, an analysand's responding associations will belie their initial resistance, forcing them to confront its falsity (ibid.: 266–9).

The elegance of Habermas's argument is that it allows us to explain both why natural-scientific and hermeneutic accounts of psychoanalysis have plausibility, but each falls short. The natural-scientific paradigm (Freud, Nagel, Popper, Solms, Kandel) responds to how symptoms, dreams and so on appear to neurotic subjects: as objective, causal determinants of behaviour. The hermeneutic stress on their meanings, by contrast (as in Ricoeur) answers to the aim of the psychoanalytic clinic: to symbolize the fatal, "split-off" representatives of the drives. What is decisive for Habermas, however, is the process of subjective transformation psychoanalysis involves, between the two epistemological stations. The specific nature of this process is captured in Freud's injunction for psychoanalysis, that "where the id was, there I shall come to be" (*Wo Es war, soll Ich werden*). Psychoanalysis, Habermas proposes, is a paradigm instance of a practice of enlightenment: an activity of critical self-reflection which, by resignifying the id as part of the I, transforms the I that undertakes the activity.

You must be having me on! Grunbaum's (critique of) suggestion

Habermas's valorization of clinical psychoanalysis as a practice of emancipatory self-reflection highlights the ethical register to psychoanalysis. The psychoanalytic analysand, confronting the truth of her desire, transforms her *ethos* or character. Psychoanalysis is closer to a practically grounded theory than a preformed science which would then be clinically "applied". Yet the clinical footing on which Habermas recentres debates on psychoanalysis's claims is hardly less controversial than the other fields in which psychoanalysis has been criticized. Indeed, whether critics assess psychoanalysis as an "Oedipal" attempt to corral desire, an unscientific mysticism or quasi-scientific brand of navel-gazing, one thing they share is a deep distrust of its institutionalized clinical forms. A 2002 Marketing Report commissioned by the American Psychoanalytic Society highlighted the ways institutional psychoanalysis is invariably conceived by non-analysts around the world:

1. Arrogance, elitism, *hauteur* . . . sense of esoteric knowledge, authoritarianism, internecine conflict, lack of openness, inability to listen, insularity . . .
2. Closed approaches, belief in psychoanalysis based on faith instead of evidence (at Kirsner 2004: 340).

Freud's defence in the 1920s of the possibility of "lay analysis" was the corollary of his conviction that a psychoanalyst can only become qualified by themselves undergoing analysis. To acquire any body of knowledge, medicinal or metapsychological, was not sufficient (QLA). This professional recommendation was motivated by Freud's ethical concern that to analyse others, analysts should be able to recognize and temper their own propensities to "transfer" unconscious wishes and identifications on to analysands. From the outside, however, this way of training analysts has invited comparisons of psychoanalytic institutions with religious sects, presided over by their own esoteric rites of passage. From the inside, it can and has encouraged sectarianism, a closure to external verification and conflicting opinions, and the defensive invocation of Freud's (Klein's, Lacan's and others') name(s) in lieu of argued validity claims. On such grounds, notably, one of Eric Kandel's principal prescriptions for any viable "future of psychoanalysis" is for a large-scale, independent investigation of the conduct of psychoanalytic institutes, with serious reforms to be considered (Kandel, 1999: 522).

Published in 1984, as new psychopharmacological medicines and therapies proliferated, Adolf Grunbaum's *The Foundations of Psychoanalysis* was intended to end debates concerning psychoanalysis's scientific, or ethical, legitimacy. Grunbaum, like Popper or Nagel, takes Freud's claim that psychoanalysis is a natural science very seriously, and for this reason criticizes Ricoeur and Habermas. Where Grunbaum differs from Popper is that he argues that psychoanalytic theory *did* generate falsifiable, risky predictions concerning human behaviour. For Grunbaum, psychoanalysis is indeed not only falsifiable; it has been falsified (Grunbaum 1994: 12–13).

Underlying Freud's metapsychology, Grunbaum argues, are two core contentions. He calls these the "tally argument" and "the necessary condition thesis". The "tally argument" asserts that only psychoanalysis can yield insights that "tally" truly with the unconscious. The "necessary condition thesis", which clinically takes all, asserts that only psychoanalysis can cure neurotic symptoms. The link between the two theses is Freud's claim that symptoms can only be "abreacted" if the analyst's interpretation "tallies" truthfully with the unconscious wishes of the analysand. Grunbaum's criticism of Freud can be framed by looking at his criticism of Freud's interpretation of an analysand's failure to recall a long-known Latin sentence: "*exoriare aliquis nostris ex ossibur ultor*" ("would that someone arise from our bones as an avenger"). The young man wanted to express his anger about the anti-Semitism his people continued to bear. However, at the spur of the moment, he could not recall the "*aliquis*". In the course of his free associations, the young man expressed his anxiety that he might have made his Italian girlfriend pregnant – a situation which meant that "*aliquis*" might, indeed, arise from his actions. It was this repressed thought, says Freud, that caused his parapraxis.

In his response to this example, Grunbaum concedes that there is a thematic or semantic connection between the thought "I wish someone would arise . . ." and the young man's memory of his illicit liaison. However, Grunbaum's point is to distinguish between such a thematic connection and the type of causal connection Freud wants between the repressed thought and the forgetting of "*aliquis*":

> There is no justification for drawing a *causal* connection between the fear of pregnancy and the memory lapse merely on the basis of the *thematic* connection between the content of the repressed wish and the desire expressed by the Latin phrase . . . thematic affinity is not evidence for a causal connection.
> (Grunbaum 1994: 24, 8–9)

Indeed, Grunbaum notes that, if one "free-associates" on any idea for long enough, its thematic connections with innumerable other ideas will emerge (*ibid.*: 25). The attribution of causal efficacy to any one such connection, Grunbaum suggests, is thus as inevitably arbitrary as it is based on a categorical confusion.

How then does Grunbaum account for the apparent successes friends claim for psychoanalytic treatment, and the type of confirmation through self-transformation Habermas defends? Grunbaum's argument is that, while Freud never backed down on his "tally argument" concerning the truth of psychoanalytic metapsychology, he did abandon the decisive "necessary condition thesis". In later works, Freud accepts that analysands may achieve a "cure through love", outside the clinic, and wrestled with the prospect that the "talking cure" might become "interminable" (ATI; Grunbaum 1994: 16–17). Grunbaum cites comparative surveys, such as Malan's, or Prioleau, Murdoch and Brody's, between psychoanalytic analysands and the out-patients from other treatments. What these analyses show, Grunbaum claims, is that psychoanalysis is no more statistically effective than "treatment" through placebos (Grunbaum 1994: 17–18). Whatever apparently beneficent effects psychoanalysis does produce, Grunbaum concludes, must arise only from psychoanalysis's own, placebo-like mobilization of analysand's suggestibility (*ibid.*: 18–20). In clinical analysis, "the search for insight is only a treatment ritual serving to strengthen the patient's therapeutic expectations". Far from being the emancipatory, truth-yielding activity envisaged by Habermas and others, that is, clinical psychoanalysis more closely approximates an elaborate confidence trick, presided over by the "suggestive, intimidating influence of the analyst" (*ibid.*: 24).

Revisiting the Symposium, in the clinic: working through the transference

Habermas's and Grunbaum's views on psychoanalysis thus seem to agree on no more than that the proof of psychoanalysis's worth lies in its clinical practice. Yet, when we read their texts alongside Freud's "Papers on Technique", Habermas's and Grunbaum's accounts of clinical practice share an important blind spot. The blind spot concerns what Grunbaum calls "suggestion", and presents as decisive evidence that clinical psychoanalysis has no distinctive therapeutic value. The problem is that what Grunbaum levels against psychoanalysis as "suggestion", far from being something whose therapeutic importance psychoanalysis denies, is what Freud's papers on technique call *transference*, and accord to it central importance (DT; RRW; TL).

We noted in Chapter 2 that, pressed to defend his conception of sexuality, Freud turned for legitimacy to Plato's "expanded" notion of *Eros*. For Plato, the *philia* (or love) involved in all *phil*osophy is an elevated species of *Eros*. It is through *Eros*, says Diotima in the *Symposium*, that we are drawn to seek the Truth. Yet just so, in another of the manifold shocks that attended the birth of psychoanalysis (see Introduction), it soon emerged that analysands undergoing psychoanalysis tend, almost "automatically", to fall in love with the analyst whose knowledge they suppose will liberate them from their malaises. Breuer literally fled rather than confront transference love when it appeared in Anna O (see Chapter 2). Freud, by contrast, proposes that psychoanalysts must openly confront the ethical and other temptations it lays at analysts' feet, and turn it to therapeutic ends (DT; TL).

The decisive thing that Grunbaum's criticism of psychoanalysis misses is Freud's repeated stress that the transference is a form of resistance to psychoanalysis. Rather than remembering his repressed wishes, shaped by his earliest relations with figures of love and authority, the analysand transfers them on to the analyst. Then he repeats the modes of conduct associated with the repressed wishes, "acting out" the truth of his desire so as not to have to consciously work it through – trying to seduce the analyst or complaining she never listens, showing up late for sessions, and so on (RRW). Freud's prescription is that the analyst must above all not play along with these repeated actings out that constitute what Freud calls the "transference neurosis". This is one reason why psychoanalysis is always conducted with the analysts seated behind the reclining analysand. In this way, as Lacan noted, they are less able to be seduced or intimated by the analysands' looks, expressions, or body language (Lacan 1993: 241). Rather than buying into the way the analysand is addressing him – in anger or with love, and so on – Freud's argument is that the analyst should maintain a near-Stoic equanimity. This equanimity has often been spoofed in films showing psychoanalysts at work. Yet its function is serious. By not responding to the "actings out" of analysands (and in this way – despite Grunbaum – not exploiting the transference), it allows the analysand to come to see, in the unmotivated emptiness of her repetitions, the extent to which their behaviour is structured by motives that can hail only from within themselves, rather than the analyst and world that they accuse.

So this is the key thing that Habermas's and Grunbaum's accounts of the psychoanalytic clinic miss. The transferential love for the analyst is truly based on an illusion – Grunbaum is right about this. Yet, if one is to achieve the type of self-transformation the end of analysis promises (whose epistemological dimensions Habermas theorizes), a subject must "work through" the transference, rather than accede to its lure – this is where Grunbaum gets it wrong. Although illusory, that is, the analysand's transferential illusion that the analyst knows the Truth is necessary. Like the proverbial ladder one must climb but can then kick away, without it, the analysand would never associate freely concerning her own intimate thoughts and affairs. The path to self-transformative truth, for psychoanalysis, is paved with this error. Yet at the end of the affair, analysands will above all *not* have come to see the world "through their analyst's eyes". The end of psychoanalysis, on the contrary, is much closer to their realizing – in a process that can be very painful, or even "depressive" (Klein) – that even the "intimidating" analyst cannot relieve them of the task of retrospectively owning the unconscious wishes and beliefs whose vicissitudes have oppressed them.

In Lacan's unpublished seminar on transference, in this light, he focuses upon the seemingly fractious, comic close of Plato's *Symposium*, rather than the "elevating", earlier accounts of *Eros* to which Freud recurred. In this part of Plato's dialogue, the petulant demagogue Alcibiades drunkenly crashes the dramatized party, and proceeds to tell all the story of his love for Socrates. Socrates is the only man in all Athens who has refused his sexual advances, and for this reason has become an obsession for him. Socrates is enigmatic, vexing and physically ugly. Yet when Socrates speaks, his words are more seductive than the music of the satyr Marsyas, as if Socrates held within himself hidden treasures and truths of incomparable virtue. How, though, does Socrates respond to this shameless transferential declaration of his lover and pupil, with all the potentials for "suggestion" it affords him? Lacan says: as a psychoanalyst ought. Socrates flatly refuses to accede to the elevated position to which Alcibiades' star-struck testimony assigns him. Rather, Socrates suggests, if Alcibiades "sees in me" such sublime things as he desires, he must be mistaken, for in truth, Socrates is "nothing". The true locus of the truth Alcibiades seeks, Socrates thereby suggests, can only lie in Alcibiades' own wishes, and it is with his own psyche, not Socrates', that he should concern himself (cf. SSD: 699–700/835–6).

Conclusion: overcoming Oedipus, and Freud

This juncture, at the end of analysis and the beginnings of philosophy, marks the conclusion of our journey in *Understanding Psychoanalysis*. Psychoanalysis begins the twenty-first century beleaguered from several sides. Outflanked in the academic humanities by new forms of cultural theory, chastened by sociopolitical critiques of its implication in social control or cultural decline, psychoanalysis is challenged as a therapy by the advent of cognitive behavioural therapy and new medications. Meanwhile, "Freud bashers" mass at the gates, declaiming Freud's, Klein's, Lacan's and others' personal lives, organizational charisma and clinical practice. In this context, the neuropsychoanalytic turn of the last decade can seem the only path available for psychoanalysis, even if it loses its clinical soul thereby.

In "The Shrink Is In," in *New Republic* (Lear 1995), psychoanalyst and philosopher Jonathan Lear has proffered a different, philosophical defence of psychoanalysis with which we can close here. Lear's article turns around Sophocles' Oedipus tragedy, which Freud placed at the heart of psychoanalysis. As we saw in Chapter 2 (and as Rieff complains), the traditional psychoanalytic reading of *Oedipus Tyrannis* sees the hero as unwittingly acting out each of our infantile sexual, aggressive wishes. Lear picks up on a different register of Sophocles' tragedy. Oedipus is the man who, returning to Thebes, solves the riddle of the Sphinx which had oppressed its people. He is thus a man whose power is based on his surpassing intellect, confident to the point of hubris that he knows all there is to know. Yet Sophocles' drama stages Oedipus' gradual coming to see, like an analysand, that for all his knowledge he has been ignorant concerning the significance of his own deeds. By aligning psychoanalysis with the Oedipal tragedy, Lear argues, psychoanalysis as originated by Freud is accordingly a unique thing. It is both a reprisal of the ancient, mythic and religious traditions that remind us of the finitude of the human condition, and a distinctly modern movement of thought that defends the possibility of our reflectively coming to terms with this finitude – and making this achievement the basis of an ethical life. What we risk if we accede too simply to "Freud bashing", Lear argues – or, we could add, if we accede to a wholly objectified, neuroscientific view of the psyche – is repeating the hubris of Oedipus: closing our eyes to the enigmatic realities of our own sexuality, aggression and subjectivity that psychoanalysis calls us to confront, instead striking out, in truly Oedipal fashion, at Freud, a flawed man long dead. Psychoanalysis cannot halt the rising plague of depression, attention-deficit hyperactivity disorder, borderline and eating disorders across first-world nations. Nor can it solve the riddle of those collective pathologies emerging today, named "fundamentalisms", which violently trouble our Oedipal hubris. Yet psychoanalytic theory would still draw us, invaluably, to reflect upon what inhumanity might lie repressed behind the short-sighted hopes that all this could be wished or medicated away. In a time of such widespread discontents of civilization, its elementary clinical and ethical commitment to the meaningfulness of human suffering and to the healing powers of speech, too, remains as salutary as ever.

Chronology of life and events

1856	Sigmund Freud is born at Freiberg in Moravia on 6 May.
1877	Freud's first publications on anatomy and physiology.
1886	Freud marries Martha Bernays. Sets up private practice in Vienna for patients suffering from nervous illnesses.
1892	Breuer's treatment of Anna O (Bertha Pappenheim) using hypnotic method.
1893–95	The publication of Freud's first "psychoanalytic" writings on hysteria (although he does not coin the term until 1896).
24 July 1895	Freud's dream of Irma's Injection. In a letter to Fliess, Freud comments that one day the event will be commemorated by a plaque: *In this house on July 24th, 1895, the Secret of Dreams was revealed to Dr. Freud.*
1897	Freud's self-analysis leads to his abandonment of the seduction theory of the neuroses, and the theory of the Oedipus complex.
1900	The publication of *The Interpretation of Dreams*; Freud's treatment of Dora.
1901	Freud publishes *The Psychopathology of Everyday Life*. Jacques Lacan born.
1905	The publication of *Three Essays on Sexuality*.
1906	Jung becomes adherent of psychoanalysis.
1908	The first international meeting of psychoanalysts at Salzburg.
1909	Little Hans and Ratman case studies; Freud, accompanied by Jung and others, delivers Clark Lectures introducing psychoanalysis to America.
1910	Formation of the International Psychoanalytic Association (IPA).
1911–15	Freud's analysis of Schreber's *Memoirs on My Nervous Illness* appears in 1911; Freud writes "Papers on Technique".
1913	Ernest Jones inaugurates the British Psychoanalytical Society.

1914	The publication of Freud's "On Narcissism" confirms Freud's break with Jung, and begins trajectory towards his later theory of the ego, and the later metapsychology; Freud writes the Wolfman case history (not published until 1918).
1914–18	World War I
1915	Freud writes twelve "metapsychological papers", of which only five have survived.
1919	Melanie Klein begins analysing children in Budapest.
1920	The publication of "Beyond the Pleasure Principle" introduces the notion of the "death drive" into psychoanalysis.
1923	"The Ego and the Id" is published, consolidating the later metapsychology of ego, superego and id.
1926	Klein moves from Berlin to London, on the invitation of Ernest Jones, and joins the British Psychoanalytical Society a year later.
1927	Publication of *The Future of an Illusion*.
1929	Klein analyses "Little Dick", publishing her findings a year later.
1930	Publication of *Civilization and Its Discontents*. Freud is awarded the Goethe Prize by the City of Frankfurt.
1933	Hitler comes to power in Germany. Freud's books are burned in Berlin.
1934–38	Freud writes the three essays comprising "Moses and Monotheism" as Europe lurches towards war.
1936	Jacques Lacan delivers a version of "The Mirror Stage as Formative of the I" at the International Congress of Psychoanalysis (he re-delivers a later version of the paper at the same Congress in 1949). Karen Horney publishes *Feminine Psychology*.
1938	Hitler takes Austria in the *Anschluss* and Freud goes into exile in London.
1939	War begins on 1 September. Freud dies of cancer on 3 September.
1939–45	World War II. Psychoanalysis's importance is underlined by American military physicians being required to know its basics after the United States enters the war in December 1941.
1944	Helene Deutsch publishes volume I of *The Psychology of Women* (volume II appears the following year).
1946	Wilfred Bion begins analysis with Melanie Klein.
1952	Lacan begins his year-long seminars in Paris, which he will continue until the year before his death. Ronald Fairbairn publishes *Psychoanalytic Studies of the Personality*.
1953	Lacan delivers his "Rome Discourse", "On the Function and Field of Speech in Psychoanalysis", at the Rome Congress of the Institute of Psychology at the University of Rome. First year in which Lacan's annual seminar is recorded for later publication.
1954	First anti-psychotic medication, Chlorprozamine, is approved for psychiatric use in the United States.
1955	Albert Ellis coins the term "rational behaviour therapy", the antecedent of cognitive behavioural therapy (CBT).

1959	Philip Rieff publishes *Freud: The Mind of the Moralist*.
1962	Lacan is expelled from the IPA.
1963	Lacan forms the *École Freudienne de Paris* (EFP).
1966	The publication of Lacan's *Écrits*.
	Paul Ricoeur's *Philosophical Interpretation of Freud* is published.
1967	Bion publishes *Second Thoughts*.
1971	Donald Winnicott publishes *Playing and Reality*.
1972	Gilles Deleuze and Félix Guattari publish *Anti-Oedipus*.
1974	Luce Irigaray publishes *Speculum of the Other Woman*.
	Juliet Mitchell publishes *Psychoanalysis and Feminism*.
1976	The American Psychoanalytic Association boasts 27,000 psychoanalysts: psychoanalysis is at the peak of its institutional success.
1980	Lacan unilaterally dissolves the EFP, forming the École for "La Cause Freudienne". David Burns publishes *Feeling Good: The New Mood Therapy*, which begins to popularize CBT in the United States.
	Sarah Kofman publishes *The Enigma of Woman*.
1981	Death of Jacques Lacan on 9 September.
1984	Publication of Adolf Grunbaum's *The Philosophical Foundations of Psychoanalysis*, and Jeffrey Masson's *The Assault on Truth: Freud's Suppression of the Seduction Theory*: beginnings of "Freud bashing", and popular decline of psychoanalysis.
1988	Prozac is sold on the US market, inaugurating the age of antidepressants and growing predominance of psychiatric treatments of mental illness.
1997	Mark Solms publishes *The Neuropsychology of Dreams*.
2000	One hundredth anniversary of Freud's *Interpretation of Dreams*.
	Formation in July of NPSA (The International Neuropsychoanalysis Society).

Questions for discussion and revision

one Where it was: Freud's biology of the mind

1. What are the systems posited by Freud in *Project for a Scientific Psychology*, and what are their functions?
2. What is the "pleasure principle"? And what is its relation to the "reality principle"?
3. Outline the differences between perception, memory and motility, according to Freud.
4. What is the "libido"?
5. What is/are the chief function(s) and characteristic(s) of the ego for Freud?
6. Can repression deal successfully with inappropriate wishes? If so, then how? If not, then why not?
7. What is the "id"? What is its relation to the ego?
8. What is the superego in relation to the ego and the id?
9. What defines "mental health" for Freud? Describe in these terms the conditions that lead to mental ill health.
10. What are the varieties of mental illness, according to Freud? What are the characteristics of each type?

two Sexuality and its vicissitudes

1. Do you find Freud's emphasis upon sexuality as the root of behaviour and culture plausible? Why/why not?
2. What are the grounds Freud provides for accepting his sexuality hypothesis?
3. Describe Freud's account, and dichotomy, of "perversion". What is the place of the perversions in Freud's greater theory of sexuality?
4. Do you agree with Freud that mental illness and the development of sexuality in the individual are connected?

5. What are the four characteristics of the drive, as described by Freud in "Drives and Their Vicissitudes"?
6. What are the "vicissitudes" of the drive?
7. Freud understands activities like thumb-sucking to be autoerotic and sexual. Why? Are you convinced by his explanation?
8. What differentiates human sexuality from sex between other animals, for Freud?
9. What are the principal features of the Oedipus complex, according to Freud? What do you think about this theory?
10. What is Freud's explanation for why some men desire only women whom they cannot love?

three To slip, perchance to dream: Freud on the unconscious

1. Do you think there is a fundamental tension between Freud's biological and linguistic (topographical) accounts of the unconscious? Or are these accounts complementary? Discuss.
2. Describe the two functions of the psyche's mnemic apparatus.
3. Explain the difference between the systems preconscious and unconscious, and how these two systems interact with one another (use examples).
4. What is the basis of all dreams, according to Freud? Do you agree, and why/why not?
5. Why do nightmares appear to contradict Freud's account of dreams? And how does Freud explain this (apparent) discrepancy? Do you find this explanation convincing?
6. What is the difference between the "latent" and "manifest" contents of dreams? How do the latent and manifest contents interact in the weaving together of a dream?
7. Freud refers to dreams as "picture puzzles" or "rebuses". What is meant by this analogy?
8. What is the purpose of "secondary revision" of dreams?
9. What is the difference between the latent contents of the dream and the "dream wish"? Do you find the concept of the dream wish compelling?
10. Explain the mechanisms of condensation and displacement.

four Precarious love: Kleinian object relations theory

1. What are the main principles of Klein's "play technique"? Do you think her adaptation of psychoanalysis for children is continuous with Freudian clinical practice?
2. Enumerate the key differences between the "schizoid" and "depressive" positions. Do you agree with the object relations theorists' contention that everyone must pass through both of these positions to become a mature, balanced individual?

3. According to Klein, schizophrenia represents a regression to the schizoid position, and depression (melancholia) to the depressive position. Do you agree with this way of framing mental illness?
4. What are the key disagreements between Klein and other Freudians respecting the Oedipus complex? Are you more sympathetic with Klein, or her opponents, in this regard?
5. Do you think that Klein's depiction of the child's fantasy life is credible? What do you make of the "good" and "bad" breast?
6. What is the "good-enough" mother?
7. What is the function of "transitional objects"? Do you think that Winnicott's theory has merit?
8. What does Wilfred Bion mean by "containment"?
9. Describe Bion's theory of communication, and relate it to Klein's understanding of "good" and "bad" objects.
10. What are Fairbairn's objections to Freud? Do you agree? Why/why not?

five Jacques Lacan: rereading Freud to the letter

1. How, and why, does Lacan position himself as a "return" to Freud?
2. What is meant by Lacan's phrase "the unconscious is structured like a language"? Discuss.
3. What does Lacan's refrain that desire is always "desire of the other" tell us about his concept of the subject?
4. What is the significance for the psyche of human children's prolonged dependence upon adults, according to Lacan?
5. How does Lacan reinterpret the Oedipus complex? What do you think is the import of this reinterpretation?
6. What is the difference between the "real", the "imaginary" and the "symbolic" fathers? What is the significance of this difference?
7. What does Lacan mean by saying that "the Father is always a dead father"?
8. What is the *objet petit a*? And what is its relation to fantasy?
9. Lacan employs the insights of linguistic structuralism to Freudian psychoanalysis. What are the important features he utilizes, and how does he do so?
10. What does a "master signifier" do?

six What does woman want? Feminism and psychoanalysis

1. Explain how psychoanalysis might provide useful tools for feminist research.
2. Do you think that, on balance, Helene Deutsch's psychoanalytic theories about women are productive for feminism? Why/why not?
3. Evaluate Karen Horney's equation of the little boy's perspective and that of the psychoanalyst. Do you think she is correct, and what would the significance of this equivalence be, if she were?

4. Do you think Karen Horney's analysis of penis-envy as just one kind of envy has merit? And what of her analysis of men's envy of women's reproductive capacity?
5. The existentialist philosopher Simone de Beauvoir opposed psychoanalysis. Why?
6. Why have feminists such as Kate Millett understood Freud to be an arch-sexist?
7. How does Juliet Mitchell respond to feminists such as Millett regarding the sex/gender distinction? How does psychoanalysis figure in this response?
8. What role is played by the Oedipus complex, according to Mitchell? And what is the family's significance within capitalist society?
9. Explain how Luce Irigaray represents her own relation to Freud. Is it an all-out rejection, or an appropriation of psychoanalytic theory?
10. What are the key points of Sarah Kofman's criticisms of Freudian psychoanalysis?

seven Freud as philosopher? Civilization, art and religion

1. Briefly describe the key features of Freud's account of civilization. Do you think it is a compelling account? Why/why not?
2. What is the significance of the incest taboo for Freud's understanding of society?
3. Max Horkheimer is critical of the concept of the death drive. Why?
4. Adorno and Horkheimer employ psychoanalysis to the task of comprehending the rise of fascism. What is their basic thesis?
5. What is the relation of "play" and creativity, according to Freud?
6. Recount what the "uncanny" means for Freud. What has the uncanny to do with works of art?
7. What is the meaning of the "gaze" for Lacan?
8. According to Lacan, what is "anamorphosis", and what does it indicate about subjectivity?
9. Distinguish Freud's different currents of thought regarding religion. Do you agree with one more than others?
10. Summarize the objections to Freud's account of religion proffered by Pfister, Strauss and Ricoeur. What is your opinion regarding these different approaches to religion?

eight Where psychoanalysis has come to be: philosophy, science, society and ethics

1. Briefly summarize the scientific grounds for criticism of Freudianism, according to Nagel and Popper. What are the chief differences between their respective objections?
2. How does Paul Ricoeur respond to objections that psychoanalysis is not a science?

3. What is "neuropsychoanalysis"? Do you think neuropsychoanalysis might achieve what Freud's "Project for a Scientific Psychology" had promised?
4. How is psychoanalysis like other sciences, and how is it unlike them? Do you think it is in psychoanalysis's best interest to pursue its connection to the natural sciences? Or do you find the alignment with hermeneutics more convincing?
5. The insights of poststructuralist theory can broadly be seen as both critical of, and as extending upon, psychoanalysis. How does each of the following negotiate their theoretical relation to Freud and Lacan: Derrida? Foucault? Deleuze and Guattari?
6. Philip Rieff suggests that Freud "democratizes" the clinic, and that this has knock-on effects for society. Summarize his argument for this claim. Do you agree?
7. Summarize Jürgen Habermas's response to Popper.
8. Summarize Adolf Grunbaum's objections to psychoanalysis. Do you agree with these objections? Why/why not?
9. How do Grunbaums's objections tally with those of Nagel and Popper?
10. What is the role of the transference for psychoanalytic practice? Do you think that the transference renders psychoanalysis's status problematic? Or is the transference an important element to the enquiry into what it is to be human? Discuss.

Guide to further reading

Full bibliographical details appear in the Bibliography.

Freud

There is a wealth of literature on nearly all aspects of Freud's work. The best introduction to Freud is still Freud himself. Arguably the best collection of Freud's metapsychological writings is A. Freud (ed.) *The Essentials of Psycho-Analysis* (1986). *The Essential Freud* (1995), Peter Gay (ed.), is also an authoritative collection. Freud wrote several classical introductions to psychoanalysis, notably "The Introductory Lectures on Psychoanalysis" and the "New Introductory Lectures on Psychoanalysis". The five Clark Lectures Freud delivered on his arrival in the United States in 1909 are also a very clear presentation of key elements of psychoanalysis (see Freud 1962). Richard Wollheim's *Freud* (1971) is a *locus classicus* in secondary literature on Freud. Jonathan Lear has also written several very good philosophical introductions to Freud (1990, 2005). *Freud for Beginners* by Richard Appignanesi (1979) is surprisingly good, given the format. Frank J. Sullaway (1979) provides a very good biographical account of Freud's life and work. *Freud's Footnotes* (Leader 2000) is an intriguing collection of essays examining many nuances in Freud's theoretical work. Readers specifically interested in the relationship between psychoanalysis and philosophy should consult *Analytic Freud: Philosophy and Psychoanalysis* (Levine 2000) and *Freud Among the Philosophers* (Levy 1996).

Klein and object relations theory

The best starting-point for exploring Kleinian theory is *The Selected Melanie Klein* (Mitchell 1987). Other authoritative texts on Klein and object relations theory include: *Melanie Klein* (Segal 1992); *Melanie Klein Today* (Spillius 1988); *Reading Melanie Klein* (Stonebridge & Phillips 1988); *A Dictionary of Kleinian Thought* (Hinshelwood 1989); and *Reshaping the Psychoanalytic Domain* (Hughes 1989). More recent works include *The Poetics of Psychoanalysis: In the Wake of Klein* (Jacobus 2005); and *Other Banalities: Melanie Klein Revisited* (Mills 2006). For an account of object relations theory's contribution to art theory, see *Freud's Art: Psychoanalysis Retold* (Sayers 2007). For a discussion of the relation between Klein and Freud, see *The Freud–Klein Controversies 1941–45* (King & Steiner 1991); and on the relation between Klein and Lacan, see *The Klein–Lacan Dialogues* (Burgoyne & Sullivan 1999). To learn more about the importance of the death drive to objects relations theory, see *Cultures of the Death Drive: Melanie Klein and Modernist Melancholia* (Sanchez-Pardo 2003). There is a growing interest in object relations theory in the humanities, particularly to explain sociological phenomena such as racial prejudice and nationalism, notable examples being *Why War? – Psychoanalysis, Politics, and the Return to Melanie Klein* (Rose 1993); and *Melanie Klein and Critical Social Theory* (Alford 1989). Information about Klein and Kleinian studies can also be found at the Melanie Klein Trust website, http://www.melanie-klein-trust.org.uk/.

Lacan

Lacan had a notoriously low regard for written publication, and the one collection of writings he did publish, the *Écrits*, is very difficult. This text has however recently been very well retranslated in complete form (Fink *et al.* 2006). Several of Lacan's seminars (numbers I, II, III, VII, XI, XII and XX) have been translated into English in editions established and authorized by Lacan's literary executor, Jacques-Alain Miller. Lacan's third seminar (1993) is arguably the clearest and most incisive of Lacan's seminars for newcomers, particularly his key notions of the symbolic, the paternal signifier and the imaginary. Students are also recommended Lacan's first published seminar (1988a). Arguably the best systematic introduction to Lacanian theory and clinical practice is *Clinical Introduction to Lacanian Psychoanalysis: Theory and Technique* (Fink 1997). *The Lacanian Subject* (Fink 1995) is also highly recommended, but more advanced. *Between Philosophy & Psychoanalysis* (Samuels 1993), *Return to Freud* (Weber 1991), and *Freud as Philosopher* (Boothby 2001) are each good, book-length examinations of Lacan's thought. *An Introductory Dictionary of Lacanian Psychoanalysis* (Evans 1996) is a helpful compendium. "Lacan and the Discourse of the Other" (Wilden 1981) is a good essay-length study of Lacan's relationship to structuralism and the French sociological tradition. Matthew Sharpe's "Lacan, Jacques" in *The Internet Encyclopaedia of Philosophy* (at http://www.iep.utm.edu/l/lacweb.htm) is a more advanced, and longer, analysis by the author than Chapter 5 here. Much of the recent interest in Lacan's work, outside clinical circles, has been generated by Slavoj Žižek's work. Several of Žižek's books are explicitly devoted to introducing readers to Lacanian theory by way of examining aspects of popular culture (see especially 1992 and 2001). Interested readers are also directed towards http://www.lacan.com, a website devoted to Lacanian theory and analysis.

Feminism

There are a number of good books addressing psychoanalysis and feminism, and recent interest particularly in Freud's position on "woman". The best of these include *Why Do Women Love Men and Not Their Mothers?* (Hamon 2000); *Gender and Envy* (Burke 1998); *Feminism and Its Discontents* (Buhle 1998); and *Female Sexuality: The Early Psychoanalytic Controversies* (Grigg *et al.* 1999). For a survey of views specifically on Freud's case study of Dora, see *In Dora's Case* (Bernheimer & Kahane 1985). For a thorough treatment of early women psychoanalysts see *Mothering Psychoanalysis* (Sayers 1991). There have been several publications dealing with French feminism and psychoanalysis, most notably *Sexual Subversions* (Grosz 1989); *Feminism and Psychoanalysis: The Daughter's Seduction* (Gallop 1982); *Luce Irigaray: Philosophy in the Feminine* (Whitford 1994); and *Yielding Gender* (Deutscher 1997). Other significant feminist engagements with psychoanalysis, of which space did not permit coverage in this volume, include Judith Butler's *The Psychic Life of Power*; Nancy Chodorow's *The Reproduction of Mothering*; and Hélène Cixous's "Castration or Decapitation?"

Civilization, art and religion

Freud's writings on civilization, art and religion have been collected in several edited volumes. These include *Civilization, Society and Religion* (1985), *Civilization, War and Death* (1939) and *On Creativity and the Unconscious* (1958). For Freud's thoughts on art and aesthetics, readers can consult *Art and Psychoanalysis* (Adams 1993). For Kleinian understandings of art, there is *Psychoanalysis and Art: Kleinian Perspectives* (Gosso 2004), which includes an essay by Klein. For material on Lacan's readings of, and debts to, literature and the arts, see *Jacques Lacan: Psychoanalysis and the Subject of Literature* (Rabate 2001); and *Lacan and Literature: Purloined Pretexts* (Stoltzfus 1996). *Psycho-analysis and Faith* (Meng, Freud *et al.* 1963) provides fascinating insights into Freud's ambivalence concerning religion, and his extraordinary friendship with Oskar Pfister. *Psychoanalysis and Religious Experience* (Meissner 1984) and *Psychoanalysis and Religion in the Twenty First Century* (Black 2006) both provide a good critical introduction to Freud's, and subsequent, psychoanalytic approaches to religion. *Freud's Moses* (Yerushalmi 1991) provides a remarkable introduction to the vexed topic of Freud's relations to Judaism, alongside Peter Gay's *Godless Jew* (1987). For excellent examinations of Lacan on religion, see Kenneth Reinhard (1999, 2005). Jurgen Braungardt (1999) is also highly recommended.

Science, society and ethics

On the history of the psychoanalytic movement, students are encouraged to consult Ernest Jones's classic *The Life and Work of Sigmund Freud* (1953–57), *Secrets of the Soul* (Zaretsky 2004), and *Fin-de-Siècle Vienna* (Schorske 1980). For a critical appraisal of psychoanalysis in the American milieu, see *Unfree Associations*

(Kirsner 2000). Key texts in the 1980s and 1990s Freud debates include *The Assault on Truth* (Masson 1984), *Why Freud Was Wrong* (Webster 1995), *The Memory Wars* (Crews 1995) and *Killing Freud* (Dufresne 2003). On Freud and science, Adolf Grunbaum's *The Foundations of Psychoanalysis* is an important text. For good essay collections on this topic, see *Psychoanalysis, Scientific Method and Philosophy* (Hook 1959) and *Mind, Psychoanalysis and Science* (Clark & Wright 1988). *Lacan and Science* (Glynos & Stravrakakis 2002) is a good, but advanced, collection of essays. Mark Solms's "Freud Returns" is the best introduction to the contemporary neuropsychoanalytic movement. Anthony Elliot (1992, 1996, 1998) has written several important analyses of the way psychoanalysis has intervened in, and been critiqued by, social theorists. Philip Rieff's *The Triumph of the Therapeutic* remains a *locus classicus*, as does Christopher Lasch's *The Culture of Narcissism*. On psychoanalysis, as a therapy, and philosophy, readers are recommended *Therapeutic Action* (Lear 2003).

Bibliography

Adams, Laurie Schneider 1993. *Art and Psychoanalysis*. New York: Icon.

Adorno, Theodor [1951] 1982. "Freudian Theory and the Pattern of Fascist Propaganda". In *The Essential Frankfurt School Reader*, Andrew Arato & Eike Gebhardt (eds), 118–37. New York: Continuum.

Adorno, Theodor 1991. *The Culture Industry: Selected Essays on Mass Culture*, J. M. Bernstein (ed.). London: Routledge.

Adorno, Theodor & Max Horkheimer [1947] 1979. *Dialectic of Enlightenment: Philosophical Fragments*, John Cumming (trans.). London: Verso.

Adorno, Theodor *et al.*, 1950. *The Authoritarian Personality*, New York: Harper.

Alford, C. Fred 1989. *Melanie Klein and Critical Social Theory: An Account of Politics, Art, and Reason Based on Her Psychoanalytic Theory*. New Haven, CT: Yale University Press.

Appignanesi, Richard 1979. *Freud for Beginners*, Oscar Zarate (illus.). New York: Pantheon.

Bernheimer, Charles & Claire Kahane (eds) 1985. *In Dora's Case: Freud, Hysteria, Feminism*. London: Virago.

Bion, Wilfred R. 1967. *Second Thoughts: Selected Papers on Psycho-Analysis*. London: Heinemann.

Black, David 2006. *Psychoanalysis and Religion in the Twenty-First Century: Competitors or Collaborators?* London: Routledge.

Boothby, Richard 2001. *Freud as Philosopher: Metapsychology after Lacan*. London: Routledge.

Braungardt, J. 1999. "Theology after Lacan? A Psychoanalytic Approach to Theological Discourse". *Other Voices, The (e)Journal of Cultural Criticism* 1(3), http://www.othervoices.org/1.3/jBraungardt/theology.html

Buhle, Mari Jo 1998. *Feminism and Its Discontents: A Century of Struggle with Psychoanalysis*. Cambridge, MA: Harvard University Press.

Burgoyne, Bernard & E. Mary Sullivan (eds) 1999. *The Klein–Lacan Dialogues.* New York: Other Press.

Burke, Nancy (ed.) 1998. *Gender and Envy.* New York: Routledge.

Butler, Judith 1997. *The Psychic Life of Power: Theories in Subjection.* Stanford, CA: Stanford University Press.

Carroll, John 1998. *Ego and Soul: The Modern West in Search of Meaning.* Pymble, NSW: HarperCollins.

Carroll, John 2004. *The Wreck of Western Culture: Humanism Revisited.* Carlton North, Victoria: Scribe Publications.

Chodorow, Nancy 1978. *The Reproduction of Mothering: Psychoanalysis and the Sociology of Gender.* Berkeley, CA: University of California Press.

Cixous, Hélène 1981. "Castration or Decapitation?" *Signs: Journal of Women in Culture and Society* 7(1): 41–55.

Clark, Peter & Crispin Wright (eds) 1988. *Mind, Psychoanalysis and Science.* Oxford: Blackwell.

Crews, Frederick 1995. *The Memory Wars: Freud's Legacy in Dispute.* New York: New York Review of Books.

De Beauvoir, Simone de 1972. *The Second Sex*, H. M. Parshley (trans.). Harmondsworth: Penguin.

Deleuze, Gilles & Félix Guattari 2004. *Anti-Oedipus: Capitalism and Schizophrenia*, Robert Hurley, Mark Seem & Helen R. Lane (trans.). London: Continuum.

Derrida, Jacques 1981. *Dissemination*, Barbara Johnson (trans.). Chicago, IL: University of Chicago Press.

Derrida, Jacques 1982. *Margins of Philosophy*, Alan Bass (trans.). Brighton: Harvester.

Derrida, Jacques 1987. *The Post Card: From Socrates to Freud and Beyond*, Alan Bass (trans.). Chicago, IL: University of Chicago Press.

Derrida, Jacques 1998. *Resistances of Psychoanalysis*, Peggy Kamuf, Pascale-Anne Brault & Michael Naas (trans.). Stanford, CA: Stanford University Press.

Deutsch, Helene 1944–5. *The Psychology of Women: A Psychoanalytic Interpretation*, 2 vols. New York: Grune & Stratton.

Deutscher, Penelope 1997. *Yielding Gender: Feminism, Deconstruction, and the History of Philosophy.* London: Routledge.

Dufresne, Todd 2003. *Killing Freud: Twentieth Century Culture and the Death of Psychoanalysis.* New York: Continuum.

Elliot, Anthony 1992. *Subject to Ourselves: Social Theory, Psychoanalysis and Postmodernity.* Cambridge: Polity.

Elliot, Anthony 1996. *Social Theory and Psychoanalysis in Transition.* Oxford: Blackwell.

Elliot, Anthony (ed.) 1998. *Freud 2000.* Carlton South: Melbourne University Press.

Evans, Dylan 1996. *An Introductory Dictionary of Lacanian Psychoanalysis.* New York: Routledge.

Fairbairn, W. R. D. 1994. *Psychoanalytic Studies of the Personality.* London: Routledge.

Fink, Bruce 1995. *The Lacanian Subject: Between Language and Jouissance.* Princeton, NJ: Princeton University Press.

Fink, Bruce 1997. *Clinical Introduction to Lacanian Psychoanalysis: Theory and Technique.* Cambridge, MA: Harvard University Press.

Forrester, John 1990. *The Seductions of Psychoanalysis: Freud, Lacan, and Derrida.* Cambridge: Cambridge University Press.

Foucault, Michel 1970. *The Order of Things: An Archaeology of the Human Sciences.* New York: Pantheon.

Foucault, Michel 1990. *The History of Sexuality.* Vol. 1. London: Penguin Books.

Freud, Anna (ed.) 1986. *The Essentials of Psycho-Analysis.* London: Hogarth Press and the Institute of Psychoanalysis.

Freud, Sigmund 1939. *Civilization, War and Death: Selections from Three Works by Sigmund Freud*, John Rickman (ed.). London: Hogarth Press and the Institute of Psychoanalysis.

Freud, Sigmund 1958. *On Creativity and the Unconscious: Papers on the Psychology of Art, Literature, Love, Religion*, Benjamin Nelson (ed.). New York: Harper.

Freud, Sigmund 1960. *Totem and Taboo*, James Strachey (trans.). London: Routledge.

Freud, Sigmund 1962. *Two Short Accounts of Psycho-Analysis: Five Lectures on Psychoanalysis and The Question of Lay Analysis*, James Strachey (trans.). Harmondsworth: Penguin.

Freud, Sigmund 1973. *New Introductory Lectures on Psychoanalysis*, James Strachey (trans.), Angela Richards (ed.), Vol. 2, *The Pelican Freud Library.* Harmondsworth: Penguin.

Freud, Sigmund 1973. "Femininity". In *New Introductory Lectures on Psychoanalysis*, James Strachey (ed.). Harmondsworth: Penguin.

Freud, Sigmund 1973. "Anxiety and Instinctual Life (1933)". In *New Introductory Lectures on Psychoanalysis*, James Strachey (ed.). Harmondsworth: Penguin.

Freud, Sigmund 1976. *The Interpretation of Dreams*, Angela Richards (ed.), Vol. 4, *The Pelican Freud Library.* Harmondsworth: Penguin.

Freud, Sigmund 1977. "Family Romances". In *On Sexuality*, Angela Richards (ed.). Harmondsworth: Penguin.

Freud, Sigmund 1977. "Fragment of an Analysis of a Case of Hysteria ('Dora')". In *Case Histories I*, James Strachey (ed.). Harmondsworth: Penguin.

Freud, Sigmund 1977. "Analysis of a Phobia in a Five-Year-Old Boy ('Little Hans')". In *Case Histories I*, James Strachey (ed.). Harmondsworth: Penguin.

Freud, Sigmund 1977. "Some Psychical Consequences of the Anatomical Distinction between the Sexes (1925)". In *On Sexuality*, Angela Richards (ed.). Harmondsworth: Penguin.

Freud, Sigmund 1977. "Female Sexuality (1931)". In *On Sexuality*, Angela Richards (ed.). Harmondsworth: Penguin.

Freud, Sigmund 1984. "Beyond the Pleasure Principle (1920)". In *On Metapsychology: The Theory of Psychoanalysis*, James Strachey (ed.). Harmondsworth: Penguin.

Freud, Sigmund 1984. "Negation (1925)". In *On Metapsychology: The Theory of Psychoanalysis*, James Strachey (ed.). Harmondsworth: Penguin.

Freud, Sigmund 1984. "Instincts and Their Vicissitudes (1915)". In *On Metapsychology: The Theory of Psychoanalysis*, James Strachey (ed.). Harmondsworth: Penguin.

Freud, Sigmund 1984. "Mourning and Melancholia (1917)". In *On Metapsychology: The Theory of Psychoanalysis*, James Strachey (ed.). Harmondsworth: Penguin.

Freud, Sigmund 1985. *Civilization, Society and Religion*. Albert Dickson (trans.) under the general editorship of James Strachey. Harmondsworth: Penguin.

Freud, Sigmund 1986. "The Development of the Libido and the Sexual Organizations (1916–17)". In *Introductory Lectures on Psycho-Analysis*, James Strachey (ed.). London: The Hogarth Press and the Institute of Psychoanalysis.

Freud, Sigmund 1991. "The Ego and the Id (1923)". In *The Essentials of Psycho-Analysis*, Anna Freud (ed.). Harmondsworth: Penguin.

Gallop, Jane 1982. *Feminism and Psychoanalysis: The Daughter's Seduction*. London: Macmillan.

Gay Peter 1987. *Godless Jew*. New Haven, CT: Yale University Press.

Gay, Peter (ed.) 1995. *The Essential Freud*. London: Vintage.

Girard, René 1977. *Violence and the Sacred*, Patrick Gregory (trans.). Baltimore, MD: Johns Hopkins University Press.

Glynos, Jason & Jannis Stavrakakis (eds) 2002. *Lacan and Science*. London: Karnac Books.

Goodchild, Philip 1996. *Deleuze and Guattari: An Introduction to the Politics of Desire*. London: Sage.

Gosso, Sandra (ed.) 2004. *Psychoanalysis and Art: Kleinian Perspectives*. London: Karnac Books.

Grigg, Russell, Dominique Hecq & Craig Smith (eds) 1999. *Female Sexuality: The Early Psychoanalytic Controversies*. New York: Other Press.

Grosz, Elizabeth 1989. *Sexual Subversions: Three French Feminists*. Sydney: Allen & Unwin.

Grunbaum, Adolf 1994. *The Foundations of Psychoanalysis: A Philosophical Critique*. Berkeley, CA: University of California Press.

Habermas, Jürgen 1978. *Knowledge and Human Interests*. London: Heinemann.

Hamon, Marie-Christine 2000. *Why Do Women Love Men and Not Their Mothers?*, Susan Fairfield (trans.). New York: Other Press.

Hinshelwood, R. D. 1989. *A Dictionary of Kleinian Thought*. London: Free Association Books.

Hook, Sidney 1959. *Psychoanalysis, Scientific Method and Philosophy*. New York: New York University Press.

Hopkins, Jim 2004. "Conscience and Conflict: Darwin, Freud, and the Origins of Human Aggression", http://www.kcl.ac.uk/kis/schools/hums/philosophy/handouts/hopkins/emotion.pdf

Horkheimer, Max 1995. "Egoism and Freedom Movements: On the Anthropology of the Bourgeois Era". In *Between Philosophy and the Social Sciences: Selected Early Essays*, Matthew S. Kramer, G. Frederick Hunter & John Torpey (trans.), 104–28. Cambridge, MA: MIT Press.

Horney, Karen 1967. *Feminine Psychology*. New York: Norton.

Hughes, Judith M. 1989. *Reshaping the Psychoanalytic Domain: The Work of Melanie Klein, W. R. D. Fairbairn, and D. W. Winnicott*. Berkeley, CA: University of California Press.

Irigaray, Luce 1981. "And the One Doesn't Stir without the Other". *Signs: Journal of Women in Culture and Society* 7(1): 60–67.

Irigaray, Luce 1985a. *This Sex Which Is Not One*, Catherine Porter (trans.). Ithaca, NY: Cornell University Press.

Irigaray, Luce 1985b. *Speculum of the Other Woman*, Gillian C. Gill (trans.). Ithaca, NY: Cornell University Press.

Jacobus, Mary 2005. *The Poetics of Psychoanalysis: In the Wake of Klein*. Oxford: Oxford University Press.

Johnson, Barbara 1988. "The Frame of Reference: Poe, Lacan, Derrida". In *The Purloined Poe: Lacan, Derrida and Psychoanalytic Reading*, John P. Muller & William J. Richardson (eds), 213–51. Baltimore, MD: Johns Hopkins University Press.

Jones, Ernest 1953–7. *The Life and Work of Sigmund Freud*, 3 vols. New York: Basic Books.

Kandel, Eric 1998. "A New Intellectual Framework of Psychiatry". *American Journal of Psychiatry* 155: 457–69.

Kandel, Eric 1999. "Biology and the Future of Psychoanalysis: A New Intellectual Framework for Psychiatry Revisited". *American Journal of Psychiatry* 156: 505–24.

King, Pearl & Riccardo Steiner (eds) 1991. *The Freud–Klein Controversies 1941–45*. London: Routledge.

Kirsner, Douglas 2000. *Unfree Associations: Inside Psychoanalytic Institutes*. London: Process Press.

Kirsner, Douglas 2004. "Psychoanalysis and its Discontents". *Psychoanalytic Psychology* 21(3): 339–52.

Klein, Melanie 1987. "The Psycho-Analytic Play Technique: Its History and Significance (1955)". In *The Selected Melanie Klein*, Juliet Mitchell (ed.), 35–54.

Klein, Melanie 1987. "Early Stages of the Oedipus Conflict (1928)". In *The Selected Melanie Klein*, Juliet Mitchell (ed.), 69–83.

Klein, Melanie 1987. "The Psychological Principles of Infant Analysis (1926)". In *The Selected Melanie Klein*, Juliet Mitchell (ed.), 57–68.

Klein, Melanie 1987. "The Importance of Symbol Formation in the Development of the Ego (1930)". In *The Selected Melanie Klein*, Juliet Mitchell (ed.), 95–112.

Klein, Melanie 1987. "A Contribution to the Psychogenesis of Manic-Depressive States (1935)". In *The Selected Melanie Klein*, Juliet Mitchell (ed.), 115–45.

Klein, Melanie 1987. "Mourning and Its Relation to Manic-Depressive States (1940)". In *The Selected Melanie Klein*, Juliet Mitchell (ed.), 146–74.

Klein, Melanie 1987. "Notes on Some Schizoid Mechanisms (1946)". In *The Selected Melanie Klein*, Juliet Mitchell (ed.), 175–200.

Klein, Melanie 1987. "The Origins of Transference (1952)". In *The Selected Melanie Klein*, Juliet Mitchell (ed.), 201–10.

Klein, Melanie 1987. "A Study of Envy and Gratitude (1956)". In *The Selected Melanie Klein*, Juliet Mitchell (ed.), 211–29.

Klein, Melanie 1987. "Infantile Anxiety Situations Reflected in a Work of Art and in the Creative Impulse (1929)". In *The Selected Melanie Klein*, Juliet Mitchell (ed.), 84–94.

Klein, Melanie *et al.* (eds) 1989. *Developments in Psycho-Analysis*. London: Karnac and the Institute of Psychoanalysis.

Kofman, Sarah 1985. *The Enigma of Woman: Woman in Freud's Writings*, Catherine Porter (trans.). Ithaca, NY: Cornell University Press.

Kofman, Sarah 1996. *Rue Ordener, Rue Labat*, Ann Smock (trans.). Lincoln, NE: University of Nebraska Press.

Kristeva, Julia 1980. *Desire in Language: A Semiotic Approach to Literature and Art*, Alice Jardine, Thomas Gora & Leon S. Roudiez (trans.), Leon S. Roudiez (ed.). New York: Columbia University Press.

Kristeva, Julia 1982. *Powers of Horror: An Essay on Abjection*, Leon S. Roudiez (trans.). New York: Columbia University Press.

Lacan, Jacques 1978. *The Four Fundamental Concepts of Psychoanalysis: The Seminar of Jacques Lacan Book XI*, 2nd edn, Alan Sheridan (trans.). New York: Norton.

Lacan, Jacques 1982. *Feminine Sexuality: Jacques Lacan and the École Freudienne*, Jacqueline Rose (trans.), Juliet Mitchell & Jacqueline Rose (eds). London: Macmillan.

Lacan, Jacques 1988a. *The Seminar of Jacques Lacan. Book I. Freud's Papers on Technique 1953–1954*, John Forrester (trans.), Jacques-Alain Miller (ed.). Cambridge: Cambridge University Press.

Lacan, Jacques 1988b. *The Seminar of Jacques Lacan. II. The Ego in Freud's Theory and in the Technique of Psychoanalysis 1954–1955*, Sylvana Tomaselli (trans.), Jacques-Alain Miller (ed.). Cambridge: Cambridge University Press.

Lacan, Jacques 1990. *Television*, Denis Hollier, Rosalind Krauss & Annette Michelson (trans.). New York: Norton.

Lacan, Jacques 1992. *The Ethics of Psychoanalysis, 1959–1960: The Seminar of Jacques Lacan Book VII*. London: Routledge.

Lacan, Jacques 1993. *The Seminar of Jacques Lacan, Book III: The Psychoses*, Russell Grigg (trans.). New York: Norton.

Lacan, Jacques 2006. *Écrits*, Héloise Fink, Bruce Fink & Russell Grigg (trans.). New York: Norton.

Lasch, Christopher 1979. *The Culture of Narcissism: American Life in the Age of Diminishing Expectations*. New York: Norton.

Leader, Dorian (ed.) 2000. *Freud's Footnotes*. London: Faber.

Lear, Jonathan 1990. *Love and Its Place in Nature: A Philosophical Interpretation of Freudian Psychoanalysis*. New York: Farrar, Straus & Giroux.

Lear, Jonathan 1995. "The Shrink is In". *New Republic*, 25 December.

Lear, Jonathan 2003. *Therapeutic Action: An Earnest Plea for Irony*. Cambridge, MA: Harvard University Press.

Lear, Jonathan 2005. *Freud*. New York: Routledge.

Levine, Michael (ed.) 2000. *Analytic Freud: Philosophy and Psychoanalysis*. London: Routledge.

Levy, Donald 1996. *Freud Among the Philosophers*. New Haven, CT: Yale University Press.

Marcuse, Herbert 1972. *One-Dimensional Man*. London: Abacus.

Markotic, Lorraine 2001. "There Where Primary Narcissism Was, I Must Become: The Inception of the Ego in Andreas-Salomé, Lacan, and Kristeva". *American Imago* 58(4): 813–36.

Masson, Jeffrey 1984. *The Assault on Truth: Freud's Suppression of the Seduction Theory*. New York: Farrar, Straus & Giroux.

Meissner, William 1984. *Psychoanalysis and Religious Experience*. New Haven, CT: Yale University Press.

Meng, Eric & Ernst L. Freud *et al.* (eds) 1963. *Psychoanalysis and Faith: The Letters of Sigmund Freud and Oskar Pfister*, Eric Mosbacher (trans.). London: Hogarth Press.

Millett, Kate 1971. *Sexual Politics*. London: Hart-Davis.

Mills, Jon (ed.) 2006. *Other Banalities: Melanie Klein Revisited*. London: Routledge.

Mitchell, Juliet 1975. *Psychoanalysis and Feminism*. Harmondsworth: Penguin.

Mitchell, Juliet (ed.) 1987. *The Selected Melanie Klein*. New York: Free Press.

Mulvey, Laura 1989. *Visual and Other Pleasures*. Basingstoke: Macmillan.

Nagel, Ernest 1959. "Methodological Issues in Psychoanalytic Theory". In *Psychoanalysis, Scientific Method and Philosophy*, S. Hook (ed.). New York: New York University Press.

Oliver, Kelly 1993. "Julia Kristeva's Feminist Revolutions". *Hypatia: A Journal of Feminist Philosophy* 8(3): 94–114.

Popper, Karl 1962. *Conjectures and Refutations*. New York: Basic Books.

Rabate, Jean-Michel 2001. *Jacques Lacan: Psychoanalysis and the Subject of Literature*. London: Routledge.

Reinhard, Kenneth 1999. "Lacan and Monotheism: Psychoanalysis and the Traversal of Cultural Phantasy". *Jouvert* 3(2), http://social.chass.ncsu.edu/jouvert/v3i12/con312.htm

Reinhard, Kenneth 2005. "Lacan on the Ten Commandments". *Diacritics* 33(2): 71–97.

Ricoeur, Paul 1970. *A Philosophical Interpretation of Freud: An Essay on Interpretation*. New Haven, CT: Yale University Press. First published in French in 1965.

Rieff, Philip 1966. *The Triumph of the Therapeutic: Uses of Faith after Freud*. New York: Harper & Row.

Rieff, Philip 1979. *Freud: The Mind of the Moralist*. 3rd edn. Chicago, IL: University of Chicago Press.

Rose, Jacqueline 1993. *Why War? – Psychoanalysis, Politics, and the Return to Melanie Klein*. Oxford: Blackwell.

Samuels, Robert 1993. *Between Philosophy & Psychoanalysis: Lacan's Reconstruction of Freud*. New York: Routledge.

Sanchez-Pardo, Esther 2003. *Cultures of the Death Drive: Melanie Klein and Modernist Melancholia*. Durham, NC: Duke University Press.

Sayers, Janet 1991. *Mothering Psychoanalysis: Helene Deutsch, Karen Horney, Anna Freud and Melanie Klein*. London: Hamish Hamilton.

Sayers, Janet 2007. *Freud's Art: Psychoanalysis Retold*. London: Routledge.

Schorske, Carl 1980. *Fin-de-Siècle Vienna: Politics and Culture*. New York: Knopf.

Segal, Julia 1992. *Melanie Klein*. London: Sage.

Solms, Mark 1996. "What is Consciousness?" *Journal of the American Psychoanalytic Association* 45: 681–703.

Solms, Mark 1997. *The Neuropsychology of Dreams: A Clinico-Anatomical Study*. Hillsdale, NJ: Lawrence Erlbaum.

Solms, Mark 2004. "Freud Returns", in *Scientific American*, May, http://www.neuro-psa.org.uk/download/SAorig.pdf

Spillius, Elizabeth Bott (ed.) 1988. *Melanie Klein Today: Developments in Theory and Practice*. London: Routledge.

Stoltzfus, Ben 1996. *Lacan and Literature: Purloined Pretexts*. Albany, NY: SUNY Press.

Stonebridge, Lyndsey & John Phillips (eds) 1988. *Reading Melanie Klein*. London: Routledge.

Strauss, L. [1958] 1997. "Freud on Moses and Monotheism". In *Jewish Philosophy and the Crisis of Modernity. Essays and Lectures in Modern Jewish Thought*, with an Introduction by Kenneth Hart Green (ed.), 285–310. Albany, NY: SUNY Press.

Sullaway, Frank J. 1979. *Freud: Biologist of the Mind: Beyond the Psychoanalytic Legend*. New York: Basic Books.

Weber, Samuel 1991. *Return to Freud: Jacques Lacan's Dislocation of Psychoanalysis*, Michael Levine (trans.). Cambridge: Cambridge University Press.

Webster, Richard 1995. *Why Freud Was Wrong: Sin, Science, and Psychoanalysis*. London: Fontana.

Whitford, Margaret 1994. *Luce Irigaray: Philosophy in the Feminine*. London: Routledge.

Wilden, Anthony 1981. "Lacan and the Discourse of the Other". In *Jaques Lacan, the Language of the Self*, 157–312. Baltimore, MD: Johns Hopkins University Press.

Winnicott, D. W. 2005. *Playing and Reality*. London: Routledge.

Wollheim, Richard 1971. *Freud*. London: Fontana.

Yerushalmi, Yosef Hayim 1991. *Freud's Moses: Judaism Terminable and Interminable*. New Haven, CT: Yale University Press.

Zaretsky, Eli 2004. *Secrets of the Soul*. New York: Knopf.

Žižek, Slavoj 1989. *The Sublime Object of Ideology*. London: Verso.

Žižek, Slavoj 1991. *Looking Awry: An Introduction to Jacques Lacan through Popular Culture*. Cambridge, MA: MIT Press.

Žižek, Slavoj 1992. *Enjoy Your Symptom! Jacques Lacan in Hollywood and Out*. New York: Routledge.

Žižek, Slavoj 1994. *The Metastases of Enjoyment*. London: Verso.

Žižek, Slavoj 1997. *The Plague of Fantasies (Wo Es War)*. London: Verso.

Žižek, Slavoj 1999. *The Ticklish Subject: The Absent Centre of Political Ontology.* London: Verso.

Žižek, Slavoj 2001. *The Fright of Real Tears: Krzysztof Kieslowski between Theory and Post-Theory.* London: BFI Publishing.

Žižek, Slavoj 2004. *Organs Without Bodies: Deleuze and Consequences.* New York: Routledge.

Zondervan, Antonius A. W. 2005. *Sociology and the Sacred: An Introduction to Philip Rieff's Theory of Culture.* Toronto: University of Toronto Press.

Index

deconstruction   5, 142, 179–80
defences   33, 43, 65, 89, 101, 130
Deleuze, Gilles   9, 179, 182, 183–5
  Anti-Oedipus   183–5
  body-without-organs   184
  desiring machines   185
  desiring production   184
  planes of immanence   184
delusion   27–9, 30, 34, 122
  delusional jealousy   107–8
  of grandeur   23
  homosexual   124
  of influence   29
  metaphysical   27
  paranoid   28–9
  theological   123–4
Democritus   162
depression   81, 196
depressive position   82, 86–9, 93–5,
  102, 194
Derrida, Jacques   5, 6, 9, 142,
  179–81, 182
  différance   180
  Dissemination   180
  The Margins of Philosophy   180
  "The Purveyor of Truth"   180
Descartes, René   6, 12, 101, 119, 160
desire   44–5, 49, 88–9, 96, 102,
  105–14, 166, 190, 193, 195
  feminine   128–31, 143–5
  as lack   24, 114, 119, 159–61,
    181–5
  and language   105, 112–14, 116,
    119, 121, 125, 176
  and motherhood   130–31
  of the other   107–10, 125
  for recognition   105
  sexual   39, 42, 52, 54–6, 81,
    106–7, 151
  see also wish
desiring machines   185
desiring production   184
Deutsch, Helene   10, 129, 130–32
diachronic theory of signification
  120
"Dick", case of   90–91

Dilthey, Wilhelm   176
disavowal   26–7, 28, 34, 52, 97,
  106–7, 145
displacement   31, 63, 68, 72, 78,
  180–81, 183, 185
  defined   74
"Dora"   37, 75, 127, 135, 188
  aphonia   134
  description of case   134
Dostoevsky, Fyodor   156
Douglas, Mary   140
dreams   7, 57, 64–76, 83, 105, 109,
  113, 179
  Anna O's   3
  anxiety   65, 67, 84
  "botanical monograph"   72
  and creativity   156–7, 170
  dream work   68, 70, 74–6
  "Irma's injection"   72
  latent content   66, 68, 72, 75–6, 78
  manifest content   66–8, 71–2,
    74–5, 78
  metapsychology of   68
  as rebus, puzzle   70
  and religion   162, 165
  as wish fulfilment   64–7, 69, 72,
    74–5, 78
  "witty butcher's wife"   107
  Wolfman's   75
drive   7–8, 20–25, 34, 37, 44–9,
  54–5, 59–61, 63–5, 76, 100–102,
  108
  active   45, 48, 53, 131
  aim   27, 42–7, 49, 52–5, 60, 65–6
  defined   45
  anaclitic   54
  and biology   46, 49, 176–7, 179
  component   43–4, 48–9, 55, 107
  desublimation of   155
  different from instinct   46, 176–7
  and language   105–6, 112, 141,
    143, 176–7, 190
  object   20–24, 27–8, 29, 34,
    40–49, 51–6, 60, 104–5, 109–10,
    112–14, 118–19
  defined   45

and language 46, 59–63, 69, 78,
   83, 92, 105–6, 115, 119–20, 141,
   179–80
and memory 62–3, 76, 105, 162
and neurosis 34, 58
as personal 172
and religion 165–6, 187
repression and 22–3, 33, 72, 115,
   175
and sexuality 40, 107, 113, 137,
   183
as somatic 59, 63, 74, 173
Unheimlichkeit see uncanny

Verleugnung see disavowal
Verneinung see repression
vicissitudes of the drives 44–6, 55,
   60, 150, 194
aim inhibition 54–6, 60, 151
repression 22–4, 26–8, 30–35,
   47–8, 60–61, 88, 108, 118, 155,
   158, 166, 184
reversal 45–6, 60
turning in 45, 55, 60, 152
Victorian era 36, 134–5, 138
Vorsagung see forsaking
Vorstellung see representation
voyeurism 41

war neuroses 84
Wilde, Oscar 158
   "Picture of Dorian Gray" 158
Winnicott, Donald W. 95–7,
   102
wish 19–25, 27, 29–35, 92, 94,
   131, 154–8, 175, 188–9,
   191–3
to be the phallus 119
to destroy the parent 83, 87, 94,
   195
dream- 58–9, 61, 63–9, 71–6, 78,
   156
fantasy 157–8, 170
jealous 107
and language 117–20, 156
for omnipotence 92, 152
to protect the parent 88–9
and religion 163, 167
Wittgenstein, Ludwig 106
"Wolfman" 49, 75–6, 114, 166
womb-envy 132, 146
word-presentations 62, 68

Zaretsky, Eli 172–3, 188
Ziel see aim
Žižek, Slavoj 72, 155, 159–61, 181,
   184, 188